Wooing, Wedding, and Power

Women in Shakespeare's Plays

Wooing, Wedding, and Power: Women in Shakespeare's Plays

IRENE G. DASH

Columbia University Press
New York

Library of Congress Cataloging in Publication Data

Dash, Irene G.
  Wooing, wedding, and power.

  Bibliography: p.
  Includes index.
  1. Shakespeare, William, 1564–1616—Characters—
Women. 2. Women in literature. 3. Feminism and
literature. I. Title.
PR2991.D27   822.3'3   81-4046
ISBN 0-231-05238-3   AACR2
ISBN 0-231-05239-1   (paper)

Columbia University Press
New York   Guildford, Surrey

*Clothbound editions of Columbia University Press
books are Smyth-sewn and printed on permanent
and durable acid-free paper.*

For
Deborah and Deena
and Martin

Contents

Illustrations

Acknowledgments

I am delighted to thank colleagues, friends, and family who have helped make this book a reality. Often, the extent of their support has been immeasurable. Modestly, I am aware that I can never acknowledge the many who have indirectly shaped my thinking—the Shakespearean scholars, the editors, the producers, and even the actors and actresses who have brought these plays to life on the stage. Nor can I name the many students whose questions in class have sharpened my thinking. It is a great privilege to express here my appreciation to the individuals who have enriched this book. For its weaknesses and errors, of course, I take full responsibility.

I want to thank my daughter Deborah who read this work in manuscript at many stages, criticizing and pushing for clarification of ideas. I am most grateful to my daughter Deena who, although living at a distance, read sections of the manuscript and offered incisive criticism and strong encouragement. From the perceptive reading of much of this book by MacDonald Moore I have profited greatly; and from the optimism and confidence of Sidney Kushner I have often regained perspective at moments of skepticism.

Moving into a new life, I have found scholars of breadth and understanding. Sighle Kennedy has offered sympathetic support when the flow of ideas seemed to stop. Debating textual interpretation with me, she has often sent me back to writing with renewed energy. When for the first time I attended a Shakespeare conference, I had the privilege of meeting a quiet scholar of modesty, warmth, and originality. I feel fortunate in having known Tommy Ruth Waldo, a courageous woman who initiated me into the complexities of this new environment. John H. Middendorf and S. F. Johnson, at Columbia University, transformed me from a student to a colleague. I am grateful to them for having taught me the research techniques underpinning all of my later work and so valuable here. I am most thankful to John Shawcross for his insightful reading of the book. His wide knowledge of literature and his sensitivity to the implications of the text uncovered layers of meaning of which I had not been fully conscious.

The Folger Shakespeare Library opened wide the world of scholarship for me. There I met others with whom I could exchange ideas, explore nuances of textual meaning, and analyze the intricacies of promptbooks: Leeds Barroll, Ruth Widmann, Tom Berger, Charles Lower, Virginia Carr, Elizabeth Hageman, Jeanne Roberts, John Velz, and Charles Shattuck. Harry Pedicord generously shared his vast knowledge of Garrick's work with me, and Barbara Mowat read a chapter of this book, offering valuable criticism.

Libraries are not impersonal places. Having worked several summers at the Folger, I want to thank O. B. Hardison, its director, and the staff for their constant, quiet, unobtrusive helpfulness. I am most grateful to Laetitia Yeandle and Jean Miller on whose expertise I relied even during the years when the library was officially closed. At the Columbia University Library, Eileen McIlvaine has tenaciously pursued my most obscure leads with enthusiasm and usually with success. I owe her thanks. A New Yorker, I am grateful to the New York Public Library where I have found rich resources and a haven in which to work.

At various moments during the progress of this book a number of people have assisted me. I appreciate the informed counsel of Miriam Sarzin. The thoughtful comments of Philip Winsor have improved this work. Two former students, Denise Fetonte and Jeannie Pool, provided that magic mirror that Virginia Woolf recognized as necessary if one is to face the unknown. I value their support as I do that of Florence Donnell. My colleagues at Hunter College have created an atmosphere free of tension and conducive to work, for which I am most grateful. Finally, I wish to thank my editors at Columbia

University Press, William Bernhardt and Jennifer Crewe, who have handled this book with care and dispatch.

Shakespeare's insights into the human condition have been observed ever since Ben Jonson's famous dedicatory poem in the First Folio. It will not be difficult for those reading this book to discover the writer's interest in the dynamics of marriage in Shakespeare's plays. To my husband, Martin Dash, for whom this work was also an adventure and who showed great patience while I explored the deeper meanings of marriage and equality between women and men, I extend my deepest thanks.

My parents provided the early nurturing that led me to question accepted patterns. For this I will always be grateful.

Wooing, Wedding, and Power

Women in Shakespeare's Plays

CLEOP. The gods confound thee! Dost thou hold there still?

MARD. Should I lie, madam?

CLEOP. O, I would, thou didst; So half my Egypt were submerg'd, and made A cistern for scal'd snakes!

Go, get thee hence; Hadst thou Narcissus in thy face, to me Thou would'st appear most ugly. He is married?

MARD. I crave your highness' pardon.

CLEOP. He is married?

MARD. Take no offence, that I would not offend you: To punish me for what you make me do, Seems much unequal. He is married to Octavia.

CLEOP. O, that his fault should make a knave of thee, Thou art not—What? Get thee hence.

The merchandise which thou hast brought from Rome Are all too dear for me; lie they upon thy hand, And be undone by 'em! [Exit MARDIAN.

CHAR. Good your highness, patience.

CLEOP. In praising Antony, I have disprais'd Cæsar.

CHAR. Many times, madam.

CLEOP. I am paid for 't now. Lead me from hence, I faint, O, Iras, Charmian,—'Tis no matter. Go to the fellow, good Alexas; bid him Report the feature of Octavia; her years, Her inclination, let him not leave out The colour of her hair—bring me word quickly. [Exit ALEXAS.

Let him for ever go—Let him not—Charmian, Though he be painted one way like a Gorgon, T'other way he's a Mars. Bid you Alexas [to IRAS] Bring me word, how tall she is—Pity me, Charmian. But do not speak to me. Lead me to my chamber. [Exeunt.

Promptbook of *Antony and Cleopatra*, 1874. Extensive cuts are indicated by

CHAPTER ONE

Introduction

Their Infinite Variety

*S*trong, attractive, intelligent, and humane women come to life in Shakespeare's plays. They not only have a clear sense of themselves as individuals, but they challenge accepted patterns for women's behavior. Compliance, self-sacrifice for a male, dependence, nurturance, and emotionalism are the expected norms. Yet independence, self-control and, frequently, defiance characterize these women. In *The Winter's Tale*, for example, Hermione disdains tears although unjustly imprisoned; her husband, Leontes, weeps in self-pity. In *Othello* and *Romeo and Juliet*, women, exercising their independence, defy their fathers as well as the mores of their society.

Shakespeare's women characters testify to his genius. They are drawn with neither anger nor condescension. In personality they vary. Some are warm, delightful, friendly; others cold, aloof, and scornful. Some speak with confidence; others with diffidence. They range in age from the youthful, joyous Juliet to the wizened, bitter Margaret. But most have a vitality; they grow and develop during the course of a drama. Their actions spring from a realistic confrontation with life as they learn the meaning of self sovereignty for a woman in a patriarchal society.

But critics, limited by their own perceptions of a

woman's role, fail to hear all the texts' cues and wrestle with interpretation. Simplification or evasion results. Some of the women are castigated as shrews; others are removed from the human sphere and their resemblances to deities or goddesses are emphasized; still others are considered as merely personifications of ideas. Occasionally a critic asserts, as one did recently, that Shakespeare's women are "the conscious sustainers of society and culture, as are Modern American Women." This critic, however, then continues:

> The prime sources of disaster in Shakespeare's plays are to be found in women who neurotically forget their biological role . . . or their social tact (like Desdemona . . .), or who attempt to seize physical supremacy from the male (like Queen Margaret or Cleopatra).[1]

The individuality of Shakespeare's portraits is buried beneath the generalizations in this statement.

Editors, too, rely on stereotypes, but they also react to the intellectual and moral climate of their era. Thus, Samuel Johnson in the eighteenth century decries the frequent use of bawdy language in *Love's Labour's Lost* and wonders how the work could have been performed before a "maiden queen."[2] The play, whose characters include outspoken, independent women, did not appear on the stage of his time. J. W. Lever, writing in our twentieth century, wonders what all the fuss is about in *Measure for Measure*. He can't understand why Isabella should refuse to capitulate to the threats of a rapist-seducer. This editor writes: "Chastity was essentially a condition of the spirit; to see it in merely physical terms was to reduce the concept to a mere pagan scruple."[3]

Actor-managers, directors, and producers have difficulty transferring Shakespeare's vision of women to the stage. Shaped by the cultural mores of their particular society, they too conform to its biases. With sometimes slight, sometimes massive changes of the text, these men of the theater reshape the woman's role in the image of the age. Promptbooks—records of plays as performed—recapture those performances. They also permit comparison of the acted play with the original. Lines are cut, roles excised, scenes transposed, and stage directions interjected. The cumulative effect of these changes is usually an altered portrait of the woman character Shakespeare had intended.

In the dramatist's age, stage props were minimal: a tree, a table, a chair, and language that cued the audience in to the exact location of the action. In later times, large stage sets were devised. Striving for grandeur, the designers created costly scenery that took time to move. The uninterrupted performance of the Elizabethan and Jacobean stage gave way to productions with long intermissions. But the cost of moving scenery also inspired producers to try to consolidate scenes occurring in one place. *Antony and Cleopatra* provides an excellent example. The scenes shift back and forth in kaleidoscope fashion between Rome and Egypt. Shakespeare's actors probably had no difficulty with such shifts. People listened to the language, looked at the costumes, and imagined. Later audiences, however, demanded verisimilitude. They wanted to see Rome and Egypt. To shift from Egypt to Rome then back to Egypt and again to move for a brief interlude in Rome before returning once more to Egypt required massive shifts of scenery. How much simpler it was to consolidate these many short scenes into a few long ones. But the intricacy of Shakespeare's method for developing a portrait was lost—and with it the subtlety of the statement.

Stage business also affects responses to a character. Ellen Terry, the famous Shakespearean actress, writing early in this century, tells of playing Beatrice in *Much Ado About Nothing*. When Beatrice's cousin swoons at being falsely slandered on her wedding day, Beatrice's suitor, Benedick, quickly goes to the aid of the fainting woman. Mr. Lacy, an old actor with the company, advised Terry to attempt to prevent Benedick from being of assistance:

> "When Benedick rushes forward to lift up Hero after she has fainted, you 'shoo' him away. Jealousy, you see. Beatrice is not going to let her man lay a finger on another woman." I said, "Oh, nonsense, Mr. Lacy!" "Well, it's always been done," he retorted, "and it always gets a laugh." I told him then that not only was it impossible for *me* to do such a thing, but that it was so inconsistent with Beatrice's character that it ought to be impossible for any actress impersonating her to do it![4]

Terry triumphed on that occasion. But not all actresses are in that commanding a position. And even she, at other times, had to bow to the wishes of Henry Irving, the renowned actor-manager of the end of the nineteenth century, when he insisted that they play for a "gag" rather than be true to Shakespeare's portrait of a woman character. The word of the director usually prevails.

M. C. Bradbrook, the contemporary critic, observes that theatrical practices today—the open stage, the swift shifts of setting, and even the absence of scenery—most nearly approximate those of Shakespeare's age.[5] The potential exists to recapture the quality of his dramas on the stage. But receptivity to Shakespeare's technique does not assure receptivity to his voice—his ideas and attitudes. A recent production of *Richard III* testified to this.[6] Audiences should comfortably enjoy hissing Richard, one of Shakespeare's unrepentant villains. Instead, a 1979 audience applauded when Richard, through guile, won for his wife a woman whose life that audience knew would be tortured and tragic. The misogynistic tone of the production indicates that technical knowledge has little to do with substance. In this production, Shakespeare's vision was ignored and his insights into women's lives lost. Instead of seeing the powerlessness of Anne, a woman tragically marked by Richard for his bride, the audience saw a cold, aloof character who seemed to deserve her fate. And the one woman character with courage enough to challenge him openly, Margaret, never appeared. Absent too was the choral lament of the wailing widows—powerless queens. The production failed to show how Shakespeare dramatized the ways in which power impinges upon and shapes a woman's life.

The sweetest power a woman can possess is that over herself. Simone de Beauvoir calls it the sense of one's self as "subject, active, free."[7] Virginia Woolf symbolizes it with the phrase, "five hundred pounds a year and a room of one's own," admonishing women to achieve economic and political independence.[8] But this power is incomplete. As de Beauvoir later notes, a woman loses this freedom when she discovers her own sexuality. She then realizes that to fulfill herself sexually, she must think of herself as "Other," or secondary, and of man as primary, for she lives in a patriarchal society. Marriage dramatizes this power of one human being over another. John Stuart Mill, the Victorian philosopher, notes that the reason the majority of men refuse to relinquish this power is that they are still too much afraid of living with an equal. He reasons for a sexual equality that will free both men and women to enjoy the full value of life.[9]

Shakespeare focuses on this inequity. Men and women confront the same experience from opposite perspectives. By creating confident, attractive, independent women whom we like, he questions the wisdom of a power structure that insists they relinquish personal freedom. Some of his dramas question accepted patterns of behavior. Some stress the value of mutual respect between a man and a woman. Some reveal the confusion in a woman's mind when she seeks to understand the limits of her world. Occasionally, a drama documents the tragedy of a woman who loses her way and her sense of self when she seeks to conform. To hear his voice, however, one must recognize the individuality and three-dimensional quality of his women characters. Like the men, the women too respond to a variety of forces in their environment and are troubled by the world they see. But that world differs from the one perceived by men.

Living at a time when a woman sat on the English throne, an artist of Shakespeare's sensitivity must have been affected by this extraordinary circumstance. Not only was Elizabeth I a remarkable woman and a person of power, but she remained unmarried, thus preserving that power. Her reign began before Shakespeare was born and extended well into his playwrighting years. C. H. Williams, the historian, describes the impact of her presence as monarch for forty-six years:

> From the moment of her accession until the time of her death Elizabeth I was a phenomenon—it is not too strong a word—in European history. She was at once a crowned monarch and an unmarried woman. To such an unconventional conjunction some of the stiffest problems of the reign must be attributed. The Queen's methods of dealing with them often bewildered her contemporaries. They have not been any clearer to historians.[10]

The Queen's life dramatized a woman's potential for greatness and the subordination that a patriarchal society mandated for her if she were to marry. With great skill, Elizabeth evaded marriage and avoided that possible loss of power. She refused to share her life or her throne with any man. As she knew by observing her sister monarch, Mary of Scotland, in a patriarchal society, marriage transforms even a queen's power. If Elizabeth is an enigma to historians, perhaps it is because they have difficulty understanding the effect of this inequity on a woman's thinking and acting. Surely the dramatist drew on this example.

Today, Shakespeare's women characters have a relevance and vitality. They offer insights into women's perceptions of themselves in a patriarchal world. They reveal the conflict women know as they move from that early awareness of themselves as "essential" to that later eroding of self-confidence when they discover that they are merely "Other." Shakespeare's plays show the diversity of the mind of a sixteenth-century man whose understanding of the human condition extended beyond his own sex and beyond his own time.

PART I

Courtship

The influence of the rococo can be seen in this illustration for Boydell's Shakespeare Gallery (1793) by Francis Wheatley. In an idealized rustic setting that occupies more than a third of the picture space, the elegantly dressed Princess of France consults with her women. FOLGER SHAKESPEARE LIBRARY

CHAPTER TWO

Oath-Taking

LOVE'S LABOUR'S LOST

"A time methinks too short
To make a world-without-end bargain in."
(V.ii.788–89)*

*I*n *Love's Labour's Lost,* Shakespeare employs oaths to reveal how men and women characters perceive the meaning of truth and honesty. During the play, oaths increase in
seriousness, progressing from the extravagantly humorous
pledge of Act I when the King of Navarre and his men swear
not to see women for three years; to the more moderate vow of
Act IV, when the gallants plan to woo and win "these girls of
France"; to the proposals of marriage of the last scene. Women
constitute the subject of men's vows, although the men swear
first to reject women, then pledge to pursue them, and finally
to marry them. The ironic progression suggests that since the
oath-takers are men, Shakespeare is mocking the male tradition of oath-taking, insisting that it be linked with honesty. In
contrast, the Princess of France and the women of her court
reject the offers of marriage of the King and his courtiers,

---

* The text used throughout is *The Riverside Shakespeare,* G. Blakemore Evans,
textual editor. Boston: Houghton Mifflin, 1974. For the sake of clarity, the square
brackets appearing in the Riverside text have been eliminated. When used in this
book, square brackets indicate interpolation by the author.

refusing to be bound by this timeless oath. One of the men objects that this is no way to end a comedy. Thus Shakespeare presents a woman's point of view on honesty and truth, endowing the play with a significance that goes beyond the limits of the comic world.

The play opens at the court of the King of Navarre moments before he and his men sign a vow to dedicate themselves solely to the pursuit of learning:

> Our court shall be a little academe,
> Still and contemplative in living art.
>> (I.i.13–14)

He promises present fame and future immortality, confident that these immodest rewards will accrue naturally to the court. "Navarre shall be the wonder of the world" (12). The King assumes his men share his aim, particularly the quest for fame. They need only dedicate themselves to study and abjure the company of women for three years. Of the three courtiers, two —Longaville and Dumaine—comply, even relishing the idea of self-sacrifice.

> I am resolved, 'tis but a three years' fast:
> The mind shall banquet, though the body pine
>> (24–25)

exclaims Longaville. Dumaine is even more extravagant in his pledge:

> To love, to wealth, to pomp, I pine and die,
> With all these living in philosophy.
>> (31–32)

However, Berowne, the third man of Navarre's court, protests. Rational and quick-witted, he finds the terms antithetical to the whole spirit of education. Moreover, he believes them too harsh:

> . . . not to see a woman in that term,
>> .   .   .
> And not be seen to wink of all the day—

When I was wont to think no harm all night,

        .   .   .

O, these are barren tasks, too hard to keep.

                (I.i.37–47)

Berowne would prefer to be excused from the pledge, explaining by most ingenious arguments that he "swore in jest" (54). His sophisticated reasoning and his rhetorical gifts set him apart from the others. He challenges the King's "study's godlike recompense" (58) with his own interpretation:

Study is like the heaven's glorious sun,
That will not be deep search'd with saucy looks;
Small have continual plodders ever won,
Save base authority from others' books.

                (84–87)

He describes those things most worth enjoying:

At Christmas I no more desire a rose
Than wish a snow in May's new-fangled shows;
But like of each thing that in season grows.

                (105–7)

Nevertheless, he capitulates when Navarre insists on a written oath to confirm the verbal pledge. "You swore to that, Berowne, and to the rest" (53). Otherwise, "Well, sit you out; go home, Berowne; adieu" (110). Almost childlike in his petulant persistence, Navarre demands total compliance. And so, threatened with exclusion from the group, the courtier relents. Peer approval overrides reason. He will not break his oath:

    . . . I have sworn to stay with you;
    . . . I'll keep what I have sworn.
            (111, 114)

Oaths, whether reasonable or not, link the men. But the play questions the wisdom of such bonding. And the Princess, Rosaline, Katherine, and Maria are the chief challengers.

    The extraordinary opening vow permits exploration of the values men and women place on oaths. Unlikely to strut

across the stage with swords or magnanimously offer king-
doms for a pledge, women make seemingly colorless vows that
lack bravado: vows of marriage. But they are timelessly binding, world-without-end bargains that will alter their lives. The
women reject oath-taking as a method of confirming a temporary agreement, skeptical about the morality of vows too easily
made and broken. When, for example, in the last act, the King
asserts, "The virtue of your eye must break my oath"
(V.ii.348), the Princess of France objects, "You nickname virtue; vice you should have spoke, / For virtue's office never
breaks men's troth" (349–50). The close relationship between
"truth" and "troth" as well as between "troth"—to pledge
one's word—and "troth" in the phrase "to plight one's troth"
in marriage cannot have been lost on Shakespeare's audience.
What makes the play unusual is that its ending confirms the
women's skepticism.

Moments after being signed, that opening vow meets
its first challenge when Berowne reminds Navarre of the forthcoming diplomatic visit of the Princess of France. She is to
negotiate the "surrender up of Aquitaine / To her . . . father"
(I.i.137–38). As we later discover, disagreement exists about
the terms of an earlier treaty. But the immediate problem is
oath-breaking. What now of an oath forbidding speech with a
woman, or of that first decision in the written proclamation
that Berowne reads: " 'no woman shall come within a mile of
[the] court . . . on pain of losing her tongue' " (119–22)?
Shakespeare exaggerates the terms for the sake of comedy.
However, his later development of the character of the men
and women around this basic plot reveals his genius. At this
moment in the comedy, Navarre concedes that he must do
something and so decides to bend his oath, welcoming the
women to the park surrounding the palace but permitting
them no entrance to the palace itself.

The argument is joined. The men must confront the
women; vows must face honest appraisal.

> I hear your Grace hath sworn out house-keeping:
> 'Tis deadly sin to keep that oath, my lord,
> And sin to break it.
> (II.i.104–6)

The Princess observes his dilemma. Lack of hospitality ("housekeeping") had not been anticipated. A simplistic oath that seemed merely a rejection of women—debasers of men's higher goals—now turns sinful. Navarre had ignored the possibility of women as equals.

Writing of the reluctance of men to grant women equality, John Stuart Mill observes that it reflects a fear of living with an equal. To support his thesis of women's potential, he cites the training of princesses, their subsequent abilities as rulers, and the effect of this training on their self-esteem:

> Princesses, being more raised above the generality of men by their rank than placed below them by their sex, have never been taught that it was improper for them to concern themselves with politics; but have been allowed to feel the liberal interest natural to any cultivated human being in the great transactions which took place around them, and in which they might be called on to take a part. [1]

The Princess of France is such a woman.

She sets the tone and provides the example for the women who accompany her. As her father's envoy to the court of Navarre, she must negotiate a delicate political solution. But this role as emissary does not compromise her. Nor does it suggest that her father adversely governs her life, as do some of the fathers in Shakespeare's plays. Rather, like the princesses mentioned by Mill, she has gained by this training. Her father has supported her strength and endorsed her as a person. Her language throughout the play and her attitude toward herself and others clearly indicate her independence. The closing scene confirms the portrait when news of her father's death arrives, interrupting the merriment. Politically and economically independent, she is a woman who knows herself.

Her independence and its exhilarating effect on her women have seldom been discussed in criticism. [2] Instead, historical parallels for her, the King of Navarre, Berowne, Dumaine, Longaville, and others have preoccupied critics. The tendency has been to justify her on a historical basis rather than a human one. However, the Princess, whose freedom is unique, expresses ideas common to women but seldom spo-

ken. Samuel Taylor Coleridge, who found traces of Shakespeare's later genius in this early comedy, observed: "True
genius begins by generalizing and condensing; it ends in re-
alizing and expanding."[3] Shakespeare's method for developing the Princess' character reveals this early genius. He
particularizes her trait of honesty; she demands it of herself as
well as others. And he never destroys her self-awareness and
self-identification as a woman.

But the play is seldom seen and the remarkably outspoken Princess infrequently heard. She is the victim of
eighteenth-century editing and of bias against outspoken,
independent women. During its early years, *Love's Labour's
Lost* was performed at court, both Queen Elizabeth's (1597 or
98) and James' in January 1605.[4] Records of performances also
indicate that it appeared "at the Blacke-Friers and the Globe"
sometime before 1631.[5] It was quite popular in Shakespeare's
time, but its subsequent stage history has been bleak. The
promptbooks of the nineteenth century and the one attempt at
converting *Love's Labour's Lost* to an opera in the eighteenth
century provide clues to its infrequent performance. Those
works owe their shape to Alexander Pope, whose edition of
Shakespeare's plays first appeared in 1723. Because of Pope's
fame, his edition had great influence on attitudes toward the
plays and on their form in the theater. Deciding that a passage
was too raucous, outspoken, or imperfectly written, Pope
would move it out of the text and place it in small print at the
bottom of the page. The result in many cases was a divided
page. Because of Pope's skill as a writer, the text at the top
could be read without interruption. One hardly realized what
had happened unless one looked at an asterisk and then
turned to the small type at the bottom. The effect on the play
and on the balance among characters was tremendous. Some
works profited from Pope's insights; others suffered.[6] *Love's
Labour's Lost* was among the latter. It became a thin comedy
whose story line alone survived.

Although most later editors rejected Pope's edition and
his method, the text, printed by the famous J. Tonson, remained in print. In 1773, when David Garrick thought he
would try a production of *Love's Labour's Lost* if it could be
converted to an opera, the adaptor Edward Thompson worked

from a Pope text.[7] In 1839, when Madame Vestris produced
the play, Pope's work still provided the skeletal basis for the
cuts.[8] Vestris herself played Rosaline. The Princess' role was
greatly abbreviated. Lines with sexual connotations as well as
those that establish the Princess as a strong character disappeared.

Samuel Johnson, commenting on the play in his edition
of 1765, indicates the general feeling of the age:

> In this play, which all the editors have concurred to censure,
> and some have rejected as unworthy of our poet, it must be
> confessed that there are many passages mean, childish, and
> vulgar; and some which ought not to have been exhibited, as
> we are told they were, to a *maiden queen*. But there are scattered,
> through the whole, many sparks of genius; nor is there any
> play that has more evident marks of the hand of Shakespeare.[9]
> (italics mine)

As a result of this protective attitude toward women, many of
the lines with sexual connotations, or lines that are direct and
bawdy, were omitted. Unfortunately, many of these lines also
help to establish the character of the Princess as a strong
woman undisturbed by direct language. Three equally self-
assertive women accompany her. Although less clearly defined, they too speak with directness. But the Princess is chief
among them. Controlling both power and wealth, she is sovereign over herself. Original in her thinking, she is unafraid
and undominated. She laughs at the Petrarchan tradition that
dictates praise of a woman's beauty and insists on truth even
in examining her own thoughts. Was she the product of her
age—an age when a maiden queen, fearing no censure of her
laughter, could listen and enjoy the language as well as the
portraits of women in this comedy?

Direct and abrupt, the Princess' opening speeches offer
the first clue to her character. She will insist on honesty, reject
flattery, and dismiss flowery, unsubstantiated words, recognizing their hollowness. She listens to Boyet, the male adviser
accompanying her party, as he praises her many endowments:

> Be now as prodigal of all dear grace
> As Nature was in making graces dear,

> When she did starve the general world beside
> And prodigally gave them all to you.
> (II.i.9–12)

Relying on Petrarchan conceits—mannerisms used in the
poetry of the period—Boyet meets a sharp reprimand. His
speech functions theatrically, triggering a response and offering an incisive character drawing of the Princess:

> Good Lord Boyet, my beauty, though but mean,
> Needs not the painted flourish of your praise:
> Beauty is bought by judgment of the eye.
> (13–15)

Refusing praise that seems unrealistic, she insists that beauty
may be easily observed and does not need words to create
what is not present. This early reference to her own physical
appearance is exploited later in her tests of the honesty of
others. Now she merely mocks Boyet's use of obviously worn
forms of flattery:

> I am less proud to hear you tell my worth
> Than you much willing to be counted wise
> In spending your wit in the praise of mine.
> (17–19)

She fails to convince him. With a last flourish, he leaves as her
emissary to the King: "Proud of employment, willingly I go"
(35). The Princess faults him once more: "All pride is willing
pride, and yours is so" (36). Compared with Navarre, who
was introduced as a man ambitiously seeking eternal fame,
she has been introduced as a woman wary of fame and aware
of the pitfalls of pride.

Shakespeare's technique for revealing her character differs from that used with the men. Berowne attempted to dissuade Navarre from his foolish vow. The Princess is never in
conflict with her women. Rather, the dramatist parades a series of different men from different economic groups before
her. With each she debates the meaning of truth; and each
encounter further reveals her point of view.

Intellectually she resembles Berowne. Like him, she enjoys exploring and exploiting verbal meaning. Like him, she delights in philosophic development of an idea. However, the Princess, even when she tends to hypothesize or, introspectively, analyze her own actions, seldom forsakes reason for peer loyalty. Berowne, despite his brilliant argument against Navarre's academy, ultimately capitulates. The Princess, however, does not yield to the pressures of others.

Virginia Woolf, in *A Room of One's Own*, suggests that a woman of independent income eventually develops an independent perspective. No longer angry or afraid, she can see the defects in the education of men just as she knows that there have been defects in her own education. Woolf describes the healing power of economic freedom and independence:

> Indeed, I thought. . . . I need not hate any man; he cannot hurt me. I need not flatter any man; he has nothing to give me. So imperceptibly I found myself adopting a new attitude towards the other half of the human race. It was absurd to blame any class or any sex, as a whole. . . . Their education had been in some ways as faulty as my own. It had bred in them defects as great.[10]

The Princess of France has this clarity and lack of animosity. When she discovers that she must camp in the park surrounding the court, she accepts and respects the King's orders. She does not, however, accept the wisdom of his choice of life style.

Upon meeting him later in this scene (II.i.), she follows the same pattern of close word analysis that she used with Boyet. To the King's "Fair Princess, welcome to the court of Navarre" (90), she responds by examining every word but "Princess":

> "Fair" I give you back again, and "welcome" I have not yet.
> The roof of this court is too high to be yours, and welcome to
> the wide fields too base to be mine.
>
> (91–94)

Continuing, she explores the meaning of "teach." Although couched in modesty—"To teach a teacher ill beseemeth me"

(108)—her speeches are spattered with words revealing her own intellectual training: "knowledge," "ignorance," and "wise."

Shakespeare includes political as well as social skills in his characterization. She knows her mission and intends to acquire the rights to Aquitaine by proving that her father had returned "The payment of a hundred thousand crowns" (129). Indulgently, the King rehearses the terms, concluding with:

> Dear Princess, were not his requests so far
> From reason's yielding, your fair self should make
> A yielding 'gainst some reason in my breast,
> And go well satisfied to France again.
> (II.i.149–52)

But the Princess knows the background of the agreement. She cites documents that go back to the time of Navarre's father. It is unnecessary to review the terms of the agreement here; it is sufficient to know that the Princess' just grasp of the details of a treaty proves her acumen. She is more than a social creature sent to appease the King through the exercise of charm. She is a competent administrator. Navarre must change his estimate.

This brief encounter with him not only enhances the portrait of the Princess, it also emphasizes the disadvantages she faces because of her sex. Despite her economic and political power, she is reduced to the status of an outsider. The equality that should exist between the men and the women does not. Handicapped, the women rely on honesty to deflate and combat the men. Whereas in Act I rustics, a pedant, and a clown mimic and burlesque the main action, suggesting the folly of the nobles, in Act II the entrance of the women signals the major contrast. Meeting the men in the Park of Navarre, each woman wins a silent admirer. Two—Berowne and the King—attempt light, insincere conversation. Each is rebuffed for dishonesty and superficiality. Conventional forms are laughed at by unconventional, free women.

"You shall be welcome, madam, to my court (II.i.95)," avers the King when he first meets her. "Conduct me thither" (96), responds the Princess. But, because of his oath, he cannot. "Did not I dance with you in Brabant once?" (114) asks

Berowne. "Did not I dance with you in Brabant once?" (115) responds Rosaline. "I know you did," the annoyed Berowne replies (116). "How needless was it then to ask the question" (117). She has forced him to admit the foolishness of conventional patterns of conversation between men and women. She has also pinpointed dishonesty. But some of their conversation falls to the bottom of the page in Pope's and later acting editions.[11] And most of the frank joking among the women after the departure of the men also joins the small print.

Flattery may sometimes defeat honesty just as honesty weakened the men's oath. For women, flattery usually concentrates on physical beauty although, as a recent writer observed, "The average woman—and that means a good 95 percent of them—is not beautiful in the way the culture pretends."[12] A realist, the Princess knows this. At the close of the first scene between the men and the women, Boyet reports to her: "All eyes saw his [Navarre's] eyes enchanted with gazes" (247). But she refuses to be lulled or beguiled by such words. Instead, her physical appearance often provides the test for honesty.

Her drive for forthright appraisal of her not-too-attractive self extends from men of the court to men of another social class. Two opportunities occur in quick succession at the beginning of Act IV: her short interview with the Forester, and her light responses to Costard.[13] In the first, the Forester directs her to an excellent vantage point for shooting deer:

> Hereby, upon the edge of yonder coppice,
> A stand where you may make the fairest shoot.

PRINCESS:

> I thank my beauty, I am fair that shoot,
> And thereupon thou speak'st the fairest shoot.
> (IV.i.9–12)

Once again she picks up the allusion to her appearance, this time creating a difficulty for the Forester by intentionally misreading his line. Unfairly, perhaps, she insists that he choose between honesty and flattery. To his, "Pardon me, madam, for

I meant not so" (13), she quickly acts astonished, "What, what? First praise me, and again say no? / O short-liv'd pride! Not fair? alack for woe!" (14–15). The poor Forester, completely confused, attempts to adopt the proper stance. "Yes, madam, fair" (16), he retracts. But the Princess will not accept his answer:

> Nay, never paint me now;
> Where fair is not, praise cannot mend the brow.
> Here (good my glass), take this for telling true:
> Fair payment for foul words is more than due.
> (16–19)

The Princess has made her point. The way she looked to herself in her "glass" was the standard she would use to test the truth of others' statements. The speech also forms an important link to the beginning of the play. In her reference to "short-liv'd pride" she reminds us of that first scene when Navarre sought to create the "wonder of the world" and dreamed of immortal fame.

But Pope moved most of this exchange and the one that follows to the bottom of the page. And when the play finally arrived on the stage in the mid-nineteenth century, many of these same lines were excised. The major woman's role, instead of belonging to the Princess, went to Rosaline.[14] Because she is paired romantically with Berowne, critics mistakenly consider her his equivalent among the women. Dark-haired, alert, bright, with many of the play's good lines, she nevertheless does not parallel him. Instead, the Princess of France, paired with Navarre romantically, most resembles Berowne. For she is intellectually and verbally the most gifted of the women.

The second example of the Princess relating honesty to a description of her own person occurs in a confrontation with one of the play's rustics. Searching for the proper addressee of a letter, Costard barges onto the scene. When he asks for the "head lady," he learns only that she is the "highest." Unwilling to accept what might be a double meaning, he persists until assured, "The thickest and the tallest" (IV.i.47). "The thickest and the tallest! . . . / Are not you the chief woman?

You are the thickest here" (48–51). For the third time, she has chosen to measure honesty by statements about her physical size. The thickest and the tallest, she is a woman who knows herself not "slimly" but well.

In Costard, the play's Clown, Shakespeare creates a character who tries people's patience. Their varying responses to him offer a measure of their personalities and their self-control. Early in the play, for example, listening to the King's reading of a letter, Costard constantly interrupts. Eventually, Navarre orders, "Peace! . . . No words" (I.i.226, 229). Later, Berowne's outbursts are less restrained. Attempting to retain the Clown's attention, Berowne explodes: "Why, villain, thou must know first" [before you can act] (III.i.159). But this reprimand does not inhibit Costard who, most respectfully, continues on his own tangent. "I will come to your worship tomorrow morning," he promises. Berowne despairs: "It must be done this afternoon. Hark, slave, it is but this" (160–63). Finally, in Act IV, Costard's errors so embarrass Berowne that he swears, "Ah! you whoreson loggerhead, you were born to do me shame" (IV.iii.200), and exclaims, "Will these turtles be gone?" (208).

Compared with the hostility expressed by words like "villain," "slave," "loggerhead," "turtle," and "fool," the Princess' language shows remarkable restraint. Reminding Costard of his errand—the delivery of the letter—she insists he focus on his business, "What's your will, sir? What's your will?" (IV.i.52). Her directions to the Clown illustrate her characteristically tenacious concentration on the business at hand, revealed as early as her first scene when she sent Boyet on his way rather than allowing him time for chatter and flattery. Her equable "sir" indicates her patience and self-control. Nevertheless, when she expresses annoyance with Costard, critics tend to misread her actions. The most recent example is Richard David's comment: "Obviously the Princess is snubbing Costard for his impertinence." David then adds a cryptic reference to an earlier editor, "Furness makes a doubt of it."[15] To understand David, one must turn to the early twentieth-century *Variorum* where Horace Howard Furness asks: "In these words of the Princess may there not be detected an impatient eagerness to cut short Costard's rather uncomplimental refer-

ences to her figure?"[16] What had been quizzical wondering
becomes definite assertion. Was David influenced by Furness?
The critic attributes vanity to the Princess, whereas the text
implies the opposite. David's comment seems to reflect the
editor's bias rather than the dramatist's intention and creates
an unnecessary inconsistency in characterization. Thus may
traditional notions of female behavior inhibit understanding
of one of the women characters. Basically, the exchange with
Costard is the last and most direct indication of the Princess'
seeking honesty in description of her own person.

Shakespeare next develops his portrait on a more complex level, extending the test for honesty from the physical to
the intellectual and the philosophical. And, finally, the value
of Boyet to the Princess becomes apparent. For it is he, not the
Forester, who challenges her statements. And it is he who acts
as a refracting glass for the varied facets of her nature. When,
following her exchange with the Forester, she ruminates on
the vanity of the human quest for fame, Boyet wonders at her
honesty. Speaking of fame, she says:

> As I for praise alone now seek to spill
> The poor deer's blood, that my heart means no ill.
>   (IV.i.34–35)

Boyet, thus far primarily a flatterer, alertly probes her words:

> Do not curst wives hold that self-sovereignty
> Only for praise' sake, when they strive to be
> Lords o'er their lords?
>   (36–38)

I am calling your bluff, he insists. To him, her seeming humility isn't quite sincere. Women too, in a very different context,
seek praise, just as Navarre in Act I hoped for fame and immortality. But women's fame, unfortunately, is built on their
wishing to be "lords o'er their lords."

Again, truth triumphs. The Princess agrees that, yes,
indeed, "praise we may afford / To any lady that subdues a
lord" (39–40). Her answer characterizes a feminist's awareness. She does not smile at his innuendo. Nor does she modestly disagree that women have no aspirations to fame. Aware

of the male world in which she moves—and made more aware by Navarre's foolish vow—she applauds any success, however slight, that women may achieve. The exchange between her and Boyet illustrates the dramatist's remarkable insight into the mind of a woman and his ability to create, as Pope observed, characters as "Individual as those in Life itself."[17] The nuances in this portrait testify to the importance of the Princess as the most fully defined of the woman characters. She is Berowne's intellectual counterpart.

Criticism of the play, however, has overlooked their resemblances. Concentrating on the romantically paired couples, it has lost sight of the variations among the women. Rosaline, because she is linked with Berowne, receives the greatest attention. But Shakespeare has invented two different types of pairing—the intellectual and the romantic. In this play they are not interchangeable. Taking their cue from the world they know, however, the critics acknowledge only the latter. Edward Dowden and H. H. Furness, for example, offer two interpretations. After crediting the women with clearer insight than the men, Dowden writes:

> And yet the Princess, and Rosaline, and Maria, have not the entire advantage on their side. It is well to be practical; but to be practical, and also have a capacity for ideas is better. . . . Berowne is yet a larger nature than the Princess or Rosaline. *His* good sense is the good sense of a thinker and of a man of action. When he is most flouted and bemocked, we yet acknowledge him victorious and master; and Rosaline will confess the fact by and by.[18]

Although Dowden mentions the Princess and Maria, he sees the major pairing as that between Berowne and Rosaline. His "by and by" takes us out of the play and into the world beyond the theater, a world where women do not set the rules. Neither the play's open-ended conclusion nor the Princess' "capacity for ideas" has relevance in such criticism. Dowden responds to the text less as a scholar and more as a man influenced by the contemporary culture.

H. H. Furness also found Berowne superior to Rosaline but arrived at his conclusion by comparing Berowne and Rosaline to other romantic couples in Shakespeare's plays. In that context, Rosaline proves weaker than other women, whereas Berowne proves superior to other men. Through a complex process of analysis and comparison of sets of romantic pairs, the editor conclusively proves Berowne's superiority to Rosaline.[19] But a close study of the text reveals that Berowne's equivalent in strength is not Rosaline—with whom he is romantically coupled—but the Princess of France.

The play continues to explore the relationship between oaths and truth. In Act IV, the first oath is challenged when the men individually—but overheard by one another—sigh for the different women of France: Navarre for the Princess: " 'O queen of queens, how far dost thou excel / No thought can think, nor tongue of mortal tell' " (IV.iii.39–40); Longaville for Maria: "Ay me, I am forsworn!" (45); and Dumaine for "O most divine Kate!" (81).

Berowne's unmasking is more extreme. He is the victim of Costard's inattention to details. The letter meant for Rosaline is misdelivered and falls into Navarre's hands. Read aloud for all to hear, it forces Berowne to acknowledge that his bond with the others has become a broken vow. He then proposes: "Sweet lords, sweet lovers, O, let us embrace!" (IV.iii.210). He forces them to confront the truth, but not for long. They now demand he exercise his rhetorical skill and intellectual ability to "prove / Our loving lawful, and our faith not torn" (280–81). In one of the longest and most magnificent speeches in the play, he convinces them that their former oath—to pursue study and lead the celibate life—was "Flat treason 'gainst the kingly state of youth" (289). Joyously, he weaves supports for his earlier thesis.

So effective is his argument that the men once more turn to oath-taking. They have learned little. Having forsaken one course of action, they swear once more, revealing their inability to temper enthusiasm with reason. Nor has the persistent Navarre, whose extravagant speech characterized the earlier movement of the play, learned to temper optimism with caution. "Saint Cupid, then! and, soldiers, to the field!" (363), he rallies them. To Longaville's query, "shall we resolve to woo these girls of France?" the King, who deals in absolutes, confidently asserts "and win them too" (368–69). He is still a man unaware of the character of the Princess.

Like the first set of vows, the second, although more reasonable, is similarly immoderate. This time the men do not plan seclusion and a life of scholarship, but action on a field of battle—specifically the wooing of the women. The King proposes entertainments. Once again, he moves with extreme self-confidence. Not scholars in a study, they are to be soldiers in the field. They have shifted from the introverted to the extroverted life. Nevertheless, once again their goal is total victory and therefore unbalanced: not fame on their gravestones, but success in the Park of Navarre. It is they, not the women, who first invent the games to be played, the tricks to be practiced in a masquerade. Their masculine egos in command, all but Berowne assume victory. He alone is skeptical:

> Light wenches may prove plagues to men forsworn;
> If so, our copper buys no better treasure.
>
> (IV.iii.382–83)

The text's lines, although consistent in their definition of character, prove a problem for Richard David, who comments: "Berowne's note of warning here comes in rather inharmoniously after his magnificent address of loyalty to Love."[20] But Berowne's verbal pyrotechnics have little to do with his underlying beliefs, as was evident in the first scene. His major role is as spokesman for the men, being the most brilliant and poetic among them. Actually the speech indicates that at least one of the men of Navarre's court has an understanding of the dignity and individuality of the women whom they plan to woo.

Resembling the Princess, the women express both their approval of the men and their skepticism about the male dedication to a cause—whether "academe" or women. "O that I knew he were but in by th' week!" (V.ii.61), exclaims Rosaline of Berowne.

> A huge translation of hypocrisy,
> Vildly compiled, profound simplicity[21]
>
> (51–52)

is Katherine's evaluation of the verses of Dumaine while Maria expresses her doubts by desiring that the pearls sent by Longaville be longer and the letter shorter. Her comment, too, is relevant. Deriding the "fool'ry in the wise" (76) as an attempt "to prove, by wit, worth in simplicity" (78), she is expressing what the audience felt at the close of Act IV when listening to the men's rather simplistic approach to wooing.

Having sent gifts and flowery words to the women, the men expect easy acceptance. Instead, convention is once again challenged. The men, having decided to mask as Muscovites, encounter masked women. Masks meet masks. Truth, like the true identity of the women, is not easily uncovered. The wooers must rely on external symbols of the women behind the masks. But the women have exchanged gifts with one another. Again the men take oaths to convince the women as well as themselves of their serious intent. Each man pledges undying love to a masked symbol.

The dramatist once again suggests the weakness of oaths as proof of conviction. For the men have wooed the wrong masked women. "The King is my love sworn," exclaims Rosaline who had posed as the Princess (V.ii.282). "And quick Berowne hath plighted faith to me" (283), returns the Princess. Although the women graciously admit, "There's no such sport as sport by sport o'erthrown" (153), the scene furnishes another example of the danger of swearing, and prepares the way for the final exchange.

In the scene of reconciliation after the Muscovite adventure, Berowne faces his most difficult moment in the play. For he is uncertain whether to reply in words and fancy phrases or whether, in the method of the women, to resort to honesty. To Rosaline's challenge, "Which of the vizards was it that you wore?" (385), Berowne retorts with questions. "Where? when? what vizard? why demand you this?" (386). He begins to close the plot's circle.

"Necessity will make us all forsworn / Three thousand times within this three years' space" (I.i.149–150), he had said in Act I after joining the others in oath. In Act V, he merely laments: "Thus pour the stars down plagues for perjury" (V.ii.394). Doubly perjured, in fact, are the men: first, for having forsworn their original oath; second, for having pretended no knowledge of the Muscovites. And they will be further perjured before the comedy ends. For oath-taking is a habit difficult to break.

The oath-maker confronts the truth-sayer in Act V. Navarre still believes in his invulnerability. To the Princess' warning, "When she shall challenge this [your overture], you will reject her" (V.ii.438), the King swiftly answers with an oath, "Upon mine honor, no" (439). His self-confidence persists. Not daunted by her "Peace, peace, forbear: / Your oath once broke, you force not to forswear" (439–40), he continues to consider himself wiser than the woman who warns him. With bravura, he exclaims, "Despise me when I break this oath of mine" (441). "I will" (442), she answers simply. When the plot unfolds, the revelation of the exchange of tokens leads to yet another forswearing. The Princess' warnings anticipate her closing words of rejection: "No, no, my lord, your Grace is perjur'd much, . . . / Your oath I will not trust" (790, 794).

What type of character is the King, and what leads him to these excessive displays? We know that he is interested in fame in the present as well as the future, fame that will survive the grave. Moreover, he is at the opening of the drama fairly certain that he can achieve this fame through dedication to study. We also learn from Boyet very early in the comedy that Navarre is a man of great reputation. Later, in the King's opening encounter with the Princess, we note his self-confidence, his certainty that he, rather than she, knows the proper path for the man of wisdom. Countering her criticism of his actions with questions of a political nature, he challenges her in the area where, supposedly, he is the wiser. Nevertheless, his wisdom lacks sensitivity and intellectual depth.

In the last scene, the dramatist draws together the two strands—oath-taking and truth-telling—that weave through this comedy. The news of the death of the King of France is a clever device for joining these elements. Once again, Navarre functions as antagonist, providing the background against which the Princess' varied talents sparkle. While she is thinking of her father and of returning to her kingdom, the King is thinking of himself. To her declaration, "I will away to-night," he responds, "I do beseech you stay" (V.ii.727–28). But he goes beyond that. He makes an offer of marriage that she doesn't understand:

> And though the mourning brow of progeny
> Forbid the smiling courtesy of love

> The holy suit which fain it would convince,
> Yet since love's argument was first on foot,
> Let not the cloud of sorrow justle it
> From what it purpos'd; since to wail friends lost
> Is not by much so wholesome-profitable
> As to rejoice at friends but newly found.
>
> (744–51)

Navarre's speech reveals an awareness of the tenuous relationship between them while at the same time minimizing, and thus distorting, the closeness of the ties between father and daughter. The dramatist cunningly gives lines to Navarre that establish a semantic parallel that does not exist, thereby emphasizing the intellectual ineptness of the King and the superiority of the Princess. She, on the other hand, unable to believe that a proposal of marriage could occur at this moment, thinks that she has suddenly lost her ability to comprehend subtle verbal meanings. For a person who has treasured her intellectual agility, this is a double blow. Not only is she bereft of father, but also of wit. "I understand you not, my griefs are double" (752), she admits.

Her intellectual counterpart, Berowne, then steps in, suggesting that "honest plain words best pierce the ear of grief" (V.ii.753). Because this second parallel has seldom been recognized by critics, Berowne's sudden intervention has been questioned. Samuel Johnson believed that the speech was "given to a wrong person."[22] Johnson suggests giving the first line (752) to the Princess; the next several, beginning "And by these badges," to the King. But Shakespeare's distribution of these lines supports the methods he has developed throughout the comedy of contrast, comparison, and parallelism to help define the portrait of the Princess.

When she does understand Navarre's meaning, she brings those two faculties—a keen mind and a desire for honest words—to her speech:

> We have receiv'd your letters full of love;
>
> . . . . .
>
> . . . rated them
> At courtship, pleasant jest, and courtesy,
>
> . . . . .

But more devout than this in our respects
Have we not been.
                                        (V.ii.777–83)

Thus does she evaluate the antics they have enjoyed. She then moves to the more complex question of oaths. Unlike Berowne who, though intellectually aware of the folly of Navarre's plot, had allowed peer pressure to override reason, the Princess remains true to her intellectual self. To the King's "Now at the latest minute of the hour, / Grant us your loves" (787–88), she responds:

A time methinks too short
To make a world-without-end bargain in.
                                        (788–89)

And she suggests that he not perjure himself again. Evaluating the type of oath now being asked of her, she knows that it requires more than a moment's consideration.

If Shakespeare was unsuccessful in retaining the comic tone, as some critics have argued, he was remarkably successful in creating, although in sketch form, the portrait of an independent woman. Writing at a time when new perceptions of women were challenging the old, the dramatist molded a character who was individual, one who drew her strength from understanding herself—a woman functioning in a man's world and questioning that world's values.[23]

In a play where vows are made and broken, Shakespeare questions this approach to swearing by introducing the vow of marriage at a serious moment in the action. Marriage is a vow whose implication women know. It will inhibit their independence; it will tie them forever. "A world-without-end bargain" implies a sense of eternity, that which the King, in the first scene, had craved through learning. The phrase has a grandeur beyond the confines of the comic world. If such bargains are not to be broken, by brilliant talk, ingenious reasoning, and clever turns of phrase, new rules for oath-taking must be found.

Truth, vows, and eternity coalesce in the comedy's last moments. Ending as it does with "Jack hath not Jill," but with the promise of reconsiderations of the men's proposals a year later, the play asks for new attitudes toward women. It suggests seeing them as full, complex individual characters. Although a romantic comedy, the play is an exploration of the meaning of words as a key to perceiving truth, particularly those words—swear and oath—which often govern our future lives.

Lynn Fontanne and Alfred Lunt are seen above as Kate and
Petruchio moments after their wedding, in the Theatre Guild
production of 1935 in New York. VANDAMM COLLECTION, THE NEW
YORK PUBLIC LIBRARY

CHAPTER THREE

Challenging Patterns

THE TAMING OF THE SHREW

"Even as a flatt'ring dream"
(Induction.i.44)

Challenging the interpretation of his title, Shakespeare tosses a mass of seemingly contradictory material at his audience and readers. He offers contrasts between Petruchio's bravado words and his sensitive actions; between wife-taming and fantasies of taming; and between two daughters of a merchandizing father—Katherina and Bianca. But theater audiences are not always made aware of these contrasts. For one thing, "Directors of *The Taming of the Shrew* corrupt its meaning when they bring Petruchio on stage cracking a whip."[1] In their interpretations, he remains a fairly one-dimensional character. Nor do audiences usually see the play's Induction, where Christopher Sly, a drunken tinker, is thrown out of an alehouse by a woman and then later watches the main comedy. Is Sly a spectator at this play? Why then does he fail to reappear at the end? His absence raises unresolved questions. Finally, the last speech of Katherina's—forty-four lines of seeming submission eventually halted by Petruchio—is so extravagantly long that it is usually abbreviated and, as a result, its irony dissipated. Worse still, for over a century—from the time of David Garrick's version in 1756—the speech was divided between Katherina and Petruchio, allowing him to dictate the proper behavior of a wife. Instead of revealing the irony inherent in the text, the speech became weighted with a moral message.

Cultural attitudes toward women in the larger society outside the theater helped shape productions of the play. Shakespeare's text was altered and trimmed to meet current ideas. How much more comfortable to present a scheming woman who, in soliloquy, vows:

> Look to your seat, Petruchio, or I throw you.
> Cath'rine shall tame this Haggard;—or, if she fails,
> Shall tye her Tongue up, and pare down her Nails.[2]

The lines are Garrick's. Shakespeare's Kate has no soliloquies —she reveals herself through her actions and speeches. Much remains ambiguous; we know only what the characters in the play know about her. How much simpler to pass judgment on Garrick's Kate, a woman who confides her inner motivation —revenge—to the audience. We enjoy seeing her tamed. It appeals to our sense of justice. Unfortunately, she conforms to contemporary concepts of woman as the schemer who needs the direction of a strong man. Shakespeare's Kate is more complex. One is less certain of the writer's intention.

George Meredith observes that the comic poet thrives best in a period of social equality of the sexes.[3] Did women have greater equality when Elizabeth sat on the English throne? Looking back to that age from the perspective of only fifty years, Anne Bradstreet, one of the first American poets, could write in 1650:

> Let such as say our sex is void of reason,
> Know 'tis a slander now but once was treason.[4]

Thus Bradstreet defines Elizabeth's impact on law. Surely having a queen as monarch must have tempered male theories about female inferiority, explaining some of the ambiguity in this play. Historians offer similar conflicting evidence about the period. The eminent scholar, Lawrence Stone, is one such historian. His recent book, *The Family, Sex and Marriage in*

England 1500–1800, provides much new information and suggests the range of ideas that persisted at the time. Writing of forced marriages such as those that face Katherina and Bianca, Stone tells of a father who tied his daughter to the bedpost because she protested marrying a mentally retarded man. But since the groom's political connections would benefit her father, the daughter was forced to consent.[5] On the other hand, Stone also quotes the new attitudes toward marriage propounded by the church: the aim was a union " 'with good consent of them both, to the end that they may dwell together in friendship and honesty' "—a marriage whose purpose was "spiritual intimacy."[6]

Shakespeare throws both ideas out to the audience: Baptista auctions his younger daughter to the highest bidder and marries his elder daughter to an unknown, seemingly wild bridegroom. But the younger daughter, Bianca, by tricking her father, marries the man of her choice, thus entering a marriage based on "good consent of both" partners. Kate and Petruchio, despite the terms of the marriage, seem to achieve "spiritual intimacy."

Critics disagree about the source of that "spiritual intimacy." Is it the result of Kate's submission to Petruchio's will, or does it grow from the mutual respect of two unconventional characters? Some consider the play misogynistic; others hear the words of the independent woman in Kate's language. But words alone do not establish a play's meaning. As the contemporary critic, Irving Ribner, reminds us, although Shakespeare's comedies express moral attitudes, these attitudes are to be found not in the didactic speeches of the characters but in the "larger dramatic context."[7] In this play on wooing and marriage, the comment by Petruchio's servant about "continency" in the bridal chamber on the wedding night has reverberations too frequently overlooked. The passage, more fully explored later in this chapter, offers insights into Petruchio's character and sets the stage for Katherina's appreciation of the man to whom she is married. It suggests the dramatist's sensitivity to those elements that contribute to mutuality in a relationship between a man and a woman and provides a valuable clue to the "larger dramatic context."

The critic must be wary—discarding, if he can, the

impressions that the acted performance has had on his uncon-
scious evaluation of the characters. He must recognize the un-
conventionality of the marriage of Kate and Petruchio—or, at
least, Shakespeare's unstereotyped understanding of a
woman's response to marriage to a wild, strange man. The
critic will also have to rise above the smug male assumptions
of a woman's expectations on the wedding night. He might
even do well to listen to John Stuart Mill who wrote:

> I am far from pretending that wives are in general no better
> treated than slaves; but no slave is a slave to the same lengths,
> and in so full a sense of the word, as a wife is. . . . [A wife
> cannot refuse her husband sexual familiarity] however brutal a
> tyrant she may unfortunately be chained to—though she may
> know that he hates her, though it may be his daily pleasure to
> torture her, and though she may feel it impossible not to loathe
> him—he can claim from her and enforce the lowest degradation
> of a human being, that of being made the instrument of an
> animal function contrary to her inclinations.[8]

Although critics may accept the fact that Petruchio did
not consummate the marriage on that first night, they have
failed to appreciate the deeper implications of such a post-
ponement for a woman. Finding parallels with the wooing
dance in folk literature, one critic writes:

> Shakespeare is very careful not to have Petruchio wrest conjugal
> rights from an unwilling bride, as one suspects the authors of
> some of the analogues would cheerfully have permitted.[9]

Michael West, then, interprets the meaning of this action as a
"teasing of Katherine," a withholding of her rights, for he
continues: "Kate must learn to behave in a way that will allow
the sexual act to take place properly."[10] This critic appears to
be unaware of the "degradation" to which Mill refers. Writing
in an age when forced marriages, arranged for economic reasons, were being questioned, and when a virgin queen, who
retained control over her physical person, ruled the country,
Shakespeare was more sensitive than his interpreters have
been to the reactions of a woman at such a moment.

Jessie Bernard, a sociologist who writes of marriage today, also refers to the folk tradition, noting that "the 'rape' of the bride on the honeymoon used to be a common folk stereotype." But Bernard's interpretation differs from West's. She not only believes that this practice survives, but that it is among "the shocks to which marriage subjects women."[11] To overlook or to minimize the obvious sexual method of taming or "training" a wife is to miss part of what the play is saying. Petruchio's respect for Kate's right to ownership of her body, while it may take time for her to appreciate, eventually becomes an important key to their relationship.

The lines that lead to this conclusion are spoken moments after Petruchio, having thrown the food to the floor, and threatened the servants, announces to his bride who is cold, tired, and starving: "Come, I will bring thee to thy bridal chamber" (IV.i.178). Immediately following the exit of Kate and her mad spouse, his servant Grumio turns to a fellow servant and asks: "Where is he?" (181). The other replies:

> In her chamber, making a sermon of continency to her,
> And rails, and swears, and rates, that she, poor soul,
> Knows not which way to stand, to look, to speak,
> And sits as one new risen from a dream.
>
> (182–86)

"Continency" in Shakespeare's time had several meanings. It included a suggestion of sexual abstinence, but it also meant restraint, as it does now. Thus the subject of the lecture is in conflict with the apparent behavior of the groom, for Petruchio acts with noise and shouting. However, the more relevant meaning of continency—chastity—is reinforced by the description of Kate moving around the room. We can visualize an independent, if distraught, person, not knowing "which way to stand, to look, to speak." No hint exists of any sexual intimacy between husband and wife.

Thomas De Quincey's thoughtful essay "On the Knocking on the Gate in *Macbeth*" analyzes a series of reactions that Shakespeare sets in motion in his audience. The critic discusses the effect of the juxtaposition of the knocking with the murder that occurs only moments earlier. He believes that the contrast Shakespeare establishes between the characters' contact with and distancing from humanity has reverberations that govern our enjoyment of the play. In *The Taming of the Shrew* the servant's report of the wedding night must also affect our responses to the play. Perhaps the lines also say different things to men and women. This may explain why women as well as men can enjoy the comedy, finding in it neither degradation nor any real signs of submission. Although in soliloquy moments later, Petruchio compares taming a woman to training a hawk—using an analogy from falconry—his actions in this scene are more relevant than his words, for he often speaks in contradictions. The last of the major characters to appear, he lunges onto the stage, vibrant, alive, and testy, ordering his servant Grumio:

PETRUCHIO: Here, sirrah Grumio, knock, I say.
GRUMIO: Knock, sir? whom should I knock? Is there any man
           has rebus'd your worship?
PETRUCHIO: Villain, I say, knock me here soundly.
GRUMIO: Knock you here, sir? Why, sir, what am I, sir, that I
           should knock you here, sir?

                                                   (I.ii.5–10)

Both men know that Petruchio wants him to knock on the gate of a friend's house. But the opportunity to play with words is too much to resist. They delight in puns and in extended misunderstanding of the most direct language. The unbending nature of Petruchio, as he refuses to clarify his meaning, and of Grumio, who refuses to concede until physically battered by his master, suggests the relationship between them—one of mutual enjoyment in words, of robustness, and of horseplay.

     Offering a perfect foil for Petruchio and his servant are Lucentio and his servant. Both masters become the successful suitors of the two sisters: Lucentio winning Bianca; Petruchio winning Kate. Again Shakespeare relies on contrast. Arriving in Padua moments before Petruchio, Lucentio confides his aim to his servant:

             . . . for the time I study,
           Virtue and that part of philosophy

> Will I apply that treats of happiness
> By virtue specially to be achiev'd.
> (I.i.17–20)

Wordy, pretentious, and naive, he resembles Navarre, but without the latter's arrogance or poetic ability. Moments later, the vision of Bianca, pursued by two suitors, alters his objective, sending Lucentio into another passionate outburst:

> . . . in plainness [I] do confess to thee,
> That art to me as secret and as dear
> As Anna to the Queen of Carthage was:
> Tranio, I burn, I pine, I perish, Tranio,
> If I achieve not this young modest girl.
> (152–56)

His quick shift from the pursuit of virtue to the pursuit of Bianca, the marvelously alliterative line, "I burn, I pine, I perish"—with its mockery of the conventions of love poetry—contrasts with the pragmatism and single-mindedness of Petruchio. "What happy gale / Blows you to Padua?" (I.ii.48–49), his friend Hortensio queries. With far less rhetoric than Lucentio, Petruchio answers, "to wive and thrive as best I may" (56). He knows his objective and states it clearly. This is the other side of Petruchio—the man who speaks with directness and honesty.

Samuel Johnson describes *The Taming of the Shrew* as a work in which the "two plots are so well united, that they can hardly be called two without injury to the art with which they are interwoven." He continues, "The attention is entertained with all the variety of a double plot, yet is not distracted by unconnected incidents." [12] Hortensio is one of many characters who help interweave the plots. A friend of Petruchio, he is also an ardent suitor of Bianca. Shortly before Petruchio's arrival, we have heard Baptista present an ultimatum to Bianca's suitors:

> . . . importune me no farther,
> For how I firmly am resolv'd you know:

> That is, not to bestow my youngest daughter
> Before I have a husband for the elder.
> If either of you both love Katherina,
> .   .   .
> Leave shall you have to court her at your pleasure.
> (I.i.48–54)

"To cart her rather" (55) is the swift response. Before Kate has uttered a word, she is exposed to her father's offensive auctioning of his daughter and to the taunting rejection by the suitor. Nevertheless, for someone described as a shrew, she is remarkably calm.

> I pray you, sir, is it your will
> To make a stale of me amongst these mates?
> (57–58)

Rationally, she wonders why her father should thus demean her. Bianca, on the other hand, is far more gently treated. Having denied the suitors' request, Baptista apologizes to her, "good Bianca, / . . . I will love thee ne'er the less" (76–77), he assures her. Kate listens. Again her father shows little affection when he dismisses her with: "Katherina, you may stay, / For I have more to commune with Bianca" (100–1). Feeling discarded and hurt, Kate responds:

> Why, and I trust I may go too, may I not?
> What, shall I be appointed hours, as though (belike)
> I knew not what to take and what to leave? Ha!
> (102–4)

Critics have variously interpreted this scene. Some have recognized the father's favoritism for his younger daughter. Others, like Robert Heilman, have chosen to interpret Katherina and Petruchio as characters in farce and therefore to dismiss this first abrupt definition of Kate's character. Heilman also turns to science to support his point of view:

Though modern, the argument that we see in her the result of paternal unkindness is not impressive. For one thing, some recent research on infants—if we may risk applying heavy science to light farce—suggests that basic personality traits precede, and perhaps influence, parental attitudes to children.[13]

Earlier in this chapter I mentioned the popular version of *The Taming of the Shrew* that dominated the stage from 1756 to 1886: David Garrick's *Catharine and Petruchio*. It continues to influence theatrical productions. Garrick omits the early scene in which Kate is contrasted with her sister, in which a father's preferences are obvious, and in which Kate exhibits no shrewish behavior but rather reveals an intellectual vigor. Her lines are bright, quick, and courageous. Bianca's are flat, dull, and coquettish. Presented as a rational woman, clearly the unfavored daughter of a merchandizing father and the unloved sister of a conventional conformist, Katherina evokes our sympathy. Garrick never presents this portrait. And even Daly, who in 1887 revived the full-length play, fails to include Katherina's speech expressing hurt and dismay at her father's seeming rejection of her. Audiences continued to see a play that weighted the evidence against her.

Since Kate later breaks a lute on the head of the music master and ties her sister's hands, demanding an answer to a never clearly defined question, we may wonder at Shakespeare's creation of this earlier scene (I.i.); or, conversely, at his withholding an exhibition of Kate's shrewish behavior until Act II. However, this is part of the larger design. For Shakespeare, whose play is called *The Taming of the Shrew*, must offer a surface exhibition of shrewish behavior if he is to challenge its meaning. He must also define a shrew. In the Renaissance such definition was easy. A standard pattern existed. The blonde, fair, beautiful woman was considered the ideal and, because outer beauty was believed to reflect inner beauty, she was also believed to be the woman of greatest worth. In contrast to her was the dark, caustic-tongued, less "pretty" woman, often characterized as the shrew. Shakespeare creates surface portraits of these two women: the blonde Bianca, whose name—"white" and "fair" in Italian—

Taming of the Shrew;

OR, KATHARINE AND PETRUCHIO.

Petruchio. There, take it to you, trenchers, cups and all.

Act II. Scene 2.

Petruchio rages at his servants in this frontispiece for an 1838 edition of the popular Kemble-Garrick version of the play. FOLGER SHAKESPEARE LIBRARY

reinforces the idea of purity, and the dark Katherina. However, even here, paradoxes prevail. For Katherine means "white" and "pure" in Greek.[14] And, although Shakespeare endows her with the outer characteristics of a shrew, he reveals her worth, forcing his audience to question the Renaissance formula of worth being equivalent to beauty.

Constructing his play like a tightly woven tapestry, the dramatist insists that we consider Kate always in relation to Bianca. Although she has only 3 percent to Kate's more than 9 percent of the speeches, Bianca is vital to our understanding of her sister. The contrast between them exists not merely at the superficial level of external beauty, but in more complicated and varied ways. For example, by presenting the types of suitors Bianca attracts, the dramatist defines Kate. Bianca's suitors prefer the compliant woman to the defiant one who seeks to preserve her individuality. Again, when Baptista tells us that Bianca loves to learn music and poetry, we must expect Kate to hate studying these subjects. As we shall see later, the question is whether or not Bianca really loves learning or whether Kate's honest, if too vehement, response also contrasts with Bianca's dissembling.

Nor can we look at Kate as a single phenomenon in Shakespeare's creative art. Among her kinfolk are the Princess of France, discussed in the preceding chapter, Beatrice of *Much Ado About Nothing*, and Paulina, that older woman who defies conventions in *The Winter's Tale*. In fact, Beatrice is frequently considered Shakespeare's modified portrait of Kate without the horseplay or the farce. And here is a further cue to her behavior: the nature of this comedy. Although an early work, it reveals a skilled theatrical craftsman. As Anne Barton, the contemporary critic, observes in her introduction to the *Riverside* text of the play, "There are undeniable elements of farce in the Katherina/Petruchio plot . . . which Shakespeare does, at moments in the play, exploit for its own, eminently theatrical, sake."[15]

Withholding evidence of Kate's shrewish behavior until Act II permits the dramatist time to establish a first sympathetic glance at her and begin a more than superficial portrait. But he must also inject characteristics of the shrew. This occurs only after Petruchio's entrance. Her behavior must match his.

For in that first scene, he had announced his aim: "To wive and thrive as best I may" (56), or, as the twentieth-century musical version paraphrases it:

> . . . to wive it wealthily in Padua—
> If wealthily, then happily in Padua.[16]

At that time, Petruchio's friend, Hortensio, could not resist suggesting Kate. But little evidence existed of her shrewishness. Thus far, she had been merely outspoken, a characteristic of the less than perfect woman, but hardly a match for the mercenary, ambitious Petruchio. Had she been maligned by a man intent on wedding Bianca?

In that early scene, Hortensio, responding to Petruchio's claim, lured him with the bait. Relying on effective literary, psychological, and theatrical devices, Hortensio hoped to convince this newcomer to woo and wed the elder sister. Hortensio's methods anticipate the far less amusing hints and innuendos by which Iago ensnares Othello—the half sentence, the withdrawal of the idea, and the enticing suggestion of an unexpressed thought:

> Petruchio, shall I . . . come roundly to thee,
> And wish thee to a shrewd ill-favor'd wife?
> · · ·
> . . . she shall be rich,
> And very rich. But th' art too much my friend,
> And I'll not wish thee to her.
> (I.ii.59–64)

Hortensio's technique, old as it is, works. Reinforcing the theme, Grumio then boasts of his master. "Marry him to a puppet or an aglet-baby, or an old trot with ne'er a tooth in her head" (78–80) he suggests, assuring them that Petruchio will handle the situation and accept the challenge. The portrait is not flattering. Money dominates the play; acquisitiveness motivates the action. But the servant's reliability is already questionable and his extravagance with language known.

In the ensuing conversation between Hortensio and Petruchio, we hear the kind of boastful bravado so frequently exhibited by young men seeking to impress their friends:

> Tell me her father's name, and 'tis enough;
> For I will board her, though she chide as loud
> As thunder when the clouds in autumn crack.
>   (I.ii.94–96)

Sexual domination as well as economic ambition are coupled. This is the portrait of an insensitive male who will tame a woman. Grumio again assures us of his master's prowess: "I'll tell you what, sir, and she stand him but a little, he will throw a figure in her face, and so disfigure her with it, that she shall have no more eyes to see withal than a cat" (112–15). By his own admission as well as the testimony of his servant, Petruchio is an unattractive, mercenary bully who enjoys practical jokes. But the question of contradictory evidence enters. How much of all this is true? How much is bravado? We have already watched the high jinks between Grumio and Petruchio. We listen now, aware of Grumio's tendency to exaggerate or misstate, imitating his master.

Shakespeare now must either create a woman to match the suitor, or modify the portrait. He does both. In the next scene we meet a truly shrewish Kate. We also hear Petruchio in soliloquy alter his stance. But a more far-reaching effect is achieved by the stage performance. Just as Garrick deducted the more favorable aspects of Katherina, he also eliminated the more extended portrait of the mercenary, bullying Petruchio. Many of the lines quoted immediately above have seldom been heard in the theater.

Presented thus far as an intelligent woman, if a maverick, Kate seems unfairly matched. To balance Petruchio's materialism, she must also become unattractive to the audience. She does. The second act opens with Bianca, her hands tied by her sister, refusing to answer Kate's questions and virtuously protesting that she knows well her "duty" to her elders (II.i.7). The subject of their debate is never really clarified; it remains ambiguous. One does, however, learn that Bianca favors neither Hortensio nor Gremio, the suitors of the first act. After this bit of violence, Kate next sends Hortensio, disguised as a music master, flying, having broken his lute over his head. Hortensio himself explains the reason for the breaking of the lute. Again we listen to Shakespeare's delight in puns:

> . . . she hath broke the lute to me.
> I did but tell her she mistook her frets,
> And bow'd her hand to teach her fingering;
> When, with a most impatient devilish spirit,
> "Frets, call you these?" quoth she, "I'll fume with them."
> (II.i.148–52)

The pun on the word "frets" is particularly appropriate here. Probably Hortensio, disguised as a music master, knew how provocative his words would be although he failed to anticipate the directness and violence of Kate's reaction.[17]

Petruchio and Kate are now well matched. Both have temporarily lost audience sympathy. Further balancing her tempestuous behavior is Petruchio's extensive bargaining for a healthy dowry, should he "win Kate's love." Boasting of his methods, he assures Baptista—this time less explicitly in sexual terms—that:

> Though little fire grows great with little wind,
> Yet extreme gusts will blow out fire and all;
> So I to her, and so she yields to me,
> For I am rough, and woo not like a babe.
> (II.i.134–37)

Unlike the earlier material, this scene of the violent, angry Kate is never omitted from stage versions. And while Petruchio's bargaining for the best settlement is also retained, Garrick and later adaptors omit the more extensive discussion of money and taming included by Shakespeare. The portrait of Petruchio is tempered.

Culminating in the wooing of Katherina, the scene introduces another element to this close interweaving of plots. Again Shakespeare develops the contrast between the sisters. For if Petruchio is to be himself and rely on verbal deception—

Say that she rail, why then I'll tell her plain
She sings as sweetly as a nightingale;
$$(II.i.170–71)$$

—Bianca's suitors consistently rely on disguise. Hortensio's skull may be slightly cracked, but it is not as Hortensio that he protests the offense. It is as Litio.

Petruchio's wooing of Katherina is a contest of wits. Alive, bright, shot through with double entendre, it establishes the relationship between them. Because, however, of the intense punning and quibbling that illuminate it, the scene failed to meet the standards of propriety demanded by eighteenth-century, as well as later, audiences.[18] Omitted are the quibbles on "women are made to bear," on "buzzards" and "turtles," on "the wasp's sting," and on "cocks" and "coxcombs." The swift retorts that Petruchio and Katherina throw at one another and the attempt of each to shock by using earthy language set these two characters apart as worthy foils for one another and demonstrate the intelligence and quick wit of Katherina.

The scene also indicates the contradictions between Petruchio's words and his actions. Having boasted to Baptista that he would meet fire with fire and having been touted by Grumio as a man who could be violent to anyone, Petruchio in the wooing scene hardly matches his reputation. For example, he taunts Kate in the following conversation—one omitted by Garrick, Kemble, Daly and most others, including the 1937 CBS radio adaptor: [19]

KATE: If I be waspish, best beware my sting.
PETRUCHIO: My remedy is then to pluck it out.
KATE: Ay, if the fool could find it where it lies.
PETRUCHIO: Who knows not where a wasp does wear his sting? In his tail.
KATE: In his tongue.
PETRUCHIO: Whose tongue?
KATE: Yours, if you talk of tales, and so farewell.
PETRUCHIO: What, with my tongue in your tail? Nay, come again, Good Kate; I am a gentleman—
KATE: That I'll try.
She strikes him.
$$(II.i.210–19)$$

The last line, a stage direction, was not inserted by later editors, but appears in the Folio. The line that follows confirms the action: "I swear I'll cuff you, if you strike again" (220), says Petruchio. She, not he, has done the striking. Although his words are sharp, his actions, in the wooing scene, are not. But this contradiction is usually lost in the theater.

In criticism, too, the interest is in Petruchio's language of assault rather than in his action. Concentrating on the double entendre and the sexual connotations, William J. Martz, in a recent book, writes of this exchange between Kate and Petruchio: "Petruchio, as if imagining them married, offers mock astonishment that she would thus interrupt the love play of the sex act. 'Come again' surely refers to a sexual climax, and it is implied that Kate's capacity for sexual enjoyment is what makes her 'good.' "[20] Continuing in this vein, Martz discusses at length the meaning of "come" and overlooks the action in the scene.

Since we are less shocked by the impropriety of Shakespeare's language today, many of these lines, so long excised, may be heard again. In Joseph Papp's recent production of the New York Shakespeare Festival at the Delacorte Theater in Central Park (1978), the entire text was retained.[21] But again the emphasis of the play was skewed because of additional action not mentioned in the text. In that production of the wooing scene, Petruchio grabbed Kate and wrestled her. He used his strength to dominate her physically and, finally, resorted to tickling her foot. All of this is additional. Because the line "I'll cuff you, if you strike again" (220) provides some insight into Petruchio's character, suggesting his restraint from physical violence, both the reading that overlooks the line and the action that negates it violate the text.

The scene itself is most illuminating because it provides a glimpse of the intellectual range of Katherina's mind. In this primarily verbal battle between them, she shifts from one strategy to another—from the bright quip, the rapier thrust attack, to the sudden straight query: "Where did you study all this goodly speech?" (262). Has Petruchio momentarily intrigued her? Perhaps. But he is not to be trapped into a simple answer. Evaluating the power of the opposition, he continues to taunt. When, finally, he breaks the news to Kate that "will you, nill you, I will marry you" (271), Shakespeare allows her no time to answer. The entrance of Baptista concludes the interview.

What will be the outcome of this marriage that a father has arranged for his daughter with a total stranger? Katherina's question to Baptista is legitimate. Confusedly she pleads:

> Call you me daughter? Now I promise you
> You have show'd a tender fatherly regard,
> To wish me wed to one half lunatic,
> A madcap ruffian and a swearing Jack,
> That thinks with oaths to face the matter out.
> (II.i.285–89)

No shouting shrew, but a rational, observant woman speaks here. In the triangle of father, daughter, and suitor, Katherina's position is both frightening and helpless. Baptista allows Kate no options. "Baptista, if taken seriously, emerges as a vicious and monstrous father figure whose perverted actions have precipitated his daughter's neurosis," writes another contemporary critic, Larry Champion.[22] Because this is a comedy, Champion's intense language is misleading. We do take the characters seriously. They help to define one another and indicate the message, if any, of the title. Like the negative areas in a painting, Baptista, as well as Bianca, offers a contrast to Katherina, helping to define her as a potentially three-dimensional character, the yellows, oranges, and reds of her portrait, contrasting with the blues, greens, and purples of the background.

In Shakespeare's play Kate is handled like "chattel and goods" long before Petruchio voices this conclusion. In Garrick's and subsequent versions, a different emphasis emerges. Although Baptista warns Kate, "Better this Jack than starve, and that's your Portion," he does allow her an opportunity to refuse. "What dost thou say, my Catharine? Give thy Hand," he asks a second time. "Here 'tis, and let him take it, an' he dare," she challenges Petruchio.[23] As her previously cited soliloquy discloses, her aim is revenge. In this version, the businesslike attitude of the father is subordinate to the viciousness of the daughter. The onus is hers alone. Bianca is married before the play begins.

Shakespeare contrasts the sisters and their suitors.

Whereas Kate is fated to marry the man of her father's choice, Bianca makes her own decision, outwitting her father. The contradictions that keynote this play and challenge easy understanding of its theme surface here. Perhaps nowhere is the distortion resulting from the omission of the second plot more evident. In the courting of Bianca deception dominates. The identity of the suitors is masked: Lucentio pretends to be Tranio, Hortensio pretends to be the music master, and Latin is used to mask the wooing by Lucentio. Unlike Kate, who is helplessly ensnared in a marriage with whatever "madman" will take up the challenge, Bianca manipulatively determines her own future. Moving from suitor to suitor, attempting to keep each satisfied, hoping to offend no one, Bianca plays the coquette. As Cole Porter's lyrics rephrase it in the musical, *Kiss Me Kate*, Bianca would accept "any Tom, Dick, or Harry . . . any Harry, Dick, or Tom." Thus the sisters differ in the options open to them, in their easy acceptance of men, and in their mental agility. For the wooing scenes are distinguished from one another in the level of verbal wit, the puns, the quick retorts, and the double entendres as well as in the contrast between truth and deception.

Moreover, the Bianca wooing scene allows Shakespeare to transfer sympathy back to Kate. All subsequent scenes intensify this. We see Kate, the bride, awaiting an absent groom. We worry with her when the man, dressed like a buffoon and acting the ruffian, does arrive. Her fate is unenviable. Commenting on Petruchio's earlier nonappearance for the wedding, Kate rationally admits:

> No shame but mine. I must forsooth be forc'd
> To give my hand oppos'd against my heart
> Unto a mad-brain rudesby full of spleen,
> Who woo'd in haste, and means to wed at leisure.
>   (III.ii.8–11)

Neither tearing off her gown nor throwing things at her father, she exits weeping. She is a woman perplexed in the extreme, who, in one line only, admits that perhaps she did assent to the match: "Would Katherine had never seen him though!" (26).

To retain this sympathy for Kate but also to assure the comedic quality of the play, Shakespeare's Petruchio must match her. Moments after her weeping exit, a broad shift of tone occurs. Overwhelmed by what he has just seen, a servant excitedly reports Petruchio's arrival. Along with Grumio and a horse that defies reality he has been spotted on the way. Description of the diseased, knock-kneed, swaybacked horse with a broken, half-attached saddle and of the grotesquely costumed men arouses audience laughter. "A very monster in apparel, and not like a Christian footboy or a gentleman's lackey" (70–71) is the awed report on Grumio.

Wildly dressed, Petruchio amazes everyone. Baptista is unmoved. To what extent he is too upset to react, we cannot tell. His response is limited: "I am glad he's come, howsoe'er he comes" (74). A conventional man, Baptista assumes that Petruchio will change his clothes for the wedding ceremony. But the father has misjudged his daughter's bridegroom. Petruchio explains:

> Could I repair what she will wear in me,
> As I can change these poor accoutrements,
> 'Twere well for Kate, and better for myself.
> (III.ii.118–20)

He too fears this marriage. Returning for the wedding on a palsied, sick, lame, swaybacked horse, himself and groom attired for a masquerade, he seems the clown. But his decision to marry Kate despite her reputation and because of her dowry reveals the opportunist. And his actions to Kate hint at still another quality, one reinforced by the fear expressed in this speech.

Which Petruchio is authentic? The punster and clown, the macho boaster, the honest man who claimed to wed for dowry, or the character who confides that he will rely on verbal contraries? The close interweaving of plots again hints at an answer. A conversation between Tranio and Lucentio interrupts two descriptions of Petruchio—the first of his fantastic entry, the second of his behavior at the marriage ceremony. Again deception permeates the discussion by Bianca's suitors. Tranio and Lucentio have woven an intricate plan to beguile

Baptista—"to steal" the marriage (140) of Lucentio and Bianca. If Petruchio's method is overt and extraordinary, Lucentio's is covert, mired in plots and deception.

Petruchio's wild attire for the wedding and the buffoonery at the ceremony raise questions in the minds of the audience. What will this bridegroom do next? Shakespeare chooses to narrate the event rather than present it on stage. As well as cuffing the priest at the ceremony and cursing him, Petruchio

> . . . took the bride about the neck,
> And kiss'd her lips with such a clamorous smack
> That at the parting all the church did echo.
>
> (III.ii.177–79)

Physical contact between the bride and groom has been limited to her hitting him during the wooing scene and his kissing her at the wedding ceremony. Any other physical contact is added by directors and not indicated by the text. In contrast, the intellectual contact between them has been more intense, resuming immediately after the ceremony. T. J. B. Spencer suggests that this heavy reliance on intellectual strength of the women characters may have been because Shakespeare was working with boys playing women's roles and therefore created attractive women by emphasizing the "verbal and intellectual, rather than the sexual."[24]

When Petruchio determines that he will depart with his bride without tasting the wedding feast, we listen to an extension of their intellectual combat even as we are given ominous signs of a physical domination heretofore not shown. A succession of people entreat Petruchio in choruslike refrain. "Let me entreat you to stay 'till after dinner," each begs. And Petruchio, choruslike, responds: "It may not be," "It cannot be." Finally Kate enters the lists. "Let me entreat you," she offers. "I am content," he answers. Keenly aware of the nuances of language, Kate recognizes the ambiguity of his statement. Picking up the word "content," she asks for a more specific assent. "Are you content to stay?" His answer confirms her suspicion. It also testifies to their intellectual compatibility.

> I am content you shall entreat me stay,
> But yet not stay, entreat me how you can.
> (III.ii.202–3)

Kate then makes a major tactical error. Relying on stereotyped conventions rather than intellectual originality, she vacillates between extremes: "Now if you love me stay" (204) and then "The door is open, sir, there lies your way" (210).

Petruchio's response is one of the strongest statements in the play. Announcing that she must accompany him, he defies the company and insists they recognize the meaning of marriage:

> . . . Kate . . . must with me.
> . . .
> I will be master of what is mine own.
> (III.ii.227–29)

He then enumerates her worth. Verbalizing what the father has been doing from the start—auctioning off his daughters —Petruchio reminds us of Stone's reference to the domination of father, then husband, over a woman:

> She is my goods, my chattels, she is my house,
> My household stuff, my field, my barn,
> My horse, my ox, my ass, my any thing;
> And here she stands, touch her whoever dare
> (III.ii.230–33)

Theatrically, this is a dramatic moment. The groom has surprised us. Has the comedy suddenly assumed a serious and unpleasant tone? Or, must we also remember Petruchio's earlier claim that he will speak in opposites? Is this an example of such inversion? He concludes by addressing those who would challenge his rights:

> . . . Grumio,
> Draw forth thy weapon, we are beset with thieves;
> Rescue thy mistress, if thou be a man.
> Fear not, sweet wench, they shall not touch thee, Kate!
> (III.ii.235–38)

Although Petruchio's words ring with the bravado of a protecting knight, the irony is heavy and lost on no one. The message is clear: he has won this round; clearer still, he owns her. However, we are dealing with words. And Kate will understand, finally, not only the nuances of his individual words, as she did when she asked him to stay, but also the larger pattern of Petruchio's language. Only through the deeper message of his actions to her will the intricacy of that language finally become clear.

Cited as keynoting the misogynistic attitude of the play, Petruchio's statement cannot stand alone but must be seen as a prologue to their relationship as newlyweds. How far will Petruchio go in establishing this mastery? Even the inference of the pun "draw forth thy weapon" raises a question. It suggests that the bridegroom who earlier had boasted he would "board" her and tame her may be planning to extend the privilege to his servant. But Shakespeare allows little time for this question to remain unanswered.

The scene that culminates in Petruchio's leading Kate to the bridal chamber and lecturing her on continency follows immediately. In *Sauny the Scot,* a 1698 adaptation of Shakespeare's play, Petruchio first orders his man to undress Kate, then relents.[25] The new husband does, however, continue to insist that she drink and smoke before she be permitted to sleep. How different from Shakespeare's text where Petruchio is "making a sermon of continency to her." According to the *Oxford English Dictionary,* "continency," a rare word today, had several meanings in the sixteenth century: the first, "self-restraint and temperance" in general behavior; the second, abstinence from "sexual indulgence." The definition is followed by an example from the 1552 *Book of Common Prayer* on "Matrimony." Here matrimony is contrasted with continency: "that such persons as have not the gift of continency might marry."

Petruchio's behavior at this time is crucial to our understanding of the play's last scenes. Delivering a speech on continency, he is also implying his own continency. It would be illogical and uncharacteristic of the dramatist to use that word in this context were he not sending messages to the audience that continency ruled in the bridal chamber. In *Kiss Me Kate,*

Kate locks Petruchio out of the room. Shakespeare is more subtle. Language indicates action. We listen to Petruchio's soliloquy:

> Last night she slept not, nor to-night she shall not;
> As with the meat, some undeserved fault
> I'll find about the making of the bed.
>
> (IV.i.198–200)

Becoming specific, Petruchio forces us to visualize the scene:

> And here I'll fling the pillow, there the bolster,
> This way the coverlet, another way the sheets.
>
> (201–2)

He also promises that noise shall keep her awake:

> And if she chance to nod I'll rail and brawl,
> And with the clamor keep her still awake.
>
> (206–7)

Her lines, when she next appears, confirm this:

> . . . did he marry me to famish me?
>
> .   .   .
>
> [I] Am starv'd for meat, giddy for lack of sleep,
> With oaths kept waking, and with brawling fed.
>
> (IV.iii.3–10)

Although Petruchio asks for suggestions for other ways to tame a shrew, he does not seem to consider sexually aggressive behavior among them. Despite his bravado, despite his extravagant claim of ownership of his wife, he rejects this method. Mill had called it "the lowest degradation of a human being"; Brownmiller, writing about the universality of rape as a method of taming, phrases it differently:

> In the cool judgment of right-thinking women, compulsory sexual intercourse is not a husband's right in marriage, for such a "right" gives the lie to any concept of equality and human dignity.[26]

Petruchio offers Kate the unexpected: a lecture on continency —respect for her physical ownership of her person.

The scenes immediately following the wedding night testify to a woman unbroken in spirit and still attempting to convince through reason. Tempted by a fancy cap and an elegant gown which are then denied her, she fails to crumple and become compliant. Her speech indicates that despite the starvation and the lack of sleep, she has retained her sense of self. Her words still challenge:

> Your betters have endur'd me say my mind,
> And if you cannot, best you stop your ears.
> (IV.iii.75–76)

Surely the phrase "your betters" betrays a woman neither tamed nor trained. Nor will she, as the lines suggest, break her heart by maintaining a silent facade. Significantly, Shakespeare understands the effect of silence on the angry person:

> My tongue will tell the anger of my heart,
> Or else my heart concealing it will break.
> (77–78)

Petruchio ignores her philosophic statement and concentrates on the cap, continuing the policy begun at the wedding. Although Kate loses both cap and gown, she survives the type of bribery described by Mill:

> In struggles for political emancipation, everybody knows how often its champions are bought off by bribes, or daunted by terrors. In the case of women, each individual of the subject-class is in a chronic state of bribery and intimidation combined.[27]

Critics, however, have great difficulty with Kate. Her challenge to her husband in this scene—

> Why, sir, I trust I may have leave to speak,
> And speak I will. I am no child, no babe
> (73–74)

—evoked the following comment from William Warburton, the eighteenth-century editor:

> Shakespear has here copied nature with great skill. Pe-
> truchio, by frightening, starving and over-watching his wife,
> had tamed her into gentleness and submission. And the audi-
> ence expects to hear no more of the shrew: When on her being
> crossed, in the article of fashion and finery, the most inveterate
> folly of the sex, she flies out again, though for the last time, into
> all the intemperate rage of her nature.[28]

Unfortunately, Warburton's reaction to women is not merely an expression of an eighteenth-century man but may be heard in contemporary criticism as well. Winfried Schleiner, teaching a course on women in literature, sees the play as the story of a "shrew cured." Applying Burton's *Anatomy of Melancholy* to Kate, he believes that she has a "distemper to which young women (notably virgins) are prone."[29] Schleiner considers Kate a sick person rather than a healthy, forthright woman.

Shakespeare aids in creating this confusion for he moves Hortensio, originally the matchmaker for Katherina and Petruchio, and later the man who loses the wager on wives, into a position of importance. Appearing at the home of Petruchio in time to witness Kate's loss of cap and gown, Hortensio becomes the voice of seeming rationality, but also of masculine superiority. The close yoking of parts that Johnson commended now illuminates the major contrast between the Bianca and Kate plots—between the conventional assumptions governing the wooing and wedding of Bianca, and the unconventional ones governing that of Kate. And Hortensio clarifies the contrast. He is the character who urges Kate's compliance and who expresses the didactic message even while Kate is slowly coming to understand her husband.

The scene teaches Kate to comprehend her husband's ways of acting. Her limited acquaintance with men, her unattractiveness to them because of her assertiveness, and her role as butt of their insults slowly alter. Listening to Grumio and Petruchio, in a pattern of quibbling that resembles their first scene—known to the audience but not to Kate—she may perceive an overall design. But she has not verbalized it; Hortensio will. She hears the brilliant farce routine between Grumio and Petruchio which includes ripples of meaning that move from sleeves and facing to threads and yards. It confuses both the tailor and the haberdasher, but it establishes a model which Kate herself will follow.

By the scene's close Kate still disagrees with Petruchio, logic still takes precedence over gamesmanship. The act, however, has given us some insight into Petruchio. He has respected Kate although trying to outwit her; he has asked Hortensio to offer to pay the tailor while himself rejecting the garment, and in the last lines of the scene he has revealed his aim, "It shall be what a' clock I say," or, as Hortensio reinterprets the lines: "Why, so this gallant will command the sun" (IV.iii.196).

In fact, it is Hortensio, not Kate who, recognizing Petruchio's objective, advises Kate on how to act. Traveling together en route to her father's home, they hear Petruchio exclaim, "Lord, how bright and goodly shines the moon!" (IV.v.2), though the sun is shining. Kate contradicts him. Hortensio advises agreement. Suddenly she understands the verbal game she has been hearing.

> Forward, I pray, since we have come so far,
> And be it moon, or sun, or what you please;
> And if you please to call it a rush-candle,
> Henceforth I vow it shall be so for me.
>   (12–15)

David Garrick evidently thought her speech was not meek enough. He changed it and Augustin Daly, in the nineteenth century, adopted his change. In those versions, the speech becomes an opportunity for self-denigration and capitulation. "I see 'tis vain to struggle with my Bonds," observes Garrick's eighteenth-century Kate who survived well into the nineteenth century and whose descendants still haunt performances of the play.[30] She is a woman beaten rather than a person who has learned a new game and who will eventually excel in it.

The irony of Shakespeare's choice of Hortensio is intensified. Having advised her to comply, he now behaves like a cheering squad leader. "Petruchio, go thy ways, the field is won" (IV.v.23), he joyously exclaims. That Hortensio has learned little from Petruchio—neither an understanding of the Katherina-Petruchio match, nor of the meaning of "taming" —becomes apparent in the last act. But here he betrays his attitude toward women in the line Shakespeare gives him when they meet the old man, Vincentio. Once again Petruchio deals in opposites. But this time Kate, having learned her husband's manner, matches him description for description. Both of them cloak the old man in the features of a youthful maiden. Hortensio, the realist, worries, " 'A will make the man mad, to make a woman of him" (IV.v.35). Is this the statement of a misogynist, or simply that of a man who believes that women are lesser beings?

As I have already suggested, the high jinks of Kate and Petruchio here are reminiscent of that earlier scene when Petruchio and Grumio entered and debated the "knocking at the door." But she outshines Grumio in her flowery, creative, extensive development of an idea. She rivals Petruchio in her description of the nonexistent "fresh gentle woman" with "white and red in her cheeks" and sparkling eyes. For Kate takes that imaginary female beyond the present into the past —"Young budding virgin" (IV.v.37), she calls the old man. "Happy the parents of so fair a child" (39). She also projects into the future: "Happier the man whom favorable stars / Allots thee for his lovely bedfellow" (40–41). Nor do these lines support the thesis that Kate believes a woman who has a husband is fortunate. She is involved in a contest of verbal wit. Her words reveal her new insights into the differences among human beings. Men are not all to be lumped into one group. They vary. Her husband, sensitive to her as an individual, is a man of imagination and humor. She is willing to accept him as an equal because of his respect for her person.

Ribner's warning, that we not accept any didactic statement, but pay close attention to the action, is well to follow. Neither Kate's assertion about women and marriage here, nor her last speech—two speeches that contradict one another—is worth reading as a straightforward statement. Both are tinged with irony. But both reveal the basic consistency in characterization of Kate as an alert, creative intelligence, rational and able to develop an idea with skill.

In the play's final act, after the many deceptions relating

to the Bianca plot are uncovered—after the false Vincentio and the true confront one another, the false Lucentio and the true are revealed to Baptista, the false Tranio and the true admit their identities, and Biondello confesses that he knows his master—Petruchio asks Kate for a kiss. Returning to the old homestead, they discover the distance between the honest relationship they are battling toward and multiple deceptions surrounding the relationship of Bianca and Lucentio. "Husband, let's follow, to see the end of this ado" (V.i.142), Kate suggests. "First kiss me, Kate" (143), he counters. "What, in the midst of the street?" she asks. "What, art thou asham'd of me?" he queries. "No, sir, God forbid, but asham'd to kiss," she admits. Once again Petruchio threatens, "Why then let's home again." "Nay, I will give thee a kiss," she concedes. "Now pray thee, love, stay." The introduction of the affectionate, intimate "love" into this line as well as Petruchio's final answer hints at their new relationship.

> Is not this well? Come, my sweet Kate:
> *Better once than never,* for never too late.
> (V.i.149–50, italics mine)

This is not a man training a hawk as some critics have suggested, but a man wooing a woman.[31] Were the word "once" to refer to kissing in the street, the next clause would be meaningless. Referring, however, to kissing in general, it suggests the end of the abstinence and continence.

Critics tend to overlook the implications of this scene. Robert Heilman, for example, writes:

> Take sex, for instance. . . . Like virtually all Renaissance lovers, Petruchio tells Kate candidly that he proposes to keep warm "in thy bed."[32]

What Heilman overlooks is that Petruchio does not fulfill his threat.

In the play's closing scene, when all the plot threads have been knotted together, the men wager on their wives. Only Katherina comes at her husband's request. To some, her response suggests Petruchio's triumph as a "wife tamer."[33]

This ignores the message of the previous scene, that they have arrived at the beginning of a relationship of mutual respect which he initiated by practicing continency. It ignores her earlier status, a woman unloved by her sister and unrespected by her father. In this frighteningly strange marriage to a seeming mad man, Kate has finally achieved status and respect. Not only has she been wooed with sincerity—"Better once than never, for never too late"—but she has also heard her husband wager on her wit against the wit of another: "A hundred marks, my Kate does put her down" (V.ii.35). Finally, she has a champion.

Virginia Woolf reflects on the advantage men have because for centuries women have been acting the magic mirror, magnifying men to twice their natural size.[34] Now Kate has someone who will act the magic mirror. No longer need she listen to the derogatory comments of a Gremio as she did at the opening of the comedy when she asked her father to defend her. Furthermore, her response, rather than being disciplined as improper, is cheered. Kate has found more than a husband in a hostile world: she has found a friend. To such a friend, compliance in a give-and-take relationship is easy. She doesn't mind expounding at length on any subject, even women's behavior. She may tend toward overstatement, as she did in turning the old man, Vincentio, into a budding young virgin, but she is merely trying out her newest skill.

When Petruchio charges she lecture the other women on their "wifely" duties, she complies with delight. How sweet to be propelled into a seat of authority and favor. Savoring this new role, she delivers a speech of extraordinary length. How delicious to reprimand her sister for unseemly behavior and jostle the smug self-complacency of both women. Noting the evanescence of beauty, Kate warns,

> Fie, fie, unknit that threat'ning unkind brow,
> And dart not scornful glances from those eyes
> (V.ii.136–37)

She emphasizes the swiftness of time in blotting out physical beauty "as frosts do bite the meads" (139). She then enumerates the many advantages of being a wife, punctuating her lecture with such nice parallels as: "A woman mov'd is like a fountain troubled," from which no one "will deign to sip, or touch one drop." She elaborates on the cost of sullen behavior, magnifying it to the rank of traitorousness:

> And when she is froward, peevish, sullen, sour,
> And not obedient to his honest will,
> What is she but a foul contending rebel,
> And graceless traitor to her loving lord?
>
> (157–60)

She graciously suggests the mode of behavior for a conventional, conforming woman:

> I am asham'd that women are so simple
> To offer war where they should kneel for peace,
>   .   .   .
> When they are bound to serve, love, and obey.
>
> (161–64)

Finally she caps the list with the directive:

> Then vail your stomachs, for it is no boot,
> And place your hands below your husband's foot;
> In token of which duty, if he please,
> My hand is ready, may it do him ease.
>
> (176–79)

Her husband, who taught her this game, can remain silent no longer:

> Why, there's a wench! Come on, and kiss me, Kate.
>
> (180)

And then he suggests:

> Come, Kate, we'll to bed.
>
> (184)

To the others he boasts, " 'Twas I won the wager," as he leaves the stage. Ironically, it is Hortensio, who learned little from watching Petruchio and Kate, who observes, "thou hast tam'd a curst shrow" (188). Are we to take his word for the meaning of the play? Shakespeare has shown us where Hortensio stands and what his myopia is. Nor does the dramatist help us in coming to any didactic conclusions. He has never given us a soliloquy by Kate; we have never learned her inner designs, her secret objectives. We, like the characters in the play, must judge her by the words Shakespeare has given her to speak in a social situation. Because he is a genius, because he could hear the words of women and transform them into language on the stage, because he did not filter these words through the screen of contemporary male prejudices, he was able to present vibrant, alive women. He recognized that women, like men, vary. He recognized women's humanity and immortalized it on the stage.

Filled with ambiguities, the play offers one final challenge at the close. The drunken Christopher Sly, for whom the comedy was performed, never returns. We have been immersed in an incomplete play-within-a-play, never knowing if Sly enjoyed the entertainment or was bored by it, as he suggests at the end of the first act. Nor do we know whether his story was meant to be excised and the opening scenes forgotten, or whether part of the text was lost. But it no longer matters. Was this meant to be the dream of a down-and-out drunk? It has expanded into a world of its own. The sisters and their father, the suitors, the rough house, the coming to terms with the meaning of marriage, the contradiction between Petruchio's "She is my chattel" and his lecture on continency have shaped into a play. Sly's absence at the close merely reinforces the sense of open-endedness.

In sharp contrast, Garrick's extreme alteration of the ending epitomizes the more usual interpretation of *The Taming of the Shrew*. Petruchio inherits most of Kate's long speech while she acquiescently listens to him preach:

> Catharine, I charge thee tell this headstrong Woman
> What Duty 'tis she owes her Lord and Husband.

Modestly Kate demurs, apologizing in the usual Garrick style, "Nay, then I'm all unworthy of thy Love, / And look with

Blushes on my former self." Petruchio then takes the reins and with them her lines:

> Such Duty as the Subject owes the Prince,
> Even such a Woman oweth to her Husband:
> And when she's froward, peevish, sullen, sower,
> And not obedient to his honest Will;
> What is she but a foul contending Rebel,
> And graceless Traitor to her loving Lord?
> How shameful 'tis when Women are so simple
> To offer War where they shuld kneel for Peace;
> Or seek for Rule, Supremacy and Sway,
> Where bound to love, to honour and obey.[35]

On this didactic note Garrick's version ends. Although infrequently performed today, the tradition it represents persists.

Despite its title, *The Taming of the Shrew*, like so many of Shakespeare's plays, questions accepted premises. Action and language, melding together, often contradict one another. Beneath the horseplay and farce, the comedy offers a remarkably mature affirmation of the potential for understanding between a man and a woman. Critics, the products of their own culture, may find here a misogynist's dream come true. Women recognize the uniqueness and sensitivity of Petruchio and the originality and courage of Kate. They delight in her triumph over Bianca—the triumph of the unconventional over the conventional—of challenging patterns of wooing over the stereotypes.

PART II

Sexuality

A Spanish influence pervades in this nineteenth-century illustration
of the balcony scene, engraved by William Henry Egleton from a
painting by Edward Henry Corbould. FOLGER SHAKESPEARE LIBRARY

CHAPTER FOUR

Growing Up

ROMEO AND JULIET

"Good father, I beseech you on my knees."
(III.v.158)

*I*n Kenneth MacMillan's ballet of "Romeo and Juliet," Juliet enters carrying a rag doll, a symbol of youth, demonstrating the attachment of a young girl to toys and the world of childhood.[1] Taking a hint from the debates that have persisted concerning the play, particularly those centering on Juliet's fewer than fourteen years, the choreographer dramatizes her youthfulness through symbol and gesture. Along with the doll, the movements—jerky, exuberant, and impulsive—establish Juliet's age. To demonstrate the transition to womanhood, gesture, symbol, and movement shift. The turn of her head, the carriage of her body, the supple, soft intensity of arms and legs when she leaps and weaves through space reveal the developing maturity. Watching this ballet, where artists in another medium recapture the essence of Shakespeare's portrait though they lack verbal language to express the depth of thought, uncertainty, and the adolescent's groping toward self-knowledge, one remains aware of Shakespeare's intention as he insistently repeats for all to remember: Juliet is not quite fourteen.

Simone de Beauvoir defines a girl's adolescence as a

difficult time because it causes a dichotomy between "her status as a real human being and her vocation as a female." Until
adolescence the girl has been able to think of herself as "subject, active, free." But then at adolescence "her erotic urges
and the social pressure to accept herself as a passive object"
conflict with this sense of self-sovereignty.[2] When, therefore,
the choreographer portrays Juliet as this young person still
attached to symbols of childhood, he captures the essence of
that freedom, that sovereignty, which de Beauvoir describes
and Shakespeare projects through Juliet's actions and language.

Critics, adaptors, and producers of the play have had
difficulty with Juliet's age. Some have explored its relevance to
the age of maturity of women in Shakespeare's time.[3] Others
have attributed her extreme youth to the dramatist's careless-
ness when borrowing from his major source, the 1561 poem,
"The Tragicall Historye of Romeus and Juliet." There, the poet
Arthur Brooke writes: "scarce saw she yet ful xvi. yeres."[4] The
nineteenth-century editor, Richard Grant White, proposed another theory. He believed that Shakespeare had neither intentionally nor carelessly altered the number, but had found "xvi"
transposed to "xiv" in the edition that he read.[5] Those who
wrote for the stage or produced the tragedy rejected the fourteen years for other reasons. They believed either that an older
Juliet would be less likely to offend accepted mores of their
own time or that the actress playing the role seemed unfit to
act a fourteen-year-old. Even today, many directors continue
to excise all references to age, so that in their productions Juliet
becomes an attractive young woman of indeterminate age.

Nor have historians arrived at a consensus about the
accepted age for marriage in England in the 1590s.[6] Lawrence
Stone, for example, in his recently published, exhaustive
study of the family, sex, and marriage during the period, offers
conflicting evidence. Preferring not to generalize, he notes
that, as a result of social stratification, one group will have a
"totally different set of familial values and behaviour patterns"
from another and therefore no simple linear or cyclical model
will work for consistent analysis of the period. Although he
finds that "the evidence about the age of marriage for the
upper landed classes" is difficult to ascertain, he estimates that

"daughters married on the average at about twenty in the late sixteenth century," and notes the general belief that "childbirth was excessively dangerous for very young girls."[7]

Because Shakespeare told us nothing about the ages of the Princess of France and her women, nor about the ages of Kate and Bianca, except that Kate was the elder sister—all women for whom he provides suitors—the emphasis on Juliet's age suggests a determination to explore the responses of a teenage girl to the process of growing up and to the meaning of marriage. "Her spontaneous tendency is to regard herself as the essential," de Beauvoir writes of the adolescent. But adolescence is also a time when the young girl is moving toward self-repression and conformity. She is "supposed not only to deck herself out, to make herself ready, but also to repress her spontaneity and replace it with the studied grace and charm taught her by her elders."[8] Struggling to understand the adult world she is about to enter, Juliet demonstrates the arrogance and uncertainty so characteristic of her age. Sometimes she exudes the confidence of youth before adopting the strait jacket of role. And as she mimics her elders, learning from her two female mentors, she also exercises her sense of herself as the essential against them.

Unusual among Shakespeare's women characters, Juliet has both her mother and the Nurse as adult women role models. Although ultimately both women fail her—victims of the generation gap as well as of adjustment to roles in a male-dominated world—at first they offer strength and solid support as she approaches maturity. Eager to learn and grow, Juliet in her first scene, confident of herself as a person, listens, questions, and complies.

Shakespeare introduces her in a particularly characteristic teenage action. Whereas characters in the plays frequently stroll onto the stage speaking, Juliet does not appear until called by the Nurse: "God forbid! Where's this girl? What, Juliet!" (I.iii.4). Although surely the young woman knows the voice of her nurse who has been calling to her since infancy, the answer, "How now, who calls?" also marks the teenager's response, challenging the caller, wanting to know more. For Juliet is well aware that the Nurse would not disturb her unless someone else were seeking her. When she discovers that her

mother is the caller—the person intruding on her privacy—
Juliet immediately responds: "Madam, I am here, / What is
your will?" (5–6). Through the formality of her address—
"Madam"—to her mother and the question that follows,
Shakespeare quickly sketches a teenage reaction. No conversation, no warmth, no joy at seeing her mother are present,
simply the query and the unstated: "You must have a reason
for being here. You would not otherwise be disturbing me."

Their opening scene establishes the formality and the
distance between them. Lady Capulet's confusion in her subsequent speeches suggests that she is uncomfortable in exchanges with her daughter. Intending at first to speak
privately with Juliet—"This is the matter. Nurse, give leave a
while, / We must talk in secret" (I.iii.6–7)—the mother
changes her mind. Intimidated perhaps by her daughter's
teenage reserve, with its slight touch of arrogance, Lady Capulet invites the Nurse to remain, "Nurse, come back again, /
I have rememb'red me, thou s' hear our counsel" (8–9). The
older woman's presence may assure a more cordial acceptance
of Lady Capulet's proposal.

The mother then launches the subject of marriage and
illustrates the accuracy of de Beauvoir's observation that, "the
daughter is for the mother at once her double and another
person."[9] First Lady Capulet speaks of Juliet's age—"a fort-
night and odd days" shy of fourteen, a "happy time," a time
for marriage, a time of sexual readiness:

> . . . younger than you,
> Here in Verona, ladies of esteem,
> Are made already mothers. By my count,
> I was your mother much upon these years
> That you are now a maid.
>   (I.iii.69–73)

Lady Capulet's first thoughts of marriage are of her own pregnancy and childbirth. The idea of Juliet's liking the man who
will be her husband comes second. Since the drama is a love
story, this inverted sequence of associations foreshadows the
tragedy to follow. And it characterizes the duality of the
mother's attitude toward her daughter. Saddling the child

with her own destiny, Lady Capulet's sequence allows her to lay "claim to her own femininity" and, in the language of de Beauvoir, to revenge herself for it.[10]

Samuel Johnson observed that Shakespeare's "characters are not modified by the customs of particular places; . . . or by the accidents of transient fashions or temporary opinions: they are the genuine progeny of common humanity, such as the world will always supply, and observation will always find."[11] Although the setting is Verona, the relationship of a teenage daughter with her elders—her mother, father, and Nurse—has a universality not limited to a particular place.

Juliet's feelings toward her mother seesaw between dependence and independence, between hostility and cordiality. Balancing the spontaneous, negative reaction to her mother's unexpected appearance is Juliet's later receptivity when her mother asks, "How stands your dispositions to be married?" (I.iii.65). Here Juliet graciously acquiesces, "It is an honor that I dream not of" (66). Her answer encourages Lady Capulet to become more expansive. After that first reference to her own early pregnancy, she now turns to the subject of love in marriage dismissing that earlier, more pragmatic emphasis on sexual readiness.

As critics have long noted, her description of Paris, Juliet's prospective suitor, abounds in Petrarchan clichés:

> Examine every married lineament,
> And see how one another lends content;
>
> .   .   .
>
> This precious book of love, this unbound lover,
> To beautify him, only lacks a cover.
>
> (83–88)

The heaviness of the rhyme and the use of the book metaphor throughout this lengthy passage betray its artificiality. Comparing Paris' love to an unbound book, she also instructs her daughter to look at Paris' face, "Read o'er the volume" (81). There, assuredly, the daughter will "find delight writ . . . with beauty's pen" (82). Of this speech, Alexander Pope writes: "In the common editions here follows a ridiculous speech, which is entirely added since the first."[12] Pope's comment is an explanation for his complete excision of the lines.

David Garrick, the actor-manager and dramatist, whose version of *Romeo and Juliet* prevailed in the second half of the eighteenth century and during most of the nineteenth, altered this scene.[13] He had promised to eliminate "as much as possible, from the Jingle and Quibble" in the play. And so he accepted Pope's judgment. Lady Capulet's speech disappeared. With it, however, went a perceptive insight into the mother's character and the example Juliet was to try to follow in her subsequent speech. When finally her mother phrases the question, "Speak briefly, can you like of Paris' love?" Juliet reveals an aptitude for imitation by punning on the word "look":

> I'll look to like, if looking liking move;
> But no more deep will I endart mine eye
> Than your consent gives strength to make it fly.
> (I.iii.97–99)

These subtleties that help define Juliet were absent from the theater.

Exchanges between Juliet and the Nurse further develop Shakespeare's portrait of the adolescent who seeks models for her actions but also regards herself as "the essential." Having been invited to remain, the Nurse breaks the intensity of the meeting between mother and daughter. The garrulous older woman disturbingly interjects her own comments. Juliet listens to her mother asking the Nurse to refrain from interrupting. "Enough of this, I pray thee hold thy peace" (49), Lady Capulet dictates ineffectually. For a moment the daughter sides with the mother, learning her position vis-à-vis the Nurse. "And stint thou too, I pray thee, nurse, say I" (58), Juliet requests. The prattling ceases. Despite its brevity, the exchange establishes the strength of the daughter, the confusion of the mother, and the intimacy between the Nurse and her young charge.

Shakespeare adds one further contrast between Juliet's two mentors that Garrick, again taking a hint from Pope, omits.[14] The scene closes with Lady Capulet formally reminding Juliet that "the County [Paris] stays" (104). But it is the Nurse who has the final words, "Go, girl, seek happy nights to happy days" (105). The differences become less sharp in Garrick's version as all three women silently exit together.

The father's relationship with Juliet is perhaps the most complex of the three. Although father and daughter do not speak with one another until their bitter confrontation in Act III, we hear his genuine concern for her early in the play. Like the mother and Nurse, he too stresses Juliet's age but has a different feeling about it. He resembles the father in Brooke's poem who protests that his sixteen-year-old daughter, Juliet, is "too yong to be a bryde."[15] Shakespeare, who changed Juliet's age, kept the father in the same mold as the father in the poem. For Capulet in the play also complains:

> She hath not seen the change of fourteen years;
> Let two more summers wither in their pride,
> Ere we may think her ripe to be a bride.
> (I.ii.9–11)

Paris, Juliet's suitor, merely glances around him: "Younger than she are happy mothers made" (12). But Capulet rejects this conclusion, realistically countering: "And too soon marr'd are those so early made" (13). Thus stressing Juliet's age and her father's early concern for her future, the poet explores not only the problem of adolescent development but also different parental responses to it.

In *The Winter's Tale,* the Shepherd, another father, offers a simple solution to the difficulties of handling an adolescent —in this case a son. "I would there were no age between ten and three-and-twenty, or that youth would sleep out the rest," says that comic character (III.iii.59–61). But Capulet, trying to protect his daughter, seeks no refuge in wishful thinking. When, later on, she challenges his authority and wisdom, he then throws up his hands in despair and acts the autocrat. Unlike the Shepherd, Capulet insists on a realistic solution: Juliet must marry the man her father chooses. Suddenly her age becomes unimportant. Between the time of these two strongly held positions of the father, his daughter grows from child to woman and his single male heir has been murdered. Capulet's altered behavior reflects his response to a new situation. Cultural, religious, and social pressures on a father's attitudes also impinge upon his daughter. Love and protectiveness of the female child yield to familiar perceptions of woman as property and procreator. The father who, in Act I, sought to postpone his daughter's marriage, must in Act III think of legality and inheritance. He must replace his murdered male heir, his nephew Tybalt, and Juliet must furnish the progeny. Or, at least, she must have a husband who will provide the male heir, preventing the property from being lost. Unfortunately, by this time, she is already married to someone else.

Growing up an obedient daughter whose sense of her own worth was never in conflict with her parents' aims for her, Juliet faces an unanticipated dilemma, one based on her awareness of the meaning of her own sexuality and on her desire to control her own body. Whereas she could easily accept her mother's suggestion of marriage to Paris in Act I, when Juliet discovers her own inner drives, she must reject her parents' choice. Retaining her sense of herself as "essential," she has married Romeo, failing to conform to the pattern of compliant daughter. But her disagreement with her parents is painful and one which she seeks, for a short moment, to escape, returning to the more open, relaxed relationship of child to parent.

As I noted earlier, language of address is one manifestation of the striving toward adulthood. Juliet's use of the formal "Madam" when speaking to her mother persists throughout the first three acts. After the wedding night, however, the word "mother" creeps into Juliet's vocabulary. First it appears in indirect address to the Nurse. The new bride asks if it is her "lady mother" who calls (III.v.65). But "mother" then disappears. The more formal "Madam" functions almost chorally as daughter interrupts mother. Staccatolike, the word punctuates the flow of Lady Capulet's message—the plan for a hasty marriage between Juliet and Paris: "Madam, I am not well" (68), "What villain, madam?" (79), and finally, the rather arrogant command, ". . . tell my lord and father, madam, / I will not marry yet" (120–21).

Juliet then turns to her father. Her knowledge of his love for her has given her strength and courage to dismiss her mother. When, to her surprise, she discovers his adamant insistence on her total obedience, she falls to her knees, imploring: "Good father, I beseech you on my knees, / Hear me with patience but to speak a word" (III.v.158–59). Calling him "father," she temporarily rejects the formal pattern of speech adopted in her groping toward adulthood. Condemned to poverty and the streets if she disobeys, she attempts to revive the close relationship implied in the early scenes of child to parent.

Only after she discovers her father unyielding does she for a moment break the barrier she has built through language and try to communicate with her mother. Hoping to create a bond between herself and this distant, formal woman, Juliet begs: "O sweet my mother, cast me not away!" (III.v.198). But her mother, like the Nurse later on, fails Juliet. Although together they represent two aspects of the nurturer, they can offer neither help, nor comfort, nor understanding for they have accepted the constraints of their roles as women in their society. But Juliet, still too young to have suppressed the sense of personal freedom in order to conform, seeks to retain the independent spirit nurtured during her years growing up.

In creating this teenager, Shakespeare alters the materials of his source to give her added stature. Critics tell us that her fourteen years make her less culpable than was Brooke's heroine of sixteen. But Shakespeare seems less concerned with culpability and more with personal initiative. Although younger than Brooke's heroine, Shakespeare's character has an option not permitted her prototype. Brooke's lovers have been married for a month or two—"The summer of their blisse, doth last a month or twayne" [16]—before the fatal duel between Romeo and Tybalt. Shakespeare shifts the sequence of events so that Juliet's decision to consummate the marriage occurs after Tybalt's death. The risks involved in marrying Romeo are no longer simply those connected with displeasing her parents. Since Romeo has already been condemned to banishment—or, if he remains in Verona, to death—Juliet may no longer dream of an easy solution. Realistically, she knows that there will be no parental acceptance of this marriage. Ironically, the sexual drive that Lady Capulet hoped she might awaken in her daughter now leads to a decision never anticipated by the parents. By marrying Romeo at this time, Juliet is also consciously rejecting the husband already chosen for her. Thus on several levels, Shakespeare's Juliet exhibits personal initiative and independence.

The contrast with Brooke's poem extends to the portrait of Paris and the timing of his offer of marriage. Unlike Shakespeare, Brooke does not have the parents propose Paris as ,a husband for Juliet until after Romeo's banishment. Tearful, weeping, the young girl seems to be sliding quickly into a depression. The poet paints a vivid portrait of the inconsolable bride. To maintain her price as a marriageable commodity as well as to prevent her complete decline, the parents quickly betroth her to Paris. Shakespeare establishes the engagement at the play's opening, thus adding an element of tension at the start.

Finally, in sharp contrast with the hero and heroine of Brooke's poem, Shakespeare's Romeo and Juliet share the decision about their future action. Although Shakespeare's Juliet momentarily protests that she will accompany her husband, she realizes that the haste of his departure allows no time for such a plan. Brooke's Juliet, however, develops a long well-reasoned argument for accompanying Romeo.[17] Resisting her pleas, he reminds her of the difference in age between them and warns her that they could both be punished:

> I, as a ravishor, thou, as a careles childe,
> I, as a man who doth defile, thou, as a mayde defilde.[18]

Brooke stresses the relative ages of the lovers and their comparative responsibilities in the eyes of society. Shakespeare declines to offer moral judgment on the lovers, presenting instead the dilemma facing two adolescents. For the text of the play implies that Romeo, too, is young. Friends, parents, and particularly Friar Lawrence, comment on his immaturity before his first stage entrance. From his father, we hear that the sorrowing son, walking with downcast eyes, closes the daylight from his room, making himself "an artificial night" (I.i.140). When Romeo enters, he reveals the source of his sorrow: love. "In love?" (165), queries Benvolio. "Out" (166), responds Romeo. "Of love?" (167) his friend persists. "Out of her favor where I am in love" (168). Thus at our first meeting with this hero, his heart is heavy with unrequited love for the "fair Rosaline."

When, after meeting Juliet, Romeo rushes to the Friar's cell early in the morning to speak of his love, the Friar asks, "God pardon sin! Wast thou with Rosaline?" (II.iii.44). Romeo answers, "Then plainly know my heart's dear love is set / On the fair daughter of rich Capulet" (57–58). The Friar, who last heard him yearning for Rosaline, voices the general skepticism about such a rapid shift of affection.

> Holy Saint Francis, what a change is here!
> Is Rosaline, that thou didst love so dear,
> So soon forsaken? Young men's love then lies
> Not truly in their hearts, but in their eyes.
> (65–68)

The exclamation, with its reference to Saint Francis and its heavy stress on rhyme, not only breaks the tone of the solemn pledge of the previous scene, the famous balcony scene, but arouses suspicion in the audience of the dependability of Romeo's love. The whole dialogue, including the Friar's lengthy description of Romeo's earlier pose of total dedication to Rosaline—"Jesu Maria, what a deal of brine / Hath wash'd thy sallow cheeks for Rosaline!" (69–70)—reminds us that the two lovers brought different backgrounds to their discovery of mutual love in one another. Samuel Taylor Coleridge, the great nineteenth-century poet and critic, rationalized this well: "It would have displeased us if Juliet had been represented as already in love or as fancying herself so;—but no one, I believe, ever experiences any shock at Romeo's forgetting his Rosaline, who had been a mere name for the yearning of his youthful imagination, and rushing into his passion for Juliet." [19]

In fact, many did blame Romeo. In the eighteenth century, Cibber eliminated Rosaline. [20] When Garrick wrote his version in 1748, he retained Rosaline, however in 1750, in response to popular demand, he eliminated all references to her when he revised his text. He also weighted the scene with a moral message. Thus, the speech that delightfully rhymes "brine" with "Rosaline" becomes:

Holy Saint Francis! what a change is this!
But tell me, son, and call thy reason home,
Is not this love the offspring of thy folly,
Bred from thy wantonness and thoughtless brain?[21]

Instead of the Friar mocking the Petrarchan convention that true love springs from the lover's eyes but not his heart, Garrick's Friar reprimands Romeo and introduces the word "wantonness." Warning Romeo against over-emotionalism, the Friar continues:

Be heedful, youth, and see you stop betimes,
Lest that thy rash ungovernable passions,
O'er-leaping duty, and each due regard,
Hurry thee on, thro' short liv'd, dear bought pleasures,
To cureless woes, and lasting penitence.[22]

Although passionate, this Romeo cannot be accused of swiftly jumping from one love to another. For with all references to Rosaline excised, his sincerity is assured. He becomes a much more acceptable romantic hero, one audiences can acclaim and critics praise. Later versions, including one by Henry Irving, follow Garrick's pattern.[23] Either through revision or excision, they omit the pointed references to Rosaline and Romeo's too recent infatuation with her. Altering the plot to retain the ball scene, Garrick provides new motivation for Romeo's attendance. No longer does the youth desire to gaze at Rosaline; instead he yearns to see the face of Juliet once more.[24] He is a young man of great constancy. Writing of Garrick's version, William Hazlitt, the nineteenth-century critic, commended the change because it narrowed the canvas and "assisted the concentration of interest."[25] It also placed the lovers on a more equal footing of first commitment.

Shakespeare's intention, however, was to show Romeo's immaturity at the opening of the play so as to reveal his growth as well as Juliet's as the drama progresses. The young man's extreme outbursts of passion for Rosaline provide the perfect foil. For he mistakes the worship of Rosaline's beauty for real love. The audience listening to him mooning because of her detects the extreme self-awareness of the adolescent in many of those early speeches.

After he meets Juliet, much of the pretentiousness and affectation disappears from Romeo's speeches, as critics have generally noted. Although his language is never as simple as hers, it takes on an intensity and a new directness that convince us of his sincerity. We therefore accept his expression of love for Juliet as true, and that for Rosaline as specious. If, like the eighteenth-century audiences, we have some slight lingering doubt about Romeo, that too may reflect the dramatist's intention of elevating Juliet to the position of major character, the one who evokes our greatest concern. Dramaturgically and psychologically, Rosaline serves an important function. Not only does she help us differentiate between Romeo and his friends, but she establishes Romeo's interest in a serious commitment to a woman. He, like Juliet, has been primed for their first meeting. The unrequited love he thought he felt for Rosaline astonishingly meets acceptance from Juliet who has also been prepared for their meeting by having been told to consider "liking" Paris and then marrying him. The young woman who at fourteen might not have entertained the possibility of marriage so soon, as hinted by her line, "It is an honor that I dream not of" (I.iii.66), is prepared to "look to like" when she meets Romeo at the ball.

"When a [female] child comes under their care, women apply themselves to changing her into a woman like themselves," de Beauvoir writes.[26] Juliet has listened to her mother and Nurse speak of the joys of marriage, has been told of her physical ripeness, and is ready to enjoy this new adventure, with little sense of its final cost. MacMillan's ballet elegantly conveys Juliet's readiness. Having entered exuberantly with that rag doll, she playfully teases the Nurse until interrupted by the appearance of mother, father, and suitor. Told of the ball that evening and of the future plans for her marriage, she play-acts a grown young woman until the adults leave. Then she bursts into ecstatic joy and grabs the doll, intending it for her confidant. But the Nurse interrupts; the time for dolls is past. She touches Juliet's breasts, the signs of the girl's becoming a woman. Following the Nurse's gesture, Juliet raises her own hands, fingers outspread, to her breasts. She discards the doll. The ballet crystallizes the statement of Juliet's age. Margot Fonteyn, the great ballerina, even at the age of forty projected the illusion of youth through gesture, movement, and symbol.

An actress, too, should be able to achieve this magic on the stage.

The ballet illustrates the importance of the interpreter's vision and the impact of contemporary cultural mores on character definition. Like Garrick's version, MacMillan's work invites comparison with Shakespeare's. Whereas the portrait of Juliet captures the essence of the original, that of Romeo is flawed. The choreographer's hero is more of a man about town than the dramatist's, and at first he is much more difficult to distinguish from his peers, Benvolio and Mercutio. The play opens with a street brawl between the servants of the Montagues and the Capulets that culminates in bloodshed and the edict of the Prince forbidding further fighting. This precedes Romeo's lovesick entrance. The ballet opens in the marketplace where Romeo, after briefly following Rosaline until she exits, participates in a large choral street number and dances unperturbedly, joyously, with one of the street whores. Whereas in the drama we know Romeo immediately, because his attitudes toward women distinguish Shakespeare's Romeo from his friends, in the dance we have to search for the lead.

One of them, Benvolio, is the first of the trio to enter. A minor character, he nevertheless provides a contrast missing from the ballet. Unlike the disconsolate Romeo, this cousin and friend believes women unworthy of men's tears. Having promised old Montague that he would unearth the source of Romeo's melancholy, Benvolio discovers it to be love of Rosaline and quickly decries his cousin's weakness. Women must not have such power. Surely there are other women around who will serve as well. As a cure, Benvolio insists:

> Compare her face with some that I shall show,
> And I will make thee think thy swan a crow.
> (I.ii.86–87)

The Romeo of the drama ardently protests:

> When the devout religion of mine eye
> Maintains such falsehood, then turn tears to fires.
> (88–89)

Romeo's intensity and seriousness alert the audience to his character even though his feelings for Rosaline evaporate when Juliet appears. The ballet fails to transmute Shakespeare's vision of Romeo into dance when it introduces the three young men as interchangeable. In the play, Benvolio is not Romeo's equal.

The contrast between Romeo and Mercutio is even greater. Unlike Benvolio, who hopes to cure Romeo by showing him a world of women more beautiful and more attractive than Rosaline, Mercutio aims to cure through pure frolic. Women are toys, playthings. This attitude glitters throughout the Queen Mab speech. Describing a fairy "no bigger than an agot-stone" (I.iv.55), Mercutio delights the mind with the exploits of this fantasy creature.

> . . . she gallops night by night
> Through lovers' brains, and then they dream of love;
> O'er courtiers' knees, that dream on cur'sies straight;
>
> .   .   .
>
> This is the hag, when maids lie on their backs,
> That presses them and learns them first to bear,
> Making them women of good carriage.
> This is she—
>
> (I.iv.70–72, 92–95)

Romeo halts the outburst of over forty lines when the fairy "no bigger than an agot-stone" becomes a hag and the images decline from the purely fanciful to the sensual. Sounding much like Juliet in her directive to the Nurse in Act I, scene ii, Romeo interjects: "Peace, peace, Mercutio, peace!" Although we are conditioned by society to admire a hero like Mercutio—the brash, imaginative male who, incidentally, denigrates women—Shakespeare creates this portrait to define through contrast a more gentle, sympathetic, youthful Romeo.

Of a certain age and temperament, he is modeled on a more human, frail frame. He is not the young man who, having sowed his wild oats, decides to settle down when he sees Juliet—as implied by the ballet. Whether or not he has had prior sexual experience we cannot be certain from the text although, in the manner of boastful youths, he, Benvolio, and

Mercutio vie with one another (II.iv.), quip for quip, and bawdy line for bawdy line. As may be expected, Mercutio triumphs. Romeo's more tentative approach becomes apparent through contrast. Nor is Romeo the perfect hero who, falling in love at first sight, has never previously thought himself enamored.

When Romeo and Juliet meet for the first time, they express the uncertainties of youth as well as its enthusiasm and brash confidence. Their speeches, each in turn, follow sophisticated adult patterns. Bantering with one another, Romeo gallantly refers to Juliet's hand as a "holy shrine" and she responds by punning on the meaning of palm in a playful exchange that continues until Romeo twice kisses her:

ROMEO: If I profane with my unworthiest hand
    This holy shrine, the gentle sin is this,
    My lips, two blushing pilgrims, ready stand
    To smooth that rough touch with a tender kiss.
JULIET: Good Pilgrim, you do wrong your hand too much,
       .   .   .
    For saints have hands that pilgrims' hands do touch,
    And palm to palm is holy palmers' kiss.
                (I.v.93–100)

In 1854 Richard Grant White, the Shakespearean scholar, observed of the above dialogue: "I have never seen a Juliet upon the stage who appeared to appreciate the archness of the dialogue with Romeo in this scene."[27] But then White had probably never seen any but a derivation of Garrick's version of this scene. Prejudiced against Juliet by what he saw, the critic then continued: "And when Romeo fairly gets her into the corner, towards which she has been contriving to be driven . . . how shyly the pretty puss gives him the opportunity to repeat the penance."[28] White found Juliet a scheming young woman. His comments illustrate the impact of the staged work on his evaluation of the total play for he combines his recollections of the theatrical experience with his responses to the literary text. Cutting for the stage affects the audience's and the critic's response. White's first observation also tells us about the production. Although Garrick's was considered the best version of *Romeo and Juliet* between 1680 and 1875, it differed from Shakespeare's text in this scene. Charles Beecher Hogan asserts that Garrick's version "with slight modifications . . . was used as late as 1875 by Charles Wyndham. It does not appear to have been abandoned until Irving's production . . . in 1882."[29] However, an undated promptbook at the Folger Library hints at a later date, possibly as late as the beginning of the twentieth century.[30] Devoid of any reference to Rosaline, stripped of Juliet's bright banter, and reduced to the exchange of two kisses preceded by a few words, Garrick's text creates a very different young woman. His scene reads:

ROMEO: If I profane with my unworthy hand
       This holy shrine, the gentle fine is this.
       [*Kiss*]
JULIET: Good pilgrim, you do wrong your hand too much,
       For palm to palm is holy palmer's kiss.
ROMEO: Have not saints lips, and holy palmers too?
JULIET: Ay, pilgrim, lips that they must use in prayer.
ROMEO: Thus then, dear saint, let lips put up their prayers.
       [*Kiss*][31]

At this point the Nurse terminates the conversation by telling Juliet that her mother "craves a word" with her. What had been an intellectual exercise in Shakespeare's drama—an extended rally in the use of metaphor—becomes primarily an exchange of kisses in Garrick's. Absent is Juliet's archness, a definite part of Shakespeare's portrait.

By the close of this fifth scene, Juliet still tends toward "quibbles." But her comment in the original, "My only love sprung from my only hate! / Too early seen unknown, and known too late!" (I.v.138–39), has an intensity that rescues it from being a mere play on words. Because Juliet herself recognizes what she is doing, she tosses off the explanation to the Nurse, "A rhyme I learnt even now / Of one I danc'd withal" (142–43). Rhetorical devices disappear from her speech when she believes herself to be alone.

At the opening of the balcony scene, unaware of any listener, she expresses her feeling in clear, intense language. Gone are the heavy rhyme and the punning heard in her conversations with Lady Capulet and later with Romeo. Instead,

The famous actress played Juliet in the 1880s. FOLGER SHAKESPEARE LIBRARY

carefully chosen words express Juliet's feelings and describe the problems she anticipates:

> O Romeo, Romeo, wherefore art thou Romeo?
> Deny thy father and refuse thy name;
> Or, if thou wilt not, be but sworn my love,
> And I'll no longer be a Capulet.
>
> (II.ii.33–36)

Unlike Kate in *The Taming of the Shrew*, whose intentions must be gleaned from watching her behavior with a variety of people, Juliet unburdens herself to the audience in several soliloquies during the course of the drama. One imagines Shakespeare saying: "Here, these are her words; these her secret thoughts. Figure her out if you can. My objective is to delineate a teenage girl, a complex individual." She combines many contradictory qualities. She has a sharp well-developed mind, and yet she is innocent and naive. She has faith in the future and an uncompromising standard of moral rectitude. And yet she is also a pragmatist. Dynamic and idealistic, she believes life holds infinite promise. Juliet's words and actions reveal this depth and intensity as well as faith. Unfortunately, productions falter when they attempt to present a young Juliet, perhaps because too often men refuse to understand that a fourteen-year-old girl may exhibit all of these qualities. Most recently, this failure by the director explains the weakness of the BBC television production of the play.[32] In that, Juliet is positively fourteen but has neither the independent spirit nor the sensitivity of Shakespeare's character. A girl with a high, squeaky voice, she appears to be somewhat of a ninny in the early scenes. This destroys the unity of the characterization because Juliet's later, strong actions then appear inconsistent with that earlier portrayal.

Not only directors, but critics, too, have difficulty with this idea of a strong, idealistic, teenage girl. Although they may recognize that Shakespeare created several strong adult women in his plays, women whose models must have existed in the Elizabethan world, they fail to see that strong girls must have lived in the world of Shakespeare's time as well. Strong women do not emerge fully grown without a childhood. Rob-

ert Ornstein, the Shakespearean scholar, in a recent work
writes:

> Whatever homilists said about the frailty and waywardness of
> women, Shakespeare . . . depicted robust, strong-minded, and
> independent women who are unwilling to suffer any indignity
> at the command of their lords and masters. Although such dra-
> matic portraits were idealized, there were many women of like
> spirit in Elizabethan society who refused to accept the depen-
> dent, submissive roles which were conventionally prescribed
> for their sex.[33]

The critic is far less sanguine about the world that fostered
teenagers like Juliet, for he continues: "Anyone as thoughtful
as Shakespeare understood that women were trained from
childhood to _docility_" (italics mine).[34] What Ornstein fails to
accept is what de Beauvoir describes about the upbringing of
a young girl and what Shakespeare's play, although written
more than three centuries earlier, seems to illustrate. An observant recorder of human behavior (and the father of two
daughters) the dramatist probably knew that very young
women savor independence. Like boys, girls too believe in
themselves as "subject," to use de Beauvoir's word for central
or primary. Only later, when these girls grow older and become aware of their own sexuality and of societal pressures to
conform, do they accept the role of "Other," of "inessential,"
relinquishing that more "spontaneous tendency . . . to regard
[themselves] as essential." According to de Beauvoir, when
the girl becomes a young woman, she finally accepts the idea
of becoming the "inessential" because she perceives docility
as the only way to accomplish her destiny.[35] Shakespeare's
insistence that Juliet be fourteen, rather than sixteen or eigh-
teen, indicates his wish to catch that wonderful, struggling age
before docility begins.

Characteristic of such teenagers are quick shifts in language.[36] Complex patterns of speech, learned from the adult
world, give way to direct questions, as we observe in Juliet's
balcony scene with Romeo. When she asks him, "What man
art thou that thus bescreen'd in night / So stumblest on my
counsel?" (II.ii.52–53), she once again sounds like the daughter who challenged her mother with: "What is your will?"

(I.iii.6). And when, during the encounter in the garden, she asks, "How camest thou hither, . . . / The orchard walls are high and hard to climb" (II.ii.62–63), her question is direct, counterpointed against Romeo's more expansively decorated language: "With love's light wings did I o'erperch these walls" (66). As they continue, the solid basic statements of Juliet are juxtaposed against the flowery words of Romeo. Only when she must respond to his flattery does a sudden change of tone occur. Admitting that a maiden blush would "bepaint" (86) her cheek were it daylight, she stubbornly insists: "Fain would I dwell on form, fain, fain deny / What I have spoke" (88–89). Not merely a young woman falling in love, she is still very much a teenager wondering how things happen, asking questions, and calling on her own good sense to help her resolve problems. Dissatisfied with his answer, she asks again: "By whose direction foundst thou out this place?" (79). Once more he evades the question, "By love" (80). This antithesis between Romeo's extravagant language—"My life were better ended by their hate, / Than death prorogued, wanting of thy love" (77–78)—and Juliet's directness continues until Romeo needs confirmation of her love with a sworn oath.

Shakespeare then raises the question posed in *Love's Labour's Lost:* What drives a man to insist on a vow to confirm a promise? For Romeo, long after he has overheard her outspoken avowal of love, queries, "O, wilt thou leave me so unsatisfied?" (125). Wondering at his meaning, she asks what he could wish "tonight." Does the directness of her question explain his answer? "Th' exchange of thy love's faithful vow for mine" (127)? Or is he wondering whether her words resemble his own less than binding vow when he thought himself in love with Rosaline? In response to his question, Juliet rationally reminds him: "I gave thee mine before thou didst request it" (128). Earlier she had rejected the timelessness of oaths:

> . . . I will take thy word; yet, if thou swear'st,
> Thou mayest prove false: at lovers' perjuries
> They say Jove laughs.
>   (91–93)

Despite her youth and naiveté, she resembles the women of *Love's Labour's Lost,* skeptical about the value of oaths. She is

willing to accept Romeo's word as honest proof of his intention. On the other hand, a realist, she believes oaths must be
translated into action. And if his word says "love," she understands that love should be accompanied by marriage. Did her
Nurse teach her this? More likely, she took her mother's words
literally.

Promising to "look to like" before marrying Paris, Juliet
finds Romeo instead. The erotic urges that de Beauvoir writes
of have been stimulated by the wrong man, but Juliet still
thinks as "subject, active, free," a fact which disturbs some
critics. After her soliloquy, her words and actions reveal that
she has not relinquished self-sovereignty. Her statement to
Romeo, "If that thy bent of love be honorable, / Thy purpose
marriage, send me word to-morrow" (143–44) springs from
this same sense of individuality. Although she insists

> . . . if thou meanest not well,
> I do beseech thee—
>
> .   .   .
>
> To cease thy strife, and leave me to my grief
> (150–52)

she little fears that he means "not well." Has she not heard his
promise of love, his insistence on swearing, his wish to exchange oaths with her? With the confidence of youth and without the passivity proscribed for the adult woman, she maps
out the logical plan for action, based on the mutuality of their
love.

Comparing the future for a young man and a young
woman, de Beauvoir writes: "The young man's journey into
existence is made relatively easy by the fact that there is no
contradiction between his vocation as human being and as
male."[37] Although the feud between the families poses a problem for Romeo on his journey into adulthood, his conflict is
one superimposed on his life; hers is essential and part of her
inevitable development as a female in society. Her tragedy
grows out of the conflict between her "vocation as a human
being" and as a woman. Because of her extreme youth, she
has not yet learned to renounce self-sovereignty. Her vocation
as a human being is to become transcendent, to fully realize

Katharine Cornell and Basil Rathbone were a mature pair of
star-crossed lovers in this 1934 production in New York.

the self, to strive for worlds unknown. She refuses to "become the inessential," to relinquish the ego.[38] Even when she thinks of exchanging her name for Romeo's love, she does not seem to anticipate a loss of personal sovereignty. Therefore, while she resembles the women of France in her sense of self-worth and in her skepticism about the validity of oaths, she does not resemble them in her attitude toward marriage. To her, marriage does not mean a loss of self-sovereignty. In fact, she initiates the idea. To retain their sovereignty, the women of France decline the offer of a world-without-end bargain by men who originally considered love and women impediments to learning. Juliet faces no such hostility from her suitor. And, because of her extreme youth, she has not yet learned to relinquish the initiative. Unabashedly, she proffers marriage.

Attitudes toward marriage vary perceptibly in this play, depending on the character and his or her background, age, sex, and experience. In some cases, the point of view shifts with the role although the character remains the same. Thus Capulet views marriage from two different perspectives—a father's and a husband's. In the latter role, he is a man of little vision, a conventional character who reminisces about the days of his youthful escapades before he was married. He bustles around the house, directing preparations for the wedding. Stuffy, self-important, he betrays his egotism when, sending his wife to announce to Juliet their plans for her hasty marriage, he asks: "How now, wife? / Have you delivered to her our decree?" (III.v.137–38). With that word "decree" he engraves his role as master—of his home, his wife, and his daughter. And yet, he believes himself a concerned father.

Had he not tried, at first, to challenge acceptable patterns in his society by withholding his daughter's hand until she was older? And then, when he capitulated, had he not defended his actions with a lengthy explanation of how Juliet's welfare had been central to him?

> Day, night; hour, tide, time; work, play;
> Alone, in company, still my care hath been
> To have her match'd.
>
> (III.v.176–78)[39]

Breaking down time into its component parts, Capulet stresses his all-encompassing dedication to finding her the proper husband. And yet he fails her. Communication between them falters and is finally destroyed. Like so many exasperated fathers of teenagers, he demands compliance to what seems to him a reasonable demand. He neither hears, nor listens. When Juliet, on her knees, attempts to dissuade him—"Good father, I beseech you on my knees" (III.v.158)—he is deaf to her pleas, accusing her of "chopped-logic" and disobedience. Finally, he threatens to disown her, to cast her on the streets, to expose her to poverty. All this is part of his concept of marriage, and of a daughter's role as wife-to-be.

In the late 1820's, Fanny Kemble, then a very young woman, first acted Juliet. FOLGER SHAKESPEARE LIBRARY

Nor is Lady Capulet capable of hearing or identifying with Juliet. Well-trained in the role of helpmate, she repeats her husband's message in more moderate language. "Do as thou wilt, for I have done with thee" (203) the mother exclaims to her daughter. De Beauvoir writes of the "complex relations of mother to daughter . . . the mother is at once overweeningly affectionate and hostile toward her daughter." [40] Shakespeare exposes some of this antagonism when Lady Capulet explodes, "I would the fool were married to her grave!" (140). Whatever temporary truce existed between them in the scene before the ball has evaporated. Dramaturgically, the line is a foreboding of the ending although the mother, of course, has no such intense feeling. Nevertheless, hostility permeates their relationship. Did this woman who was a mother at fourteen ever sparkle with enthusiasm and passion? Has marriage been reduced to childbirth and a classic ceremony about which one says "The County Paris . . . / Shall happily make thee there a joyful bride" (114–15)? The two modifiers, "happily" and "joyful," are positive recommendations from a very unimaginative, joyless woman who, if she ever resembled Juliet, is positive testimony of the calming, oppressive effect of marriage on a woman.

Appearing to offer Juliet a healthy attitude toward marriage, the Nurse lacks any sense of moral values. Shuttling easily from praise of Paris to praise of Romeo to praise of Paris again, she considers all men attractive, particularly those who become Juliet's suitors. Nourishing Juliet's easy acceptance of her own sexuality, the Nurse demurs from any deeper commitment. Love in marriage is irrelevant. Religious scruples must not interfere with the joyous sexual experience. In his source, Shakespeare found the Nurse acting the bawd on the wedding night, hurrying the lovers, who are engaged in conversation, into the bridal bed. Instead of giving her that role in his play, the dramatist awaits a more dramatic moment to expose her limitations and to lift Juliet to a plane of terrible aloneness. Distraught at her father's ultimatum, she begs for advice and hears to her horror the Nurse's pragmatic recommendation:

> I think you are happy in this second match,
> For it excels your first; or if it did not,

Your first is dead, or 'twere as good he were
As living here and you no use of him.
(III.v.222–25)

Physical proximity becomes the final measure for a successful marriage. Incredulous, Juliet repudiates this mentor, seeking counsel from the Friar, who also has a limited vision of marriage. He fancies himself a hero in joining the lovers, foreseeing the end of a feud and laurels for his wise political gesture.

Only Romeo and Juliet approach the ideal of marriage, albeit briefly. Critics have noted that Shakespeare presents a new vision here. He alters the traditional pattern, where romance exists in one category and tragedy in another, by combining the two—probably a revolutionary change at the time.[41] Rather than the marriage of convenience or the love relationship that culminates joyously in comedy, *Romeo and Juliet* ends in tragedy, a seeming contradiction. Shakespeare is also thought to have created a new ideal: the love marriage.[42] Discarding his source, he forges a relationship of great mutuality between the lovers, one that begins with her challenge, "If your thoughts be honorable," and ends in her farewell: "My lord, my love, my friend!" (III.v.43).[43] The ideal of marriage created by this play remains, perhaps because the protagonists are destroyed so quickly. Or, perhaps it remains because the mutuality born of youth and an equal sense of the I, the ego, of both partners has not yet shifted so that he becomes the I and she the Other, in de Beauvoir's terms. Could this ideal have survived time? Could Juliet have sustained her perspective or would she, like her mother, have succumbed to societal pressures? Shakespeare allows no time for these questions to be answered. The play's strength lies in its poetry and the individuality of its two principal young people who, in a world of cynicism, have not yet felt the full pressure of that environment. But the play's uniqueness lies in its portrait of a young girl who remains strong during her swift growth to womanhood.

Critics have had difficulty with this concept. Some resemble Harley Granville-Barker, the dramatist-actor-producer whose life spanned the late nineteenth and early twentieth centuries. Although they agree on the importance of Juliet's

being accepted as a fourteen-year-old, they have strange notions of what a fourteen-year-old girl is like. Do they retreat to
their own notions of fourteen-year-old girls, those mysterious,
ethereal beings that peopled their own youths? Or do they
incorporate that idea with a larger one that encloses all women
in a shell of Otherness? Granville-Barker's estimate of Juliet
combines his responses to womankind in general with his pity
for the fate of a child bride whose life is cut short:

> One day a child, and the next a woman! But she has not grown
> older as Romeo has, nor risen to an impersonal dignity of sor-
> row. Shakespeare's women do not, for obvious reasons, so de-
> velop. They are vehicles of life, not of philosophy. Here is a life
> cut short in its brightness; and it is a cruel business, this
> slaughter of a child betrayed.[44]

Irving Ribner, the contemporary critic, worries less
about Juliet's age and more about the necessity for a single
hero in a tragedy. Unlike Granville-Barker, Ribner admits that
women have the capacity for growth. Nevertheless, he too
believes Romeo the more logical protagonist, observing:

> Both Romeo and Juliet mature greatly as the play unfolds,
> but to demonstrate the particular progress of the human
> life journey, Shakespeare concentrates upon Romeo. The
> exigencies of drama required that he concentrate upon
> one figure, and Romeo, of course, was the natural one.[45]

A close examination of the division of lines and
speeches suggests that Shakespeare sought to give equal
weight to the fortunes of the two principals. According to the
Concordance, Romeo has approximately 19 percent of the lines
and Juliet 17 percent.[46] But statistics prove illusory when a
work of literature is being judged for its emotional and psychological effect. Since Romeo tends to longer, more expansive
speeches, the division of lines merely records that fact. It does
not record the intensity of the speeches, or the impact of the
total characterization on the observer. Although the role of
Juliet may present difficulties for an actress who is herself
older than fourteen, it nevertheless offers a range and lyricism
that makes it an enviable part. Juliet moves the audience, not
with "pity for a child betrayed" but with admiration for a

courageous person attempting to fight her destiny as a woman. She is recognizable as a person caught in a web—a tragic figure who expresses a human predicament.

Although Romeo matures during the play, Shakespeare uses several devices to weight the tragedy in favor of Juliet as the major figure. He retains Rosaline from the source; he emphasizes Romeo's irrationality; and, in the scenes in which they can be compared, he gives the lines of greater depth and beauty to Juliet. Probably one of the sharpest contrasts is that between Romeo's response to the news of his banishment and Juliet's to the news of her forthcoming marriage to Paris. In the scene in the Friar's cell, when learning of his banishment Romeo throws himself on the floor and threatens suicide. Faced with a far more complex challenge—bigamy rather than banishment—Juliet, although considering suicide herself, seeks advice, listening hopefully for some solution.

The scenes between Romeo and the Friar, and Juliet and the Friar illuminate the contrast. In the former, we hear:

ROMEO: . . . "Banished"?
O friar, the damned use that word in hell;
. . .
FRIAR: Thou fond mad man, hear me a little speak.
ROMEO: O, thou wilt speak again of banishment.
FRIAR: I'll give thee armor to keep off that word:
Adversity's sweet milk, philosophy,
. . .
ROMEO: Yet "banished"? Hang up philosophy!
(III.iii.46–47; 52–55; 57)

Their conversation continues with this intensity until the Nurse's arrival. The decision to proceed with plans for the wedding night, with its offer of only momentary solace, calms Romeo. In contrast, Juliet—alone, rejected by her parents, ill-counselled by the Nurse, and even forced to speak politely to Paris before hearing the Friar's advice—retains control of herself. To the Friar's offer of sympathy, she responds with a warning:

Tell me not, friar, that thou hearest of this,
Unless thou tell me how I may prevent it.
(IV.i.50–51)

Anxious to allow him no opportunity for advice resembling the Nurse's, Juliet continues at length, disclosing the alternatives she has considered so as "to live an unstain'd wife" (88) to her sweet Lord. Prompted by the desperate tone of Juliet's decision, the Friar offers another alternative: a potion that will stop the warmth and breath, thus seemingly the life, in her veins. When Juliet agrees, the Friar approvingly asserts in one of the more ironic lines in the play:

> And this shall free thee from this present shame,
> If no inconstant toy, nor womanish fear,
> Abate thy valor in the acting it.
>
> (118–20)

Throughout the play Shakespeare introduces the word "womanish" in the Friar's speeches. When this man of the cloth unthinkingly warns a woman against being womanish, he reveals his insensitivity. Because of his subsequent actions in the tomb scene, his lines here have a great poignancy. He is directing Juliet to take a most unusual potion and picturing to her the moment of her awakening. She is womanish indeed in the deepest sense of the word—in love, and married, and seeking to remain true to the man she has married. If, however, womanish is to be interpreted as fearful and cowardly, then the Friar, who may have chosen his vocation in order to be unwomanish all his life, ultimately proves himself cowardly at the one moment when his courage is tested. Anxious to leave the tomb, worried about the magnitude of his own responsibility, he urges Juliet: "Come go, good Juliet, I dare no longer stay" (V.iii.159). Instinctively "womanish," according to his own definition of the word, he flees, and must be considered directly responsible for Juliet's suicide when, no restraining hand present and abandoned by the Friar, she believes herself without an alternative.

Courage and directness of action more truly characterize Juliet than Romeo. Compared with his thrashing about on the floor of the Friar's cell in self-pity, she moves on her own behalf. Later, going to the Friar for help and warning him against suggesting acquiescence to marriage with Paris, she reveals strength and determination. The loss of her parents' and Nurse's support intensifies Juliet's tragedy by stressing her terrible aloneness. Although Romeo's parents know nothing of his attachment, either to Rosaline or to Juliet, they are unconcerned about his marrying, fail to connect his melancholy with thoughts of love, and are never in open conflict with him. Juliet's parents, on the other hand, assert their right to determine her husband from the moment the play begins. When she chooses another, she must confront their anger and hostility. Once again Shakespeare stresses the challenge to a woman to govern her own life. Juliet, like Kate and Bianca, must accept the husband of her parents' choice. She is expected to be compliant chattel in a good business arrangement. Whereas the feud magnifies Juliet's problem and leads to tragedy, it also asserts Shakespeare's awareness of the humanity of women.

He not only contrasts the strain that parents impose on sons and daughters, but compares the responses and the sense of personal commitment of the two lovers to each other. Fearing the unadvisability of their sudden contract, Juliet exclaims:

> It is too rash, too unadvis'd, too sudden,
> Too like the lightning, which doth cease to be
> Ere one can say it lightens.
>
> (II.ii.118–20)

Romeo fears merely that "Being in night, all this is but a dream" (140). She seems more aware of the far-reaching effects of this agreement. Her lines indicate insight into her own actions and forebodings about the outcome. Another comparison occurs in their actions moments after the wedding. Romeo proves unable to withstand the societal pressure to conform despite his knowledge that participating in the duel with Tybalt must be disastrous. Invoking the word "effeminate" to his own attempts at maintaining the peace, he challenges Tybalt after Mercutio's death. Loyalty to family and male code of honor prevail over reason. His mind fails to govern his action.

In comparison, Juliet, in the scene in which she hears of Tybalt's death, wrestles with the unexpected dilemma. For a moment she wonders whether she has been duped into marrying the wrong man. The list of epithets that spout from her

mouth—"Beautiful tyrant! fiend angelical! / Dove-feather'd
raven! wolvish ravening lamb!" (III.ii.75–76), passionately
linking opposites in this series of pictures—reveals a sharp
imagination and an intensity of spirit. Although, upon hearing the news, she momentarily exclaims "O serpent heart, hid
with a flow'ring face! / Did ever dragon keep so fair a cave?"
(III.ii.73–74), she quickly relents. When the Nurse, following
Juliet's lead, derides Romeo, Juliet vehemently reprimands
her:

> Blister'd be thy tongue
> ·   ·   ·
> Upon his brow shame is asham'd to sit;
> For 'tis a throne where honor may be crown'd.
> (90–93)

Choosing her husband over mother, father, and family, Juliet
decides:

> Why followed not, when she said, "Tybalt's dead,"
> Thy father or thy mother, nay, or both,
> Which modern lamentation might have moved?
> ·   ·   ·
> . . . "Romeo is banished"!
> There is no end, no limit, measure, bound,
> In that word's death.
> (III.ii.118–20, 124–26)

Despite these examples of Juliet's strength and of her
struggle to control her own future, critics have been reluctant
to accept her as the major tragic protagonist. Some, like Ribner, have theorized that if there is to be a single protagonist,
Romeo should be the choice. Others have even suggested that
"the two great protagonists of the drama are the two families"
and that the lovers are "only part of the design."[47] Since we
are deeply involved with the Capulets—Juliet, Tybalt, Lord
and Lady Capulet, and the Nurse—and only peripherally
aware of the Montagues, this seems a questionable proposal.
The families function as they relate to Juliet and her parents.
The only other major character in the play, Mercutio, is friend,
not family, to Romeo, and is distant enough to enunciate the

final ominous curse, "A plague a' both your houses!" (III.i.106).

Michael Langham, Artistic Director of the Shakespeare Festival in Stratford, Ontario, from 1956 to 1968, offers an interesting analysis of the closing moments of the play and then suggests still another alternative. He reminisces about his directorial approach:

> A theme which the passage of years now reveals as significant to me, and which I ignored in my previous interpretation, is a favorite of Shakespeare's—learning responsibility through adversity, learning the answer to the time-honoured question asked by bewildered parents, "Where did we go wrong?" This, I now realize, is the dramatic meaning, well prepared for throughout, of the play's long final movement following the lovers' deaths.[48]

Langham then admits that he cut a great deal from the ending where the people in authority, the Prince as well as the parents, ask themselves, "Where did we go wrong?"

Langham, of course, was following a tradition going back to the eighteenth century when the last act was greatly altered and much of the material after the death scene was omitted. Like Langham's production the ballet, too, closes with the death scene. There, however, one can almost forgive MacMillan because, working in another medium, he strives to capture the major feeling of the play and successfully retains the centrality of Juliet. His closing scene is devoted to a long dance in which Romeo, clasping the dead Juliet, dances with her, reluctant to accept the finality of her death. It is a remarkable tour-de-force on the part of both dancers—the man playing Romeo as he swirls her through a series of turns; the woman dancing Juliet, the lifeless corpse.

Langham's observation, however, while it reminds us of the long speeches of the Friar and the shorter comments of the Prince and Montague, again seeks to divide the play equally between the two young people. I believe he is right in noting that the parents would tend to ask themselves, "Where did we go wrong?" Yet this obscures the difference in responsibility between the parents of Romeo and those of Juliet. It

overlooks the deep involvement of Juliet's parents in precipi-
tating her dilemma, and it fails to accept the greater intensity
of her problem.

One can cope with banishment; bigamy and the pros-
pect of rape in marriage are more threatening for a woman.
Although Clifford Leech, a contemporary critic, writes, "Juliet
knows that the man is possessed by the woman while he
merely penetrates her"; women know that this is a male myth
to justify the invasion of the inner, private personal space of a
woman without consent.[49] Turning upside down what "Juliet
knows," this critic distorts the meaning of the play and depre-
cates the importance of sexual chastity and fidelity to this
young woman. I agree with Philip Edwards, the distinguished
contemporary scholar, when he says that "Juliet, after all, is
the truest being in the play as well as the most important."[50]
For while the feud between the families leads to the death of
Tybalt and the banishment of Romeo, the decision of the parents to catapult Juliet out of childhood into marriage with little
thought of her responses as a person leads to the ultimate
tragedy.

The young Peggy Ashcroft portrays an innocent, serious Desdemona to Paul Robeson's adoring, naive warrior-husband in this 1930 production in London. BILLY ROSE THEATRE COLLECTION, THE NEW YORK PUBLIC LIBRARY

CHAPTER FIVE

A Woman Tamed

OTHELLO

"Be as your fancies teach you;
What e'er you be, I am obedient."
(III.iii.88–89)

*M*arried to Othello before the drama opens, Desdemona is a woman slowly tamed in the crucible of marriage. Bright, intelligent, and courageous, she is endowed with qualities that should assure her success. Nevertheless, these strengths become handicaps when she seeks to adjust to a new role. Continuing where *Romeo and Juliet* ended, *Othello* raises questions left unanswered by the swift deaths of those youthful star-crossed lovers. It asks whether the passion and idealism of two lovers who have courageously crossed color lines and defied conventions can be sustained in marriage. It asks whether the patterns of marriage are stronger than the individuals, even the most outstanding individuals. Arguing for the success of Desdemona and Othello are their maturity, their long friendship and love preceding marriage, her managerial skills, and his gentleness. Arguing against their success are miscegenation and villainy feeding passion. Holding the balance are marital conventions—conventions that demand more of women than of men.

The regulations that limit a woman's activity in marriage are greater than those limiting a man's; despite the advantages of security and protection that marriage assures her, the woman actually loses more and gains less than does the man, reasons the late nineteenth-century sociologist, Emile Durkheim.[1] John Stuart Mill denounces the relationship because "it confers upon one of the parties to the contract, legal power and control over the person, property, and freedom of action of the other party, independent of her own wishes."[2] Even more significant to *Othello* is Mill's conclusion that this arrangement is demoralizing for both parties.

Although the play examines marriage, it is not a domestic tragedy, for, as Helen Gardner reminds us, any evaluation of *Othello* must begin with our first responses to the drama— our sense of its grandeur and soaring beauty.[3] Domestic tragedy usually presents characters of limited power in imagination and background. The magnificence of Othello, the range in Desdemona as a woman, including her intelligence, originality, and defiance of convention, belie this designation of the work. But it is the tragedy of a woman, of women, pummeled into shape by the conventions that bind. For Shakespeare takes not one, but two marriages—one new and fresh, one old and worn—to give us a double vision of the experience. Some critics tend to prefer Emilia, the wife of Iago, to Desdemona because Emilia's story ends defiantly on a positive note, offering hope for women. But the extremity of the force that breaks her submission to her husband hardly argues for her independence. Desdemona's tragedy is the more usual—a slow wearing away of the resistance, a slow imposition of patterns—a slow loss of confidence in the strength of the self, always with the aim of adjusting to marriage. Coleridge believed that she was just the woman every man "wishes . . . for a wife."[4] How sad that this should be a man's dream.

Shakespeare presents Desdemona in all of her power at the beginning of the play. To heighten our curiosity, he offers three different perspectives of her before she ever appears. The first is from Iago who, hidden by the dark of night, coarsely taunts her father, "An old black ram / Is tupping your white ewe" (I.i.88–89). The next is from her adoring father who, describing the Desdemona he knows, refuses to believe she has married Othello:

> A maiden, never bold;
> Of spirit so still and quiet that her motion
> Blush'd at herself.
>> (I.iii.94–96)

Finally, we listen while Othello adds still another dimension to the portrait, suggesting that she was not merely a passive woman entrapped by him:

> My story being done,
> She gave me for my pains a world of sighs;
>> .   .   .
> She wish'd she had not heard it, yet she wish'd
> That heaven had made her such a man.
>> (I.iii.158–63)

Thus claims Othello. We anxiously await Desdemona's entrance.

When, at last, she appears, she speaks with dignity and self-possession. Her first words are addressed to her father, Brabantio. Standing before the Venetian Senate, she listens when he asks:

> Come hither, gentle mistress.
> Do you perceive in all this noble company
> Where most you owe obedience?
>> (I.iii.178–80)

Neither weepingly begging her father's approval, like Juliet, nor angrily fighting his treatment of her, like Kate, Desdemona rationally answers him. Admitting her obligation to him for "life and education" (182), she then insists:

> . . . so much duty as my mother show'd
> To you, preferring you before her father,
> So much I challenge that I may profess
> Due to the Moor, my lord.
>> (186–89)

Her words are terse; her approach direct. Aware of her father's prejudice, she chooses her language with precision. Unwilling to equivocate, she challenges him with her phrase, "The Moor, my lord."

Father and daughter duel with words. While the senators stand on the sidelines, time-keepers and referees in this combat, Desdemona and Brabantio carry on their battle, focusing on the naming process surrounding the word "Moor." "Valiant Othello" (I.iii.48), says the Duke. "Brave Moor" (291), asserts a senator. But Brabantio admits neither. He converts "Moor" from a term of approbation to one of disgust by omitting the definite article or any descriptive adjective from his words of address. "Look to her, Moor," the father warns in his final words, "She has deceiv'd her father, and may thee" (292–93).

Nor are these Brabantio's only words as we tend to believe from stage productions that often cut his earlier anguished interchange with his colleagues. The senators, having decided to send their most capable general, Othello, to repel the Turks, and hoping to defeat the enemy, are immersed instead in a family dispute. Faced with a political and military as well as a social problem, the Venetians attempt mediation between Brabantio, one of their members, and his daughter, who has married their most able general. Speaking on Desdemona's behalf, the Duke reprimands her father with "Your son-in-law is far more fair than black" (I.iii.290). But Brabantio knows only a father's loss, "He bears the sentence well that nothing bears / But the free comfort which from thence he hears" (212–13). In this vein, the father rejects solicitude or kind words. "But words are words; I never yet did hear / That the bruis'd heart was pierced through the ear" (218–19). The speech, searing in its intensity, helps define Desdemona. Frequently, however, this speech dwindles to a few lines. Desdemona, then, loses some of her specificity, for drama relies on the interaction of characters. A colorless father diminishes the intensity of the daughter. The full text, however, vibrates with the challenge of youth to age, of daughter to father.

The victim of neither magic nor drugs, Desdemona convinces the court of her love for Othello. Nor will she willingly remain behind when he must depart for war. "I crave fit disposition for my wife" (I.iii.236), Othello requests. Insensitively, unimaginatively, the Duke suggests she reside in her

A self-confident Desdemona confronts her father and the Venetian
Senate in this 1821 illustration by Richard Cook. FOLGER
SHAKESPEARE LIBRARY

father's home. Swiftly all three—Desdemona, Brabantio, and Othello—reject the proposal. In comparison with the almost monosyllabic responses of Othello and Brabantio, Desdemona speaks at length, offering several reasons against the Duke's plan. Among her arguments, she cites the strain such an arrangement would be on her father—how repugnant to him. Finally, she proposes an alternative. She would accompany Othello to Cyprus. Speaking in direct language once again, she refers to conjugal rights—the joys of marriage that include sexual fulfillment:

> That I did love the Moor to live with him,
> My downright violence, and storm of fortunes,
> May trumpet to the world.
>
> (I.iii.248–50)

Although the language obscures exact meaning, the individual words convey the speaker's intensity: "violence," "storm," and "trumpet" as a verb. Desdemona speaks for youth, sexual honesty, and passion.

At Cyprus, she continues to surprise us with her freshness and vigor, as well as her sensitivity to those around her. With Iago, she parries in verbal quips. With Lieutenant Cassio, her husband's second in command, she acts the solicitous friend. To all, waiting anxiously with her for Othello's arrival, hoping that his ship has not been lost in the storm, she reassures with her gaiety, confiding to the audience:

> I am not merry; but I do beguile
> The thing I am by seeming otherwise.—
>
> (II.i.122–23)

Thomas Rymer, writing in 1693, denounced Desdemona's behavior in this scene, accusing her of crudeness.[5] But Shakespeare was expanding his earlier portrait of an independent, bright woman, worthy of audience interest. "Come, how wouldst thou praise me?" (124), she laughingly challenges Iago, then matches him witticism for witticism. She recognizes the "fond paradoxes" he sports "to make fools laugh i' th' alehouse." (138–39). She accuses him of inaccuracy in the way he praises (actually denigrates) all but the worst women. She listens to his puns and double entendres. "O most lame and impotent conclusion" (161) she asserts of his last quip in a series of descriptions of women, introducing her own pun. Most of these lines usually disappear from stage productions. The excision may seem slight—a mere thirty-six lines of quick banter—but it alters the portrait of Desdemona, simplifying her character.

Desdemona's activities on the quay at Cyprus prior to Othello's arrival illustrate her skill and training as a hostess as well as her sophistication. In the scene where he addresses the senators, Othello had described her activities in the days when he came courting. He spoke of how she alternated between listening to his tales of adventure and acting the housewife for her father:

> . . . These things to hear
> Would Desdemona seriously incline;
> But still the house affairs would draw her thence,
> Which ever as she could with haste dispatch,
> She'ld come again, and with a greedy ear
> Devour up my discourse.
> (I.iii.145–50)

The scene at the dock verifies Othello's report, reveals the self-confidence nurtured by her early experience, and provides additional background on the youthful Desdemona before she attempts to adjust to marriage. On the quay at Cyprus she is testing her old skills in a new setting. Verbal agility, outspokenness, honesty—they all seem to work.

In an excellent essay on *Othello,* Susan Snyder compares the endings of the comedies, which, she claims, insist that interdependence in marriage is a way of completing oneself, with the ending of *Othello,* which challenges such a postulate.[6] Snyder believes Shakespeare to be saying that, since separateness is part of the human condition, when two people who love each other become interdependent they are bound to meet tragedy. Upon this concept of the separateness of people, I wish to offer a further theory for consideration. In *Othello,* Shakespeare is dealing with two people who have known and loved each other for some time. Until they marry, the tragedy does not occur because until that time they do not have to conform to any set roles; they function as two individuals. With marriage, they receive a new set of rules, new patterns for behavior. Desdemona, in Act III, reminds Othello of how often they disagreed. Attempting lightness, she speaks of:

> . . . Michael Cassio,
> That came a-wooing with you, and so many a time,
> When I have spoke of you dispraisingly,
> Hath ta'en your part—
>
> (III.iii.70–73)

Implicit here is the idea that disagreements between them could lead her to disparage Othello. Her lines also suggest that these disagreements were an integral part of their relationship.

We hear an example of this disagreement and mutual respect when they reunite at Cyprus. "Oh my fair Warrior" (II.i.182), exclaims Othello joyously. "My dear Othello" (182), returns Desdemona, her speech tempered while his words continue to soar in hyperbole. "If after every tempest come such calms, / May the winds blow till they have waken'd death" (185–86), he begins, continuing uninterrupted until he ventures to speak of the absolute comfort and contentment achieved at this moment:

> If it were now to die,
> 'Twere now to be most happy; for I fear
> My soul hath her content so absolute
> That not another comfort like to this
> Succeeds in unknown fate.
>
> (189–93)

Vehemently, Desdemona protests. She envisions marriage as an ongoing process, one that promises continued growth.

> The heavens forbid
> But that our loves and comforts should increase
> Even as our days do grow!
>
> (193–95)

They have disagreed before. They disagree now. He accepts her semantic correction, her meticulousness with words that she exhibited in the interchange with her father. "Amen to that, sweet powers!" (195), Othello responds. Although his words prove prophetic within the context of the drama, his willingness to alter his views underlines the uniqueness of their early relationship.

Marriage will impose new forms. Mutual respect will give way to an aloneness created by one party holding the power, the other being powerless. Shakespeare offers an immediate illustration in the lines of Iago and the interaction between him and Emilia. Despite her sullen protest that her husband has "little cause" to complain, Iago, in a few swift strokes, blocks in the basic forms of his marriage:

> Bells in your parlors, wild-cats in your kitchens,
> Saints in your injuries, devils being offended.
>
> (II.i.110–11)

For Iago, women's voices clang like dissonant bells in the parlor and rise to the level of screams in the kitchen, the word "wild-cat" even implying a physical tearing at one another by women. But try to stop such behavior, he suggests, and women will act the injured saints. Hardly a pretty picture of women or of marriage emerges from these lines. Although spoken in jest, they hint at the interaction between him and Emilia. More revealing are her weak protests of innocence, confirming Iago's description. In this glimpse of a marriage long suffered by a man and a woman, he emerges as the dominant person. Nevertheless, he has no illusions about the potential for happiness in marriage but speaks with the bitterness of a misogynist. Later, in an aside about Othello and Desdemona, he sneers: "O, you are well tun'd now! / But I'll set down the pegs that make this music" (199–200). His words are those of skeptical humanity to the joy and hope of new found love. The guest at the wedding wishes the bride and groom joy but thinks of the disappointments that lie ahead for them. Othello, too, will discover reality; Iago promises to guide him to it. Thus Shakespeare contrasts the mutual respect between the newlyweds with the imbalanced relationship in a long standing marriage.

As the drama progresses, Desdemona continues to exhibit the self-confidence fostered during her youth. She assumes that the virtues of rationalism and forthrightness will prove natural supports. Instead, she finds they trap her. Her first semi-defeat occurs when she appeals for the reinstatement of Cassio who has been stripped of his position because of fighting when drunk. Desdemona appeals to Othello, not on the basis of his arbitrarily pleasing her, but on the basis of reason. She questions the wisdom of his extraordinarily harsh punishment for Cassio's comparatively harmless offense:

> And yet his trespass, in our common reason
> (Save that they say the wars must make example
> Out of her best), is not almost a fault
> T' incur a private check.
>
> (III.iii.64–67)

Conceding that some reprimand is necessary, she believes that in time of joyous celebration her husband is applying measures reserved for wartime.

Othello refuses to argue with her. Accustomed to discussing their disagreements, she is surprised by his answer. "I will deny thee nothing" (76), he asserts. But she is not asking blind assent. She then lists all of the normal processes of living to which Cassio's return to his former position might be compared. Finally, Desdemona distinguishes between a reasonable request, such as she here presents, and a favor of great weight:

> Why, this is not a boon;
> 'Tis as I should entreat you wear your gloves,
> Or feed on nourishing dishes, or keep you warm,
> Or sue to you to do a peculiar profit
> To your own person. Nay, when I have a suit
> Wherein I mean to touch your love indeed,
> It shall be full of poise and difficult weight,
> And fearful to be granted.
>
> (76–83)

Arguing with him, as she had previous to marriage, she expects a rational answer. Instead, Othello repeats his earlier statement, learning the ways of a husband:

I will deny thee nothing.
(83)

Role playing has begun. Othello's vulnerability to convention not only leads him to permit Iago to malign Desdemona in the scene immediately following this encounter, but also marks the beginning of the decline in the relationship between Othello and Desdemona. Prior to her appeal for Cassio, Iago's innuendo had been limited to a few comparatively inoffensive lines. After it, he freely muddies Desdemona's reputation. Striving to conform to a role, Othello dams the easy flow of talk between himself and his wife. The man who had prided himself on her independence, asking the senators to "Let her have your voice" (I.iii.260), now begins to think in terms of power and powerlessness. This precedes only briefly the thought of a wife as a possession.

Because her appeal for Cassio in this scene so clearly reaffirms her strength, the stage history offers interesting insights into attitudes toward Desdemona. Both the longer speech, beginning "Why, this is not a boon," and the shorter one, on the subject of Cassio's trespass, tend to disappear, whole or in part, from productions. As I have previously indicated, I believe an inter-relationship exists between textual excision or emendation and attitudes toward women in the larger society of the time. *Othello* has always been a popular play; it has also frequently been cut. Fairly extensive records exist of acting texts since 1761. A few characteristic texts suggest the treatment of these speeches. In 1761, both disappear from the stage.[7] In 1804, Kemble eliminates both although retaining the longer speech in the printed text (it is crossed out in the promptbook).[8] The same formula holds as late as 1871. One of the speeches appears in the text but both disappear in the theater.[9] In the twentieth century—and here I cite the 1930 Paul Robeson production—stage business offers a valuable key to Desdemona.[10] Again only the longer speech appears in print. A fountain on stage provides the focus for the major

A man that languishes in your displeasure.
Oth. Who is't you mean?
Des. Why, your lieutenant, Cassio. Good my lord,
If I have any grace or power to move you,
His present reconciliation take;
For if he be not one that truly loves you,
~~That errs in ignorance and not in cunning~~,
I have no judgement in an honest face: 50
I prithee, call him back.
Oth.   Went he hence now?
Des. Ay, sooth; so humbled,
That he hath left part of his grief with me,
To suffer with him. Good love, call him back.
Oth. Not now, sweet Desdemona; some other time.
Des. But shall't be shortly?
Oth.   The sooner, sweet, for you.
Des. Shall't be to-night at supper?

Oth.   No, not to-night.
Des. To-morrow dinner then?
Oth.   I shall not dine at home;
I meet the captains at the citadel. ————   *X. L. move slowly round fountain. followed by Des.*
Des. Why then to-morrow night; or Tuesday morn; 60
On Tuesday noon, or night; on Wednesday morn:
I prithee, name the time; but let it not   ————   *Oth Sits on R corner of fountain*
Exceed three days: in faith, he's penitent; ————   *Des sits back of fountain*
~~And yet his trespass, in our common reason—~~
~~Save that, they say, the wars must make examples~~
~~Out of their best—is not almost a fault~~
~~To incur a private check.~~ When shall he come?
Tell me, Othello; I wonder in my soul,   ————   *Des shakes water from Lily on othello head, he rises*
What you would ask me, that I should deny,   69   *and moves R.*
Or stand so mammering on. What! Michael Cassio,
That came a-wooing with you, and so many a time
When I have spoke of you dispraisingly
Hath ta'en your part; ~~to have so much to do~~
~~To bring him in~~! Trust me, I could do much— — *Rise X. to Othello*
Oth. Prithee, no more: let him come when he will;
I will deny thee nothing. ┗————   *Xing L. to fountain and sit.*
Des.   Why, this is not a boon;
'Tis as I should entreat you wear your gloves,
Or feed on nourishing dishes, or keep you warm,
Or sue to you to do a peculiar profit
To your own person: nay, when I have a suit   80
Wherein I mean to touch your love indeed,
It shall be full of poise and difficult weight,
And fearful to be granted. ————   *X to Oth and kneel.*
Oth.   I will deny thee nothing:
Whereon, I do beseech thee, grant me this,   *Rise and lift Des*
To leave me but a little to myself.
Des. Shall I deny you? no; farewell, my lord. —   *X. L. and curtsey*
Oth. Farewell, my Desdemona: I'll come to thee straight.
Des. ~~Emilia, come.~~ Be as your fancies teach you; — *X up to othello*
Whate'er you be, I am obedient.
[*Exeunt Desdemona ~~and Emilia~~.* ┗ .
Oth. Excellent wretch! Perdition catch my soul,   90   *watching them go*
But I do love thee! and when I love thee not,
Chaos is come again.
Iago. My noble lord,— ————   *Xing to C.*
Oth.   What dost thou say, Iago?

Directions for Desdemona to sprinkle water on Othello's head
appear in this promptbook of the 1930 Robeson production. FOLGER
SHAKESPEARE LIBRARY

action. From it Desdemona plucks a lily, sprinkling the water from the lily on Othello's head. At the conclusion of her appeal, she crosses to Othello and kneels. Accompanying his second "I will deny thee nothing," he rises and lifts Desdemona from her kneeling, suppliant position. Finally, when she departs, the stage directions "cross left and curtsey" accompany her lines "farewell my lord." There can be little misinterpretation of the role of Desdemona in these acting versions. Either she is denied the power of reasoning, appearing submissive and begging, or she is transformed into a coquette, whose coy gestures, rather than her words, form the focal center of the action.

Anyone seeking to understand Desdemona's attitude toward herself vis-à-vis Othello must carefully scrutinize her response after his second "I will deny thee nothing" followed by his request to "leave me but a little to myself" (III.iii.85). She picks up his phraseology and skillfully converts it into the interrogative, "Shall I deny you? No. Farewell, my lord" (86). Before leaving, however, she makes one final comment: "Be as your fancies teach you; / What e'er you be, I am obedient" (88–89). Is this the statement of a compliant wife, or does the word "fancies," with its negative connotation in the Elizabethan era, suggest a challenge? (The word "fancies" at that time included "delusive imagination" and "caprice" among its many definitions.) Loaded with ambiguities, the speech has ironic overtones. When, however, excisions occur, or stage directions dictate coquettish, compliant actions, a new meaning emerges. Then, the meekness implicit in the individual words dictates a straight reading.

As the play progresses, we watch Desdemona attempting to understand her role but inevitably exhibiting—although with less frequency—the strength that characterized her at the start. One of the last examples occurs in Act IV. Already convinced of her infidelity, Othello listens incredulously while she speaks to the Ambassador from Venice. Unfortunately, the subject is Cassio, the person with whom Othello believes her unfaithful. The lines have a double edge. "How does Lieutenant Cassio?" (IV.i.222), Lodovico, the Ambassador asks. Iago noncommittally responds, "Lives, sir" (223). Desdemona gives the more complete explanation "Cousin, there's fall'n between him and my lord / An unkind breach; but you shall make all well" (224–25). When Othello challenges "Are you sure of that?" Desdemona, stunned, answers "My lord?" But when Lodovico pursues the questioning, Desdemona volunteers to explain, using the unfortunate phrase, "for the love I bear to Cassio" (233). Still not fully aware of the demands on a wife, she fails to be silent.

Throughout the play, we hear echoes of the voice that defied her father and society to marry Othello, the Moor. Dynamic and verbal in the early scenes, she resembles many of Shakespeare's strong women—particularly Juliet, who defied her parents, and Beatrice, who knew that wooing is not smooth. Like them, Desdemona is "half the wooer." Unlike them, her story begins with marriage, and her tragedy derives from the testing of premarital ideals against the reality of marriage. Jessie Bernard writes of woman's being "ciphered out" in marriage—losing her identity as an individual; Simone de Beauvoir speaks of woman accepting the role of "Other" where man is the "Subject."[11] Virginia Woolf offers still another perspective when she describes woman as the magic mirror in which man sees himself at twice his normal size.[12] Like Gulliver in the land of the Lilliputians, man then sees woman as a diminutive being. For a person like Desdemona, such a swift transformation is difficult although she thinks she understands her new role. "So much duty as my mother show'd / To you," she claims to her father, she will give to Othello.

Shakespeare forces the audience to recognize her strength in the first act where two conflicting qualities surface: her sense of self-confidence and her belief in woman's dedication to her husband. After addressing her father, she offers her reasons for loving Othello:

> I saw Othello's visage in his mind,
> And to his honors and his valiant parts
> Did I my soul and fortunes consecrate.
> (I.iii.252–54)

Charles Lamb cites this speech when presenting his own reason for preferring to read the play in the privacy of his study rather than seeing it on the stage where miscegenation would be obvious. "I appeal to everyone that has seen Othello played, whether he did not, on the contrary, sink Othello's mind in his colour."[13]

The lines are important not only because they challenge those present to acknowledge Othello's blackness, but because of the religious connotations of the language: "valiant parts," "honors," "souls," and "consecrate." The words betray an almost holy dedication to the man she has married. Desdemona is willing to subordinate her life to his, illustrating de Beauvoir's thesis of the male as "Subject," or major focus of attention, and the woman as "Other." But this new bride does not comprehend the full implications of such self-denigration, believing rather that reciprocity and mutual respect, elements that animated their relationship before marriage, will continue to prevail. She little realizes that these words will conflict with the person behind them—the woman who had been certain of her self.

Othello's reasons for marrying have nothing to do with gods and super-beings. "She lov'd me for the dangers I had pass'd" (I.iii.167), he tells the senators before her arrival. "And I lov'd her that she did pity them" (168). In greater detail, he explains how their relationship grew, his tales of adventure eliciting her pity:

> She swore, in faith 'twas strange, 'twas
>   passing strange;
> 'Twas pitiful, 'twas wondrous pitiful.
>   (160-61)

The words "pitiful" and "pity" ring through his speech, offering a verbal portrait of Desdemona as an emotional woman highly influenced by romantic tales. Was this Othello's impression of her—was he hoping that the words would appeal to his auditors—or was he, perhaps, transferring to her some of his own perceptions of what a woman's role should be? The word "pity" never enters Desdemona's vocabulary when describing her love, just as "duty" never enters Othello's. Nor does he express views similar to Desdemona's on the relationship of sex to marriage. Compared with her healthy, outspoken desire to accompany him to Cyprus, he protests little interest in the "light-wing'd toys / Of feather'd Cupid" (268–69), insisting that his obligations to the state supersede all others. Seeming to dismiss romantic love and sexuality, he refers to "wanton dullness" (269) that can result from love interfering with business. The irony of his statement vibrates through the tragedy.

Finally, Desdemona and Othello present different visions of the future. Early in the play, he confides privately that were it not for Desdemona's unusual qualities, he would never have married:

> But that I love the gentle Desdemona,
> I would not my unhoused free condition
> Put into circumscription and confine
> For the sea's worth.
>   (I.ii.25–28)

Marriage confines; no vast horizons exist here. The most illuminating contrast, however, occurs in the exchange already cited when he and Desdemona disagree during their reunion at Cyprus.

Despite their differences, they promise an original marriage for it will include an interchange of ideas; it will even allow for disagreement. Othello's lines when they leave the senate acknowledge a multifaceted role for Desdemona:

> Come, Desdemona, I have but an hour
> Of love, of worldly matter and direction,
> To spend with thee.
>   (I.iii.298–300)

But something happens to their relationship that is not attributable merely to the machinations of Iago, a character who probably grew out of the medieval Vice figure and reveals elements of evil in men.[14] Whether he exhibits, as Coleridge suggests, "motiveless malignity," personifies evil within Othello himself, as others believe, or is a valid, recognizable character, Iago contributes to the tragedy and arouses our pity for Othello, his major victim. Nevertheless, Shakespeare goes beyond the relationship between these two men to delve into that between Othello and Desdemona. The tragic portrait is one we still recognize of a man and a woman who have entered an unconventional marriage but lack the creativity and strength to nurture it. Divided by their cultural backgrounds as well as by their self-perceptions as male and female, they discover marriage to be more complex than either had anticipated. Their racial differences, which helped emphasize their strengths in the early section of the drama, exacerbate their problems of adjustment. Othello, unfamiliar with Venetian ways, enters a foreign territory both emotionally and socially. False reports of Venetian patterns of marriage delude and confuse him. Desdemona, too, clings to conventions, believing that mutual respect can coexist in a relationship where a woman owes "duty" to a husband and considers him almost godlike. Slowly, unwillingly, she discovers the contradiction implicit here. Finally, Othello's attempt to conform means a retreat to a male world, setting another network into operation, one that supersedes the intimacy between husband and wife. As a result, he becomes vulnerable to Iago's description of Desdemona. This willingness to allow another man to speak of her as Iago does reveals Othello's inability to create new patterns of marriage.

In the medieval morality plays, good and evil battle for the soul of mankind. The Vice figure, or Devil, frequently triumphs until the last moments before death when Virtue finally convinces the protagonist to repent, saving his soul, if not his life.[15] Because of Othello's anguished choice between believing Desdemona and accepting Iago's word as truth, some critics consider Iago the representative of evil and Desdemona that of good in a conflict for Othello's soul. But this formula fails because the play transcends the simple battle between the personifications of two abstract ideas for a soul. Although Iago is the quintessence of evil—whether a Satan figure or evil in mankind—Desdemona is far more complex than a simple representation of good. Nor are the two characters exact opposites.[16] Any neat equation balancing them distorts, minimizing the strength of Shakespeare's portrait of this new bride. Compared with Iago, she has stimulated far less in-depth critical analysis—perhaps because evil is more flamboyant and more easily discernable than good.[17] Nevertheless, close explication of her lines reveals a well-developed character guided by reason, complementing her intense love for her husband in a tragedy exploring the impact of marriage on a woman of courage and independence.

That Shakespeare was concentrating on marriage rather than just discussing love seems apparent from the references to the long courtship of Othello and Desdemona, indicating an extensive period of love before marriage. Mutuality of respect and affection could survive then. Marriage alters this. The demoralizing effect of its conventions and institutions may be observed in Othello's new attitude toward Desdemona as property:

> O curse of marriage!
> That we can call these delicate creatures ours,
> And not their appetites!
>
> (III.iii.268–70)

Desdemona too feels the effect of the inequality in the power relationship, becoming confused as to obligations to self and obligations as wife. Finally, Shakespeare expands his canvas by his portrayal of Emilia who is explicable as a consistent character only if one constantly reminds oneself of the meaning of adjustment to the role of wife for a woman.

Rymer mockingly called this play the "tragedy of the handkerchief." But Shakespeare merely uses the device of a handkerchief to expose the fragility of marriage and to question the standards that govern the behavior of a husband and a wife. Treasured by Desdemona as the first gift from Othello, the handkerchief is the key to his other life. Dropped by Desdemona in a moment of confusion, the handkerchief is stolen by Emilia and given to her husband. It becomes the symbol of fidelity and infidelity, of a woman's obedience and disobedience, of the cultural gap between Othello and Desdemona. Asking Desdemona for the handkerchief after she has lost it, Othello entwines it in a tale of magic and mystery. An enchanted token, given him by his mother on her deathbed that he in turn might give it to his wife, the handkerchief has special powers governing marital felicity. Its loss "were such perdition / As nothing else could match" (III.iv.67–68). Listening, Desdemona is terrorized by the intensity of Othello's emotion. While we as audience know that Othello has already been victimized into believing his wife unfaithful, she, knowing nothing of this, is repelled by his words. "Is't possible?" (68), she asks, wondering that he could accept such a myth. But her question is ambiguous. To Othello, it merely challenges the authenticity of the story. "Then would to God that I had never seen't" (77) she passionately concludes. The magic in the web of the handkerchief—the charmer, the furies—suddenly reveals to Desdemona a world she does not know. She is meeting a stranger: the man she married.

In this scene, Desdemona counterpoints Othello's references to the handkerchief with her second request for the reinstatement of Cassio. Rosenberg cites the scene as an example of Desdemona's dishonesty, noting that "She 'meddles' in her husband's business, presses him to reinstate his dismissed officer—presses him at the worst moment, when he most needs understanding. Finally, she lies to him, and destroys their hope of love. Is this quite a heroine?"[18] That depends, of course, on whether one considers supportiveness of a husband to be a necessary component of a heroine or whether one judges a hero/heroine as a character of unusual strength and moral fortitude striving to achieve a particular goal, aware, eventually, that he/she may be destroyed in the quest. Desdemona continues to strive for success in an unusual marriage, relying on her two major supports: her intelligence and her ideal of a wife's role. At this moment in the play, however, she faces tremendous disappointment.

One is reminded of Hamlet's sudden explosion at Ophelia in his "Get thee to a nunn'ry" (III.i.120) scene. Unlike the comments on that scene, where critics do not worry about the truth or falsehood of Hamlet's, "I lov'd you not" (118), they worry a great deal about Desdemona's honesty in the handkerchief scene. Nevertheless, in both instances, Shakespeare is presenting the emotional response of one character to qualities previously unknown in a loved one: Hamlet to Ophelia, Desdemona to Othello.

Desdemona's concept of her role is shaken. Othello's intense response to the seeming loss of the handkerchief forces her to rethink her expectations. What are the dimensions of her husband? Is he a mere man, not a god after all? Having rationalized excuses for Othello's behavior—attributing his unreasonableness to worries about affairs of state—she concedes:

> Nay, we must think men are not gods,
> Nor of them look for such observancy
> As fits the bridal.
>
> (III.iv.148–50)

Reality presses her to reevaluate the man she married.

Writing of the "shocks" a woman faces in marriage, Bernard includes the wife's discovery of the fallacy of the sex stereotype that women have been "socialized into accepting."

> Her husband is not the sturdy oak on whom she can depend. There are few trauma greater than . . . the wife's discovery of her husband's dependencies; than the discovery of her own gut-superiority in a thousand hidden crannies of the relationship. . . . These trauma are the more harrowing because they are interpreted as individual, unique, secret, not-to-be-shared with others, not even, if possible, to be admitted to oneself.[19]

Desdemona follows the pattern described above. No sooner has she come to the awful realization that her husband is but a man than she backtracks. The thought must be obliterated, pushed aside. For a woman brought up to think of man as superior, the shift requires too much psychological energy. Before she completes her speech, Desdemona begins to blame herself—retrogressing—becoming forgiving and apologetic.

> I was . . .
> Arraigning his unkindness with my soul;
> But now I find I had suborn'd the witness,
> And he's indicted falsely.
>
> (III.iv.151–54)

Does she really believe that she has been dishonest in her evaluation of Othello? Bernard's explanation sounds more valid.

This retraction by Desdemona marks her first major decline. John W. Draper, a critic writing in the nineteen-thirties, suggests that in creating the contrast between the Desdemona of Act I and the Desdemona of the other acts, who "becomes increasingly naive and innocent," Shakespeare was combining English and Venetian mores of the period—the free versus the restricted life for women.[20] But Shakespeare's portrait has a remarkable consistency as the story of the decline of a woman from a single, self-confident person to an uncertain, married woman still attempting to understand her role.

Demonstrating the decline and confusion in a woman's value system, Shakespeare contrapuntally presents Emilia in the scene where she hands her husband the stolen handkerchief. Rationalizing that she hopes to "please his fantasy" (III.iii.299), she is aware of the immorality of the act. No sooner has she handed Iago the handkerchief than she seeks to retreat from the deed, desiring to absolve herself of responsibility by weakly demanding the handkerchief's return. Since she knows that it will not be returned, her action merely characterizes a woman who, although she has not lost her ability to discern right from wrong, finds it simpler to be guided by her husband's moral code than her own. She prefers not to confront him. Iago knows this. Observing the intensity of his reaction to the handkerchief, she momentarily reconsiders what she has done. "If it be not for some purpose of import, / Give't me again" (316–17), she protests, knowing he will refuse. Unfortunately, Emilia has learned her role too well. In actions she conforms to her husband, hoping to evade responsibility and rid herself of guilt. In many ways, she presents the syndrome of the battered wife. "The psychological costs to women of the happiness achieved by thus adjusting to the demands of marriage have been not inconsiderable," writes Bernard.[21]

When, therefore, in subsequent scenes, Emilia fails to admit the theft of the handkerchief, despite being witness to Othello's tirade against Desdemona, we realize the extensiveness of this domination by a husband of his wife. After Othello leaves, having shocked Desdemona with the story of the magic in the cloth, Emilia can rant about men:

> 'Tis not a year or two shows us a man:
> They are all but stomachs, and we all but food;

"The Moor's abus'd by some most villainous knave" (IV.ii), confides Emilia (Margaret Webster) to Desdemona (Uta Hagen) and Iago (José Ferrer) in this 1943 Robeson production in New York.

> They eat us hungerly, and when they are full
> They belch us.
>
> (III.iv.103–6)

Emilia speaks from her deepest knowledge and experience but loyalty to her husband supersedes all others. The images in the quote above are ugly and sensual, indicating man's attitude toward woman as object rather than person. They also fairly accurately suggest what has happened to Othello. Trying to conform to the societal patterns for a husband's behavior, he has allowed all former interchange with Desdemona to be wiped out by this new relationship: marriage.

We witness his further sense of ownership of his wife in the famous brothel scene (IV.ii) where he considers her offenses insults to his own name. Desdemona, already broken by a hostility she cannot fathom in a marriage to which she cannot adapt, clings to the one strength she still retains—her ability to reason. "Am I the motive of these tears?" (43), she queries early in the scene, hoping that Othello's anger is directed against the Venetian Senate, not herself. And then reminding us of the third scene when she challenged her father, she mourns the loss of Brabantio's love: "If you have lost him, / Why, I have lost him too" (46–47). Not hearing her, Othello speaks only of his own anguish. "But, alas, to make me / The fixed figure for the time of scorn" (53–54), he exclaims.

Still unknowing and inexperienced in the new art of wifely compliance, Desdemona attempts neither to soothe nor to placate him. Rather, she returns to her earlier theme, "I hope my noble lord esteems me honest?" (65). Not a question, but a plea, the words nevertheless arouse his anger, reminding him of the original purpose of the interview. From "chuck" and "Desdemon," the affectionate names he called her at the scene's opening, he spits out the epithet, "O thou weed" (67). And still Desdemona persists, as Emilia would not. This new young bride has not yet learned the lesson that wives must know—to absorb insult without responding. "Alas, what ignorant sin have I committed?" (70), she insists, hoping for a rational answer. But reason has fled. Othello names her "whore" and "public commoner" (72–73). Automatically she rebels, "By heaven, you do me wrong" (81).

After he leaves, Desdemona recognizes that "his unkindness may defeat" her life (160), but concludes that it will
"never taint" her love. Because of these lines, Desdemona's
critics hail the noble, selfless, Desdemona—constant, forgiving, loving. By then, however, she is a woman defeated by
marriage. Even were she not murdered at the drama's close,
her tragedy has occurred. A. C. Bradley found her "helplessly
passive . . . because her nature is infinitely sweet and her love
absolute." Desdemona, however, is not helplessly passive
when she decides to marry Othello. Her love is absolute but
her nature seems more varied than Bradley would grant. He
continues to say that, although we may pity Othello more, we
are aware that he is "a man contending with another man; but
Desdemona's suffering is like that of the most loving of dumb
creatures tortured without cause by the being she adores." [22]
Unable to see a woman as a full-blooded person, the critic fails
to realize how accurately Shakespeare portrays the transformation of a woman, even a strong woman, by marriage.

John Stuart Mill, writing more than two centuries after
Othello was composed, suggests a major reason for critical inability to recognize this conflict facing Desdemona. "Many a
man thinks he perfectly understands women, because he has
had amatory relations with several, perhaps with many of
them." But such an observer, while he may learn something
about the sexual nature of woman, will not learn about the
other aspects of woman because she carefully hides her true
self from him. On the other hand, a man who is a husband
may think he knows women well because he may know one
woman very well, the woman to whom he is married. Mill
continues:

> And in fact, this is the source from which any knowledge worth
> having on the subject has, I believe, generally come. But most
> men have not had the opportunity of studying in this way more
> than a single case: accordingly one can, to an almost laughable
> degree, infer what a man's wife is like, from his opinions about
> women in general. [23]

Thomas McFarland, writing today, applies contemporary philosophical ideas to his analysis. "Desdemona's virtuous purity

is not only an existentially unique event, but a youthful idealism and unawareness of the exceeding worldliness of the world."[24] In this comment, we find Desdemona's innocence partly responsible for her fall. Again the tendency is to consider a force acting for good rather than evil as being passive. Here the early religious tradition of the psychomachia for the soul of mankind may have contributed to Shakespeare's development of Desdemona as a more vital character than usually believed. However critics, seeking to understand her, continue to think primarily in terms of "Other." Is she unaware? Or is she, like Hamlet, aware but unwilling to compromise her ideals?

As well as innocence and naiveté, the word "unaware" may also carry negative connotations. Listen to D. A. Traversi, another twentieth-century critic. He finds that, "like Isabella and even Ophelia before her, Desdemona has the power to exercise upon men an influence of whose nature and strength she remains until the last moment very largely unaware; and this power, given a logical basis and a perverse interpretation in Iago's 'philosophy' of 'nature,' becomes a principle of dissolution and destruction."[25] Where is this power of which she is unaware? Surely she has confidence in her ability to sway the senators and to match wits with Iago at Cyprus. Nor does she believe herself lacking in power when she promises Cassio:

> My lord shall never rest,
> .　　.　　.
> I'll intermingle every thing he does
> With Cassio's suit.
> (III.iii.22–26)

But how does her power become a principle of dissolution unless Traversi, too, is asking for a completely compliant Desdemona? Somehow, Desdemona here sounds evil despite her inherent goodness.

Then there are the almost classic interpretations of the woman's role as forgiver or supporter of men. We are told that Desdemona learns the depths of her love through suffering. Bernard McElroy, in his recent study of tragedy, offers a version of this approach when he observes that Desdemona comes eventually "to know her love only by discovering the powers of loyalty and forgiveness with which it endows her."[26] Did she misunderstand loyalty before? Had she no perception of the meaning of forgiveness? I find it difficult to accept the theory that woman is enhanced by her ability to be the constant "forgiver" in an inequitable arrangement. She may also be destroyed by suppressing the self and continually accepting others' affronts. Too often, a woman painfully adjusts to a vision of marriage that she had never anticipated.

Whereas many critics have idealized Desdemona, others have found her responsible for the tragedy—usually because she did not fulfill her role properly. Both types of criticism are based on expectations about women's behavior and both have persisted into our own time. J. A. Bryant in a recent work comments, "Othello represents the figure of God. . . . Desdemona is the ideal—truth, goodness, beauty—made flesh, an incarnation of her creator's ideal excellence."[27] If to Bryant Desdemona represents the ideal, to other critics writing today she falls far short of that perfection. Hugh Richmond, for example, finds her guilty of forgetting her social tact and H. A. Mason, another of our contemporaries, believes her cold, observing:

> As soon as we see that Othello is blind and ignorant we hope that Desdemona will be able to save him by a love both clairvoyant and active. We are consequently appalled to find her with her warm-blooded nature, in matters of intelligence about life so cold, inert and self-contained.[28]

We continue to read Shakespeare's plays and to enjoy them in the theater, not because the characters are idealizations but because they capture human elements that we recognize. Helen Gardner suggests that the reason for the strong disagreement about *Othello* is that the ideas it explores are still alive: "The conflict of attitudes on such subjects as 'jealousy, fidelity, chastity, the quality of desire between a man and a woman, the illicit or degenerate forms of it, the rights that lovers have over each other, the proper response to amorous treachery' is one reason for the conflict of views about the play and its hero."[29]

It is also the reason for the conflict of views about Desdemona. Tillie Olsen may offer the answer when discussing the oppression of women. She sees the problems women face as unique: "The oppression of women is like no other form of oppression (class, color—though these have parallels). It is an oppression entangled through with human love, human need, genuine (core) human satisfactions, identifications, fulfillments."[30]

When in the last scene, after Desdemona's death, Emilia finally blurts out the truth, she first throws off the yoke of marriage: "My husband?" (V.ii.146), and again two lines later, "My husband?" until she expands on this question, "My husband say she was false?" (152). Only after challenging Iago and discovering his villainy does she finally break loose, but not before indicating the long force of habit—submission. " 'Tis proper I obey him; but not now. / Perchance, Iago, I will ne'er go home" (196–97). Only the murder of a woman she treasured could finally break the chain that had dictated Emilia's relinquishing of responsibility for her own actions.

By examining not one, but two marriages, Shakespeare records the effect of "adjustment," of being a "proper wife," on a woman. Emilia follows the formula. Did she ever rebel when first married? We do not know. No remnant of rebellion remains until the death of Desdemona shocks the long-married woman into action. It is as if the hypnosis of role were suddenly broken.

Othello is one of Shakespeare's studies of the complexity of marriage and of the pressure of conventional patterns on even the most unusual characters. The play examines the many qualities demanded of a man and a woman to succeed in marriage. It contrasts the mutual respect between a man and a woman with the more usual power-versus-powerlessness relationship. It contrasts a long standing marriage with one newly consummated, recording the corrosion of value systems in a woman long dominated by her husband. By creating in Desdemona a woman of intelligence, courage, and self-confidence, Shakespeare intensifies the tragedy of her disintegration. Unable to discard her habits of thinking and speaking, she fails to adjust to marriage. Although Shakespeare creates in Iago a powerful agent for the destruction of Othello and Desdemona, the lack of communication between them and the inability to transfer to marriage patterns of mutual respect practiced when they were single made their tragedy inevitable. In this play, Shakespeare suggests the dangers of attempting to conform to stereotyped ideals of marriage, and the cost to husband and wife. In *The Winter's Tale,* he offers other, extreme alternatives.

Mrs. Pritchard,
In the Character of Hermione in the Winters Tale.

Eighteenth-century audiences marveled at the actress's performance
as the statue-come-to-life, recaptured here in the illustration by
Robert Edge Pine. FOLGER SHAKESPEARE LIBRARY

CHAPTER SIX

Courageous Wives

THE WINTER'S TALE

"Do not you fear. Upon mine honor, I
Will stand betwixt you and danger."
(II.ii.63–64)

Within the framework of the story of a man's jealousy and his suspicions of his wife's infidelity, Shakespeare, in *The Winter's Tale*, develops two strong, attractive, rational female characters who learn the limits of marriage and the importance of their own sense of personal value. He also introduces, although more briefly, a third female character who, through contrast and comparison, helps to define the other two. By presenting these women characters at different stages of self-knowledge, by comparing them with accepted norms for the men, and by allowing for rational explanations of even the most extraordinary happenings within the text, Shakespeare reveals his understanding of women. Once again he indicates a skillful manipulation of accepted stereotypes for men and women. Once again he blurs their distinctions. This drama deserves a searching reexamination as a work probing and exposing the actions of mature women as they work to revise their lives.

The two older women differ from one another in their sense of self and in the values they place on marriage. Hermione, the Queen, introduced in her ninth month of pregnancy, appears happy in her own sexuality. A model woman, wife, and mother, she is comfortably committed to her role. Paulina, the other woman, wife of the King's adviser, is also satisfied with her marriage and confident of her relationship with her husband. Unlike Hermione, however, her behavior is less conforming; she challenges conventions even at the start. Reputed for her forthrightness, she is told that orders have been given to inhibit her anticipated actions. Although bold and bright, she too must alter her expectations.

By the drama's close, both women have learned to defy the dominance of male rule and find their own human worth. The Queen develops these attitudes slowly, discovering her hidden fortitude when she realizes that conformity to role does not assure happiness. Paulina's knowledge derives from a deeper understanding of the limits of marital partnership. When her husband compromises his beliefs and later rationalizes the validity of his actions, she knows that she must forge her own value system—that she must function as a human being, alone.

Forerunners for both Hermione and Paulina appear in Shakespeare's other plays. The Queen, who asserts "The Emperor of Russia was my father," is a descendant of the Princess of France of *Love's Labour Lost* without the Princess' options.[1] Unlike the Princess, Hermione, a married woman, is not free to determine her own destiny or reveal her decision in open forum. She is also related, although more as a wise older sister than as a descendant, to Desdemona, both having been unjustly accused of infidelity by their husbands. Paulina's predecessors are many: all the outspoken girls of Shakespeare's plays and the women whose marriages hold the promise of mutual respect betweeen a husband and wife.

Evaluation of the women, two of whom rebelled against the system as it existed, has usually been limited to male expectations of female behavior. As early as 1733 for example, Lewis Theobald, an editor of Shakespeare, suggested emending a line of Paulina's because it seemed out of character for a woman. Theobald challenged the propriety of Paulina's calling the King "a fool" (III.ii.186) although the King had just been responsible for the death of his son and the seeming death of his wife and daughter:

It is certainly too gross and blunt in Paulina, tho' She might impeach the King of Fooleries in some of his past Actions and Conduct, to call him downright a Fool. And it is much more pardonable in her to arraign his Morals, and the Qualities of his Mind, than rudely to call him "Idiot" to his face.[2]

Thus we find that the editor is less interested in the text as a source of character description and more in his own preconceived notions of proper female behavior.

Later in the century, Samuel Johnson was to interpret Paulina's apology to Leontes after her strong condemnation of his actions as illustrative of "the sudden changes incident to vehement and ungovernable minds" although irrationality seldom characterized Paulina's behavior.[3] Like Theobald, Johnson looked at the individual speech rather than the plot in its totality. As a result, Johnson was satisfied to find parallels between this woman and the mentally unbalanced King whose rash actions had led to tragedy.

Other criticism of Paulina has ranged between extremes. She has been considered a shrew in the tradition of Noah's wife in the mystery plays. Anna Jameson, in the nineteenth century, wrote "Though a very termagant, [she] is yet a poetical termagant."[4] Among contemporary writers, Joan Hartwig believes that Paulina combines shrew and goddess. This critic suggests that Paulina and Leontes "characterize each other throughout the play." To Hartwig, both retain the elements of the stock figures of drama. "Paulina plays the shrew to Leontes' tyrant in the first half of the play; in the last half, she plays confessor to Leontes' humble penitent."[5] Reverting to the earlier opinion of Paulina, Hartwig here also acknowledges the more recent estimates by such critics as G. Wilson Knight and R. G. Hunter. The former writes of the "aptly-named Paulina" who functions as "conscience, guide and priestess to Leontes."[6] The latter describes this remarkable woman as the "instrument" of the gods and the "personification of Leontes' conscience."[7] For none of these critics does Paulina really acquire a developing human form. Nor do they find in Shakespeare's characterization fresh insights into human behavior and an understanding of the particularity of the plight of women. Accepting stereotypical descriptions of "woman," they tend to overlook the humanness of Paulina.

Nor have Hermione and Perdita escaped comments that, while varied, deny them their humanity. Critics have found in this mother and daughter symbols of Demeter and Proserpine, parallels with Ann Boleyn and Queen Elizabeth and even, in Hermione alone, the figure of Shakespeare's noble long-suffering wife.[8] Finally, Hermione, because she disappears for sixteen years, and because she falls into Leontes' arms at the play's close, has been compared with the Patient Griselde of legend although, as I shall illustrate, she uses the only weapon possible against Leontes—hardly behaving in a passive manner.

The drama begins with the swift, tempestuous flaring of Leontes' suspicion and concentrates on the impact of jealousy as it affects a man, his wife, his children, his court, and his own life. Unlike *Othello, The Winter's Tale* omits the long study of the growth of jealousy in a man and centers on the responses to his aberrant vision:

> Is whispering nothing?
> Is leaning cheek to cheek? is meeting noses?
> Kissing with inside lip? stopping the career
> Of laughter with a sigh?
>   `        .      .      .`
> Is this nothing?
> Why then the world and all that's in't is nothing,
>   . . . Bohemia nothing,
> My wife is nothing, nor nothing have these nothings,
> If this be nothing.
>
>   (I.ii.284–96)

Misreading his wife's cordiality to Polixenes, his dearest friend, Leontes suspects her of adultery. Not only does he sentence her to prison, but he disowns their infant daughter born in prison and orders Antigonus, his counselor and husband of Paulina, to take the babe to some unknown land and there abandon it. Following instructions, Antigonus leaves, never to return. The infant, named Perdita, is found by a shepherd who raises her as his own daughter.

A period of sixteen years divides the first three acts from the last two. Disguised as a shepherd, Florizel, Polixenes' son, having fallen in love with Perdita, announces their betrothal at the sheepshearing scene of Act IV. His father, also disguised, unmasks, denounces the engagement, and threatens the young woman. Escaping Bohemia, the young people seek shelter in Sicilia. In the closing scenes the lost child is found. At the same time Hermione, believed dead for sixteen years, reappears in a dramatic scene in which, posing as a statue, she comes to life. The plot skeleton has many of the features of a fairy tale. However, the characterizations of the women as well as the men, the method of hiding Hermione and killing Antigonus, and the realism of the language indicate a depth far beyond the simple, surface plot.

The jealousy that destroys so much, particularly the accepted patterns of relationships between men and women, has a constructive aspect as well. It forces the women to rethink their priorities: children, husband, the right to make decisions about one's own body, procreation, companionship. They learn that dependency, while it may be comfortable, is also threatening. Unlike the women in *Othello*, Hermione and Paulina take over the management of their lives.[9] It is significant that the latter, rather than mourning the loss of her husband, functions positively as a persistent voice of truth and reason. The scourge of Leontes, she constantly reminds him of the wife, son, and daughter lost to him through his unnatural jealousy.

Perhaps the strength of personality these women had may also have contributed to the drama's limited existence in the theater. During the days of neo-classical criticism, *The Winter's Tale*, because it spanned a period of sixteen years and moved from Sicilia to Bohemia, was denigrated for its lack of unity of time and place, and therefore not performed. When the play finally reached the stage for a sustained period, in Garrick's version, the first three acts and the self-possessed women had disappeared.[10] During the nineteenth century, when the sensibilities of the audience became a major concern, the intense vocabulary and combative quality of the early scenes were softened.[11] The drama's appeal centered on the last scene where an actress' skill in standing trancelike and immobile drew applause. During the closing years of the last century and the beginning of this one, when the work was considered characteristic of Shakespeare's golden, and therefore waning period, the work was seldom produced. More recently with new interest in the romances, the mythic quality of *The Winter's Tale* has stimulated productions bathed in a mystical or an ethereal atmosphere.

Were these women to appear on the stage as fully developed characters, they would serve as exciting models, exhibiting many of the qualities of the "liberated woman." At the same time, their development within the context of the play offers an excellent example of Shakespeare's method—his varied techniques for challenging preconceived notions of acceptable actions for women and for questioning the validity of limited patterns of behavior.

A 1970 work on sex-role stereotypes explores the impact of these societal norms on our expectations. It documents the conflicts between standards for mental health for men and women. Applied to Shakespeare's dramas, they could provide a new base for judging its women. The subjects of the study were clinicians in mental hospitals who were asked to describe "a healthy, mature, socially competent (a) adult, sex unspecified, (b) a man, [and] (c) a woman." [12] Although the clinicians were men and women, their conclusions did not differ. Not only did they have different standards of mental health for men and women, but those for men correlated with those for "adult, sex unspecified." Moreover, the clinicians tended to agree that healthy women differed from healthy men by being

> more submissive, less independent, less adventurous, more easily influenced, less aggressive, less competitive, more excitable in minor crises, having their feelings more easily hurt, being more emotional, more conceited about their appearance, less objective, and disliking math and science. [13]

Commenting on this, Phyllis Chesler, in her study of madness in women, notes that "for a woman to be healthy, she must 'adjust' to and accept the behavioral norms for her sex even though these kinds of behavior are generally regarded as less socially desirable." Agreeing with the authors of the study that "this constellation seems a most unusual way of describing any mature, healthy individual," Chesler concludes: "The ethic of mental health is masculine in our culture." [14]

Shakespeare defies this ethic in *The Winter's Tale* by applying to adult women as well as men the standards for healthy "adults, sex unspecified."

How do we know this? And how, one may ask, can such a statement be made when the play itself opens with such a flagrantly female manifestation of woman as Hermione in the ninth month of pregnancy? Because Shakespeare, like a skilled debater, first presents his characters in traditional roles before he chips away at their sex-linked differences, he masks his intention. Thus, he introduces the Queen as an exemplary woman. She is not only a testimony to a physical relationship between man and woman and to the specifically female aspect for which nature has determined her, but, in the intimate conversations in the first act, she seems delighted and happy in her female role. Significantly, her first words are spoken in response to her husband's command "Tongue-tied our queen? Speak you" (I.ii.27). Following acceptable protocol, she acts the role of the perfect wife. Her invitation to Polixenes, too, conforms to the accepted pattern. Charming, solicitous, slightly teasing, she threatens,

> How say you?
> My prisoner? or my guest? By your dread "verily,"
> One of them you shall be.
> (I.ii.54–56)

Although in their bantering quality her words do not suggest a woman fearful of her husband, they do reinforce the first impression that this is a female who sees her primary role as wife to her husband, and hostess for his home and kingdom.

Her wit and ingenuity are in the service of Leontes. Ironically, her success as wife and hostess leads to her personal failure in these roles. For, employing coquetry, charm, and the familiar skills expected of a woman, she convinces Polixenes —but loses Leontes. The charm of her request and the warmth of her pursuit illuminate her womanliness. And it is this womanly loveliness that Leontes wants to possess wholly.

As the scene progresses, Shakespeare gives lines to Hermione that also suggest a sexuality and passion capable of further arousing the jealousy of her husband. Although the following passage is considered one of the cruxes of the play, defying absolute comprehension, it evokes images that, while fleeting and temporary, emphasize her easy delight in her female role. Persistently begging for a series of answers to her questions with, "What? have I twice said well? When was't before?" (90) she admits enjoying flattery:

> Our praises are our wages. You may ride's
> With one soft kiss a thousand furlongs ere
> With spur we heat an acre.
>
> (I.ii.94–96)

The images are there: kiss, ride, spur, heat; and they suggest the sensuality of the woman.

Shakespeare next explores the validity of the stereotypes for the terms "masculine" and "feminine," "male" and "female" in the actions and language of the male characters. Again, he begins with accepted patterns. Dramatically he rejects them; he presents close friendship and everlasting loyalty, courage, freedom from self-pity, and rationality as the tests. Leontes, Polixenes, Camillo, and Antigonus offer the examples. Before the entrance of Polixenes and Leontes, Camillo touts their friendship, speaking of them as intertwined roots of the same tree—raised as friends and maintaining their close ties with one another over the years. Polixenes, on his entrance, reminisces about the dreams they shared:

> We were, fair queen,
> Two lads that thought there was no more behind
> But such a day to-morrow as to-day,
> And to be boy eternal.
>
> (I.ii.62–65)

A friendship tied through mutual ideals as well as close companionship, nevertheless, cannot withstand the suspicions of a jealous husband. It turns to gall. Close friendship does, however, grow between two members of the same sex: Hermione and Paulina. Thus Shakespeare focuses on one stereotype. Another supposedly male characteristic closely scrutinized at the opening is "courage." Again the dramatist offers an illustration—this time in Camillo, the adviser to whom

Leontes discloses his suspicion of Polixenes and Hermione. Ordered by Leontes to poison Polixenes, Camillo faces a series of complex choices, first between expediency and morality, then between self-preservation and courage, including protection of the "weaker sex." Telling Polixenes, King of Bohemia, of the plot against his life, Camillo rejects regicide but opts for self, accepting the proposal that they both depart from Sicilia at once:

> Good expedition be my friend, and comfort
> The gracious queen, part of his theme, but nothing
> Of his ill-ta'en suspicion! Come, Camillo,
> I will respect thee as a father, if
> Thou bear'st my life off. Hence! Let us avoid.
> (I.ii.458–62)

Fortunate Camillo and Polixenes. But who will be the "father" to Hermione? What, more than "comfort," a rather weak substitute for "expedition," may she expect? And yet her own courage as well as the friendship of another woman do sustain her.

Further confusing the gender of courage are the two scenes immediately following the departure of Polixenes and Camillo: Hermione's bedroom scene in which Leontes accuses her of adultery, and Paulina's confrontation with the jailer. The former opens with a classic portrait of female behavior. The latter portrays the challenges to a strong woman in a male world. In the bedroom scene, Hermione, restlessly awaiting the birth of her infant, has little patience with her son. "Take the boy to you; he so troubles me, / 'Tis past enduring" (II.i. 1–2), she complains to her ladies-in-waiting who observe, "The Queen your mother rounds apace" (16), as if in explanation of her petulant dismissal of Mamillius. Having thus established the specifically female quality of her actions, Shakespeare then reveals the depth of courage and self-control of which Hermione is capable.

Her husband accuses:

> . . . I have said
> She's an adultress, I have said with whom:
> More—she's a traitor . . .
> (II.i.87–89)

Hermione quietly objects,

> Should a villain say so,
> . . .
> He were as much more villain: you, my lord,
> Do but mistake.
>
> (78–81)

Since she has, only moments before, querulously protested her son's presence, Hermione's words illuminate the contrast between the woman acting out her role, and the woman responding from the depth of her being. As the scene progresses, Shakespeare questions other behavioral norms for women.

Among the many definitions in the *Oxford English Dictionary* for "woman," "female," and "feminine," one that is not based on the physical differences between the sexes describes woman "with allusion to qualities generally attributed to the female sex, as mutability, capriciousness, proneness to tears: also to their position of inferiority or subjection." Hermione considers aloud the reason for "proneness to tears" in this scene of accusation. Just as she understood and delighted in her role as a woman in the second scene of Act I, she now begins to reject some of the characteristics, or behavioral patterns, expected of her. Tears are among the first:

> . . . Good my lords,
> I am not prone to weeping, as our sex
> Commonly are, the want of which vain dew
> Perchance shall dry your pities.
>
> (II.i.107–10)

Acknowledging the sex-linked character of tears, Hermione knows their effectiveness: "to evoke pity." She, however, will not rely on such emotional devices. More than that, she also analyzes the power of tears and their implications for the auditors in her speech to her women:

> . . . Do not weep, good fools,
> There is no cause. When you shall know your mistress
> Has deserv'd prison, then abound in tears
> As I come out.
>
> (118–21)

Weeping must be for true tragedy, not to evoke pity for the woman falsely accused. Tears should not be shed for the innocent, according to Hermione. The dramatist does not then dismiss "tears," attributed by the *Oxford English Dictionary* to women. While not mentioned explicitly in the next court scene, they would seem to characterize, in part, Leontes' behavior. "Nor night, nor day, no rest. It is but weakness / To bear the matter thus—mere weakness" (II.iii.1–2), rants the King. Later we are informed that "he hath not slept" (31), having bathed himself in anger, frustration, and tears of self-pity.

Shakespeare continues to erase sex-linked definitions of roles in the trial scene. No longer the compliant woman who awaited her husband's invitation to speak, Hermione, although she realizes the ultimate futility of challenging the King, persists:

> . . . it shall scarce boot me
> To say "Not guilty." Mine integrity,
> Being counted falsehood, shall (as I express it)
> Be so receiv'd.
>
> (III.ii.25–28)

Nevertheless, with remarkable calm and self-possession she faces Leontes' constant and furious attack. Standing before a court of men and a hostile husband, she understands the impossibility of winning a just verdict. "My life stands in the level of your dreams" (81), she offers. "Your actions are my dreams" (82), he counters. "You had a bastard by Polixenes, / And I but dream'd it" (83–84). "Sir, spare your threats," Hermione finally retorts, then lists the pleasures that had once enhanced her life: her marriage, her young son, and her infant child. But still she insists,

> . . . no life
> (I prize it not a straw), but for mine honor,
> Which I would free—
>
> (109–11)

For honor alone she wishes to live.

Rather than seek to manipulate the response of the men through tears, she relies only on words and reason. Did adversity kindle this inner strength? Or was it a quality belonging to the daughter of a king but submerged to help her conform to the female role she was physically destined to play? "The Emperor of Russia was my father" (119), she asserts, implying that she should be respected and honored as an equal. The qualities of heredity and the pride of person, supposedly male characteristics, are exhibited by a woman to whom, ironically, the female "privilege" of childbed has been denied.

Compared with Hermione, in whom we witness the slow shift from a female encased in her womanliness to one willing to challenge the world of men, Paulina, at her first appearance, shortly after the Queen's imprisonment, functions like the "healthy adult, sex unspecified," exhibiting self-confidence, rationality, and courage. Introduced in a scene of her own, she requests an audience with the Queen. But the jailer refuses. He has "express commandment" (II.ii.8) to bar her entry. Surprised by his refusal, she nevertheless persists. Contrasted with the muted humble character of the jailer, her brilliance, wit, and sophistication sparkle.

Thus introduced, not as a lady-in-waiting to the Queen or as a member of Hermione's staff, Paulina functions as an independent, a woman with a staff of her own. "So please you, madam, / To put apart *these your attendants*" (II.ii.12–13, italics mine), he insists. Acquiescing to this demand, she pursues her goal. Although her mission is specifically that of a woman—concern for and protection of a mother and newborn infant—her methods are those usually ascribed to a man—rationality and fearlessness. Relying upon her tongue "if wit flow from't" (50), she exhibits her intellectual power:

> This child was prisoner to the womb, and is
> By law and process of great Nature thence
> Freed and enfranchis'd, not a party to
> The anger of the King, nor guilty of
> (If any be) the trespass of the Queen.
> (II.ii.57–61)

Through reasoning, she has convinced the jailer who then relinquishes the infant. Her ingenuity and mental acumen have defined the legal limits of the jail.

In her next scene, in the King's chamber, rationality as a sex-linked trait is further explored. After the moderate attempts of the gentlemen of the court to dissuade the King from his rash behavior, and following their earlier capitulation to his censuring command "Cease, no more" (II.i.150), Paulina appears. Hoping to arouse their moral sense while dismissing their injunction that she not enter Leontes' chamber, she exhorts them:

> Nay, rather, good my lords, be second to me.
> Fear you his tyrannous passion more, alas,
> Than the Queen's life?
> (II.iii.27–29)

When they fail to respond, Paulina continues, characterizing their behavior:

> 'Tis such as you,
> That creep like shadows by him, and do sigh
> At each his needless heavings, such as you
> Nourish the cause of his awaking.
> (33–36)

But neither reason, wit, threat, nor scorn moves them. Although, to a greater extent than any of the men, Paulina is willing to defy the King, because she is a woman her words are not seriously weighed. Rather they irritate the men, marring the surface calm. Finally, when Leontes orders her husband to "Take up the bastard" (76), she explodes:

> For ever
> Unvenerable be thy hands, if thou
> Tak'st up the Princess by that forced baseness
> Which he has put upon't!
> (77–80)

The ultimate, irrational, but most convincing response (to a male) springs from Leontes: "He dreads his wife" (80).

Critics interpret this speech of Paulina's as either the ranting of a shrew or the awful sentencing of a priestess. Dramaturgically, however, Shakespeare would seem to be making another point. Not only does he contrast the irrationality of Leontes with the rationality of Paulina, he also contrasts the irrationality of the more reasonable males with the rationality of Paulina. By giving these specific words to Leontes—words packed with emotional force—the playwright weakens the effectiveness of Paulina's earlier arguments: that the infant resembles the father, that the Queen's past record is irrefutable, and that the general illness of Leontes distorts his thinking. All rational discussion fails. Nor do Leontes' epithets—"Thou dotard" (II.iii.75), "Dame Partlet" (76), "crone" (77), and "gross hag . . . worthy to be hang'd" (108–9), damage the effectiveness of his inference that Antigonus is "ruled" by his wife. Shakespeare perceives the inability of a man, even a seemingly rational man, to dismiss the scorn of his peers that he is "less than a man" when confronted by his wife. The counselor who might otherwise have persisted in Hermione's defense succumbs to male pressure. Antigonus' decision later in the play to dispose of the infant, while it may or may not reveal his inhumanity to a fellow creature, certainly discloses his inability to differentiate between right, when expressed by Paulina, and wrong, when dictated by Leontes.

Nor is he able to separate emotional from rational argument. Antigonus, then, is Shakespeare's more subtle counter-portrait to Paulina. As she assumes more and more the qualities ascribed to the male, he assumes more and more the weaknesses supposedly characterizing the female. Finally, when he accepts his dream as reality, we leave the area of rational thought:

> Come, poor babe.
> I have heard (but not believ'd) the spirits o' th' dead
> May walk again. If such thing be, thy mother
> Appear'd to me last night . . .
>
> . . . . .
>
> "Good Antigonus,
> Since fate (against thy better disposition)
> Hath made thy person for the thrower-out
> Of my poor babe, according to thine oath,
> Places remote enough are in Bohemia,
> There weep, and leave it crying."
>
> (III.iii.15–32)

Having seen a vision of Hermione and heard her command that he leave the infant in Bohemia, he decides that the child is probably Polixenes' offspring. The scene is particularly ironic since it occurs after the audience has already heard the report of the oracle that Hermione is innocent, and listened to Leontes' admission of guilt in plotting to poison his friend Polixenes. Since to the audience Hermione at this point appears to have died, the scene cleverly reinforces the reality of her death. More important, however, is what this soliloquy reveals about Antigonus' thinking and, in the larger context, the contrasts between men and women in the play. To justify his abandonment of Perdita, Antigonus substitutes intuition, a faculty usually attributed to a woman, for rationality.

Unlike his behavior, Paulina's actions always have a rational base. Although they may sometimes appear rashly courageous, they are never guided by dreams. We may listen to her retort to Polixenes' threat to have her burned:

> I care not:
> It is an heretic that makes the fire,
> Not she which burns in't.
> (II.iii.114–16)

Or we may observe the dueling metaphor that creeps into her language when her words seem to carry her into the male world:

> Good queen, my lord, good queen, I say good queen,
> And would by combat make her good, so were I
> A man, the worst about you.
> (II.iii.60–62)

Her courage persists throughout the play. At the beginning of Act V, she dares more than all the men, jostling Leontes with:

> If, one by one, you wedded all the world,
> Or, from the all that are, took something good
> To make a perfect woman, she you kill'd
> Would be unparallel'd.
> (V.i.13–16)

Although sixteen years have elapsed since those false accusations by Leontes resulting in the deaths or seeming deaths of
his son, wife, and infant daughter, Paulina continues to remind him of his culpability. She remains the same forthright,
critical person who in Act II invited the Lords of the court to
imitate her behavior, "be second" to her. And she continues
to evoke the same response. Cleomines remonstrates in Act V:

> You might have spoken a thousand things that would
> Have done the time more benefit, and grac'd
> Your kindness better.
>
> (V.i.21–23)

Thus, while she displays the supposed virtues of the male,
behaving according to acceptable patterns for an adult "sex
unspecified," the men who judge her, the men with whom she
interacts in the play, find these behavior patterns highly unacceptable for a person whose sex is specified as female. In a
positive sense, she is Shakespeare's creation of the strong,
resilient, mature, and rational woman functioning without
any supportive male for sixteen years.

The third woman, Perdita, provides a contrast with the
two older women. In many ways she exemplifies the accepted
patterns of female behavior. In love with Florizel, the disguised son of Polixenes, she defers with humility to her lover
during most of the sheepshearing scene. Although her speech
describing the gifts she would give him—the garlands of flowers "to strew him o'er and o'er! / . . . like a bank, for love to lie
and play on" (IV.iv.129–30)—sounds remarkably forthright,
her immediate retraction, attributing her arrogance to the cos-
tume she wears, nullifies its force. She does, however, exhibit
some qualities which link her with the older women: self-confidence and individuality. Acting the hostess for her supposed
father, the shepherd, Perdita refuses to agree with Polixenes,
her disguised guest, when he suggests she plant "gillyvors,"
known as "bastard" flowers in her garden.

> I'll not put
> The dibble in earth to set one slip of them;
> No more than were I painted I would wish

This youth should say 'twere well, and only therefore
Desire to breed by me.

(IV.iv.99–103)

Although the issue is minor, her refusal to be an agreeing, acquiescent hostess indicates her independence. In the debate between them—frequently referred to as the art-nature debate —her willingness to defend her own ideas offers a brief insight into her character. Later in the scene, her reaction to Polixenes' threat "I'll have thy beauty scratch'd with briers" (IV.iv.425) with the generalization "The self-same sun that shines upon his court / Hides not his visage from our cottage" (444–45) further emphasizes the self-confidence of this young woman.

In creating these three women who differ in their attitudes toward themselves, marriage, and the larger world around them, Shakespeare developed characters solidly based in reality. However, despite their straightforwardness and honesty as well as the occasional earthiness of their language, these characters have failed to be recognized as prototypical. Critics have been reluctant to remove such women from the distant sphere of myth and fantasy. The extraordinary nature of the plot has been the excuse for considering these women as beyond the human. Recently, however, critics have begun to approach Shakespeare's late plays not as any excursions into the world of fantasy, but as possible new experiments in dramaturgy. As Barbara Mowat, for example, observes, "The strangeness in these plays . . . could not be accidental, nor the result of Shakespeare's boredom, inexpertness, or senility."[15] Other critics have discussed Shakespeare's possible interest in expanding the limits of drama, seeking to erase the division between audience and actor in a new theatrical experience.[16] In such a theater realistic explanations for much of the action exist, although *The Winter's Tale* defies some accepted dramatic conventions.

In this play Shakespeare carries his study of the meaning of sexuality to a woman, to her role as procreator. Hermione survives the trauma of childbirth only to lose both her children shortly therafter. Paulina, herself a mother, empathizes with the Queen and becomes her major support. In the earlier plays, the Princess of France could reject her suitor, and Kate, although she had no choice but marry, discovered that the man she married respected her self-sovereignty. Hermione, a married woman, does not have the option that the Princess of France had; she realizes that her husband has become overwhelmed with sexual fantasies. Does such a woman have choices? Or do her choices exist only in myth? If Shakespeare was exploring the new limits of drama, he was also relying on valid psychological observations.

Karen Horney, the famous psychologist, discusses the effect of a woman's pregnancy on her husband and notes the possibility of male envy of the woman's capacity for childbearing. Although Leontes' jealousy has frequently been thought to be inexplicable, twentieth-century psychology provides a reasonable answer, apparent in the first act of the drama. Horney's comment appears in response to some of the theories of her contemporaries, psychologists like Sandor Ferenczi and Helene Deutsch. Rather than believing that "the only thing in which she, the woman, ultimately has the advantage over the man is the, surely very questionable, pleasure in the act of childbirth," Horney offers an expanded discussion of the implications of motherhood. Here she includes references to the attitudes of some of her male patients as well as to those of women. Writes Horney:

> At this point, I, as a woman, ask in amazement, and what about motherhood? And the blissful consciousness of bearing a new life within oneself? And the ineffable happiness of the increasing expectation of the appearance of this new being? And the joy when it finally makes its appearance and one holds it for the first time in one's arms? And the deep pleasurable feeling of satisfaction in suckling it and the happiness of the whole period when the infant needs her care?
>   . . . Moreover, we explain penis envy itself by its biological relations and not by social factors; on the contrary, we are accustomed . . . to construe the woman's sense of being at a disadvantage socially as the rationalization of her penis envy.
>   But from the biological point of view woman has in motherhood, or in the capacity for motherhood, a quite indisputable and by no means negligible physiological superiority. This is most clearly reflected in the unconscious of the male psyche in

the boy's intense envy of motherhood. . . . When one begins, as I did, to analyze men . . . one receives a most surprising impression of the intensity of this envy of pregnancy, child-birth, and motherhood, as well as of the breasts and act of suckling.[17]

According to Horney's observation, then, both Hermione's joy in herself and Leontes' jealousy could spring from a physically obvious source. Shakespeare had probably observed the mixed emotions of a man to his wife's pregnancy and incor-porated these observations into this drama.

Thus *The Winter's Tale*, rather than being pure fantasy, seeks to illuminate another aspect of the human condition. It presents women at different stages of self-knowledge who ma-ture and discover their own strength. Paulina and Hermione challenge the wisdom as well as the domination of them by their husbands. Hermione disappears. Paulina, like many of Shakespeare's attractive, heroic male characters, discovers that women, too, must function alone, relying on their own intel-ligence and power. The woman who originally had the confi-dence to answer Leontes' taunt: "What? canst not rule her?" (II.iii.46) with the statement:

> From all dishonesty he can. In this,
> Unless he take the course that you have done—
> Commit me for committing honor—trust it,
> He shall not rule me.
>
> (II.iii.47–50)

discovers that even a husband as compatible as Antigonus may compromise standards and bow to male pressure. Al-though some critics have tended to see Paulina as a priestess, and others to condemn her as a shrew, she represents the best in woman. She and Hermione, both strong and perseverant, offer two different insights into the female experience.

In this play, Shakespeare questions the stereotypes for human behavior. Thematically the play is dominated by the conflict between the irrational and the rational where women represent the latter. Thus the language of Paulina and the qui-etly combative action of Hermione are vital to an understand-ing of the play. Although it opens with "We were as twinn'd lambs" (I.ii.67)—children frolicking, men alone—it concludes with the exultant cry that more is required of the men. They must "awake" their "faith" (V.iii.95), not in imagination, in which they have recklessly indulged, but in reason and the wisdom of Paulina. Only then will she command "Music" and Hermione acquiesce to "awake" (98).

PART III

Power

C. GREEN PINXT   C. GOLDBERG SCULPT

PENANCE OF THE DUCHESS OF GLOUCESTER.

Glo. Be patient, gentle Nell, forget this grief.

This moving scene of the Duchess walking barefoot through the
staring crowd, her husband standing by in silence, was engraved in
the late nineteenth century from an illustration by Charles Green.
FOLGER SHAKESPEARE LIBRARY

CHAPTER SEVEN

The Paradox of Power

The HENRY VI–RICHARD III Tetralogy

"Am I a queen in title and in style,
And must be made a subject to a duke?"
(*2 Henry VI*, I.iii.48–49)

*Q*ueens and duchesses stalk through these plays, commanding, ordering, sweeping officiously in and out of the English court, but also walking alone, powerless—for they are women. Married to men of power, these women rule by fiat. They dazzle when in power, arouse sadness and terror when out. In their experiences, in the uncertainty of their power, women recognize the anomalousness of their own lives. When, near the close of this tetralogy, Margaret, the deposed, widowed Queen turns to her alter ego, Elizabeth, and mocks, "Vain flourish of my fortune. . . . A queen in jest, only to fill the scene" (*Richard III*, IV.iv.82,91), the elder woman has begun to achieve self-knowledge. The ambiguous and uncertain limits of her own power have taught her the condition of women. For she has, at moments, reached the zenith of power, but she stands now powerless. In exaggerated form, her experience and those of the queens and duchesses in these plays illustrate the dilemma of most women. Sexual politics molds their lives, distorts their perspectives, and damages their relationships with women as well as men. Kate Millett defines sexual politics as the process by which women have been socialized into accepting the values of a patriarchal society where men control "every avenue of power."[1] She then describes the destruction of a woman's self-esteem by this system, observing that it leads to woman's "self-hatred and self-rejection, a contempt both for herself and for her fellows—the result of that continual, however subtle, reiteration of her inferiority which she eventually accepts as a fact."[2]

Shakespeare presents a range of women in this tetralogy, one of whom, Margaret, provides the overall arch, giving this boldly spreading group of dramas a unity. Although she does not dominate any single play, she links the works from the end of *I Henry VI* through *Richard III*, provides continuity, and allows one to observe how women must contend with the power structure in a patriarchy. Not included in this chapter are Joan of Aire and the Countess of Auvergne, two women prominent in *1 Henry VI*. Rather, the women chosen for discussion interact with one another and reveal Shakespeare's gift for reiterating elements in women's experiences and yet showing the individuality of each life.[3] Shakespeare dramatizes the meaning of power for women—its nearness and infinite distance. By creating portraits of women who are mature and thoughtful, he also challenges the idea of woman's innate inferiority and shows how sexual politics destroys her ability to see life whole.

Married to wielders of power, these women find weakness, greed, and incompetence and they wonder at the validity of the system. Nevertheless, they must accept it. Discovering the powerlessness of their titular authority, the women become angry, irrational, self-doubting, self-denigrating and, ultimately, denigrating of all women. Unlike Hermione and Paulina of *The Winter's Tale*, these queens and duchesses have great difficulty liking or sympathizing with others of their sex. In an attempt to cope with powerlessness, they imitate the actions of the men. Margaret Fuller, in the nineteenth century, logically explained:

> Ye cannot believe it, men; but the only reason why women ever assume what is more appropriate to you, is because you

prevent them from finding out what is fit for themselves. Were they free, were they wise fully to develop the strength and beauty of Woman; they would never wish to be men, or man-like. The well-instructed moon flies not from her orbit to seize on the glories of her partner. No; for she knows that one law rules, one heaven contains, one universe replies to them alike.[4]

Shakespeare's characters, too, have difficulty "finding out what is fit for them," as he illustrates through the material he chooses to dramatize and the limited options he allows the women.

Margaret, who spans the tetralogy, falls in love, marries, becomes a mother, and, later, a widow. Unlike most women, however, she becomes a queen. Endowed with power and confronted by powerful enemies, she arouses an extra measure of hatred and contempt. Her sorrows and joys, her vulnerability to sexual approaches and derisive slurs on her womanliness: these she shares with others of her sex. Her right to exercise power and to lead armies—these are hers alone. During the course of the plays, the handsome young woman of *1 Henry VI* becomes the Cassandra-like older woman of *Richard III*, foreseeing the doom of those who mock her. To acquire this skill, however, Margaret must make mistakes, be trapped by her vanity and ambition, react unwisely to personal affronts when deciding on political moves, and come to understand the ambiguities of her position as a woman and political figure.

The life of Elizabeth, the other woman who marries a king, imitates Margaret's. Wives of rivals for the English throne, the queens themselves bitterly oppose each other during most of the tetralogy, taunting each other, cursing each other, and identifying with rival male camps. Elizabeth's husband usurps the throne from Margaret's. Nevertheless, Shakespeare replicates elements of Margaret's life in Elizabeth's, reinforcing the sense of repetitiousness, of the basic powerlessness, even of women who are queens. Elizabeth is propositioned before being offered marriage. Like Margaret's husband, the King who marries her defies the advice of counsel, arbitrarily entering a politically disastrous marriage. Like Margaret, she seeks to protect her progeny. Unlike Margaret, who adopts warlike male behavior, Elizabeth chooses the role of compliant woman. Neither approach assures the survival of the woman's offspring. Both women must function in a world where women are subordinate to men, where women's power is tenuous, where respect for women's leadership seldom occurs. Both women, too, tend to accept the stereotyped patterns for male and female behavior. They believe that men should be strong, that if women exert power it must be in the classic role of "power behind the throne," and each reserves her greatest scorn for other women until the tetralogy's closing moments.

Taken out of historical context, the third woman, Eleanor, the Duchess of Gloucester, appears in this play as a foil for Margaret. Although the Queen arrived in England more than four years after Eleanor had been accused of treason, Shakespeare places them in direct opposition with one another—power is the prize for which they vie. Opening the play with one scene for each, the dramatist creates two strong women characters who, in different ways, must cope with the concept of rule and the limits of power. Eleanor also illustrates the problem women have in convincing men that women should be treated as equals rather than as children. Even her husband, known as the "Good Duke Humphrey," fails to address her as a mature fellow human being. Mary Wollstonecraft, in the eighteenth century, suggests the permanent effect of such treatment:

> My own sex, I hope, will excuse me, if I treat them like rational creatures, instead of flattering their *fascinating* graces, and viewing them as if they were in a state of perpetual childhood. . . .[5]

Eleanor responds too readily to flattery. Having been dismissed by her husband as foolish, she finds solace in the praise of those who call her clever, and falls into their trap.

The fourth woman who tries to walk successfully through the maze of deception in the male world is Anne. She appears briefly in *Richard III* and is the victim of Shakespeare's clever hunchback king. Anne offers still another illustration of the impact of sexual politics on a woman's self-image. She also most closely conforms to the stereotypes describing women.

Confronted by Shakespeare's notorious arch villain, Richard, she reacts positively to his suggestion that a beloved woman can reform even the worst of sinners and that a woman's beauty (her own) can lead a man to kill for love. Despite its brevity, the portrait is convincing.

Popular during Shakespeare's lifetime, this cycle of history plays has infrequently appeared on the stage since then. Explanations for this absence vary, the primary one being that editors and critics had long questioned Shakespeare's sole authorship of all of these plays. Another, and perhaps equally pertinent, explanation is that the *Henry VI* cycle offers no male "star" roles. Sir Barry Jackson, discussing his experience in producing these dramas in 1953, wondered why "no major actress ever discovered the tremendous character of Margaret of Anjou, surely one of the greatest feminine roles in the whole gallery?"[6] Since men control the means of production, even theatrical production, in a patriarchal society, a work with no male stars would hardly inspire a male actor-director, like the producers of Shakespeare's plays—usually men—to venture a *Henry VI* cycle whose logical emphasis should be on Margaret.

Young and beautiful, the most controversial of the women characters, she first appears in the last act of *1 Henry VI*. The daughter of an impoverished French king, Margaret is prisoner of the successful English Earl of Suffolk. Concerned about how she will be treated, she thinks:

> Perhaps I shall be rescu'd by the French,
> And then I need not crave his courtesy.
> (V.iii.104–5)

While she is assessing her situation, Suffolk is assessing her beauty and his chances for a liaison:

> She's beautiful; and therefore to be wooed:
> .   .   .
> Fond man, remember that thou hast a wife.
> (78,81)

Reassuring herself that her situation is not hopeless, Margaret observes: "Tush, women have been captivate ere now" (107).

She thereupon resolves to ask Suffolk the price of her ransom. He, meanwhile, deep in his own thoughts, decides to woo her for Henry, King of England.

Publicly, and rather ambiguously, he begins his suit: "Madam, I have a secret to reveal" (V.iii.100). "What though I be enthrall'd," she wonders, then decides, "he seems a knight, / And will not any way dishonor me" (101–2). The audience, of course, knows better. Alternating direct address with the aside—a particularly valuable theatrical device to illuminate the different objectives of the characters—Shakespeare reveals the cross purposes of captor and captive. Because in an aside, as in a soliloquy, a character speaks what she or he truly believes, Margaret's asides allow insights into her character. She sincerely fears being dishonored, or raped, by her captor.

Suffolk, meanwhile, wondering exactly how to tell her his plan, finally phrases his proposal:

> Say, gentle Princess, would you not suppose
> Your bondage happy, to be made a queen?
> (V.iii.110–11)

She does not anticipate a joyous life as a "queen in bondage" and therefore demurs. When, however, he specifies, "I'll undertake to make thee Henry's queen" (117) and describes the advantages, "To put a golden sceptre in thy hand, / And set a precious crown upon thy head" (118–19), Margaret listens silently. This is an elegant proposal until Suffolk concludes with an if clause: "If thou wilt condescend to be my—" "What?" interrupts Margaret. Suffolk alters the conclusion to "His love" (120–21). Nevertheless, he has propositioned her.

Rape in war is "a familiar act with a familiar excuse," observes Susan Brownmiller.[7] Her recent study of the implications of rape on the overall relationship between men and women challenges old myths and provides valuable new historical data. Relevant to Margaret and Suffolk is Brownmiller's reference to "one of the earliest surviving Articles of War . . . proclaimed by Richard II of England in 1385. Among the twenty-four articles governing the conduct of his soldiers, King Richard decreed 'that none be so hardy as to . . . force any woman, upon pain of being hanged.' "[8] Margaret was not an ordinary woman, but a princess. Nevertheless, her thoughts pertaining to the conduct of her captor reflect the concern of a woman about the possibility of rape—even if the rapist is a politically powerful person and his technique veiled in grandiose offers. The document of Richard II precedes by less than sixty years the war in which Margaret is hostage.

Having listened to Suffolk alter the close of the sentence from "my love" to "his love," and aware of her position as a prisoner, Margaret answers with political wisdom and "feminine" conformity: "And if my father please, I am content" (V.iii.127). After her father most willingly assents—for his daughter is to bring him undreamed of wealth—Suffolk once again indicates his intention while Margaret expresses openly the thoughts she spoke privately in an aside. Asking her whether she wishes to send a "loving token to his Majesty" (181), he dismisses her answer:

> Yes, my good lord, a pure unspotted heart,
> Never yet taint with love, I send the King.
> (182–83)

Suffolk had something else in mind. Kissing her, he shrewdly explains, "And this withal" (184). Margaret knows what Juliet and Romeo knew, and what even Kate knew—that kisses go no farther than to the kissed:

> That for thyself; I will not so presume
> To send such peevish tokens to a king.
> (185–86)

This speech acknowledges that she understands Suffolk's meaning; it does not indicate compliance.

In this brief introduction Margaret appears composed while expressing some fairly standard moral precepts. She should evoke our admiration and sympathy. Some critics, however, believe that she acts the seducer because her position shifts from one of weakness to one of strength, from being a captive to the promise of being a queen. Neither her open statements nor her asides convince them of her concern about her plight. Rather, such critics note primarily her composure and self-possession in a difficult situation. Men "show too much surprise" at women's strength, Margaret Fuller writes.[9] The strength of the young Margaret of Anjou in this first play of the trilogy evokes not surprise but a more negative response from one recent critic: David Bevington writes, "Men do not faze her, though she knows how to appeal to their sense of masculinity and possessiveness."[10] But the text suggests that men do faze her. She wonders apprehensively about Suffolk's intention. Fuller further observes that "Self-dependence . . . is deprecated as a fault in most women."[11] Shakespeare, creating a historical character who will eventually lead an army, must reveal her self-confidence. Surely this is an admirable quality, whether in a man or a woman.

As for Margaret's beauty, Bevington believes that she "muddles the senses" of those who behold her.[12] Although Suffolk is smitten with her beauty when he first sees her, offering to make her Henry's Queen, he later considers her primarily a pawn to help him win personal power. The man who, in scene three, speaks with longing—

> O, wert thou for myself! but, Suffolk, stay,
> Thou mayest not wander in that labyrinth,
> There Minotaurs and ugly treasons lurk
> (V.iii.187–89)

—in scene five thinks only of his own political career. He has changed into a wily, ambitious courtier seeking total domination of the country:

> Margaret shall now be Queen, and rule the King;
> But I will rule both her, the King, and realm.
> (107–8)

Nor does she confound the senses of others in this play or in *2 Henry VI* when she arrives at the English court as Queen. Welcomed by Henry, for whom Suffolk, as surrogate, married her in France, she is transferred to the King in a scene that opens with pomp and ceremony and closes with acrimony. Only Henry is overwhelmed by her beauty. The others consider her either a political liability or a possible ladder to their own success. Accepting her from Suffolk, Henry establishes a transition with the previous play by requesting a kiss:

> Welcome, Queen Margaret,
> I can express no kinder sign of love
> Than this kind kiss.
>
> (I.i.17–19)

The King then continues his formal welcome. Margaret, with equal formality and graciousness, responds. The members of the court hail her with "Long live Queen Margaret, England's happiness!" (37). But Humphrey, the Duke of Gloucester, quickly mars this surface hospitality. The King's uncle and official Protector—given this title originally when Henry, a child, inherited his father's realm but was obviously not yet capable of ruling—the Duke of Gloucester, finds this marriage abhorrent.

Reading aloud the marriage contract which specifies the return of "the duchy of Anjou and the county of Maine" (I.i.50–51) to Margaret's father, Gloucester lets the agreement fall—a dramatic gesture of disapproval. Nor will he continue reading. Instead, he offers the transparent excuse that his eyes are "dimm'd" by "some sudden qualm" that struck him at the heart. Henry, in this first moment when he might act the hero for his wife, does nothing, merely asks the Cardinal to continue the reading. After the departure of the bride and groom from the stage, Gloucester expresses his hostility more openly, concluding with a warning to his fellow lords:

> Fatal this marriage, cancelling your fame,
>
> . . .
>
> Undoing all, as all had never been!
>
> (I.i.99,103)

Because of his position as second in the realm, a man whose power has seldom been challenged by his nephew, Gloucester appears to be the most threatening of Margaret's enemies. His speech seems to warn of her potential powerlessness unless she should actively move against him.

But the audience quickly discovers what Margaret fails to learn until much later—that men of greed and jealousy surround Henry. She is not privy to the plots and counter-plots of the characters as one by one, or in groups, they leave the stage. Nor does she hear the strategy of the Duke of York, who will prove her greatest antagonist. Alone, in soliloquy, sounding much like Iago, York confides his plan to grab the throne after Henry:

> . . . surfeiting in joys of love
> With his new bride and England's dear-bought queen,
> And Humphrey with the peers be fall'n at jars.
> (I.i.251–53)

Ignorant of these machinations, the Queen has a skewed vision of the political alignments in the English court. She knows that she has one friend, Suffolk, whose powers seem tremendous because he converted a prisoner into a queen and acquired lands for her father. She believes Gloucester, not York, to be her greatest enemy. Politically naive, and scorned as a dismissable commodity, she eventually stumbles into the traps laid by Henry's enemies. First, however, she will seek to exercise the power—the command over others, the authority, the ascendancy—that she thinks she has.

Gloucester, the man against whom she hopes to practice this power, challenges easy evaluation in this play. Although called the "Good Duke Humphrey" and known from the chronicles by that title, he is presented in this first meeting with Margaret as an arbitrary, self-righteous, and impolite man. Smugly, he flaunts his power before the new Queen declaring his own private war against her although never thinking in terms of actual war. Dramatically, the scene raises the question of Humphrey's right to the title "good." Jealously guarding his power to govern and perhaps jealous of his nephew's shift of first allegiance from uncle to wife, Humphrey appears insensitive to the feelings of a woman.

Juxtaposing against this scene one in which Humphrey appears with a woman he likes, Shakespeare next presents a confrontation between Humphrey and his wife. Aware of her husband's unhappiness, Eleanor, the Duchess of Gloucester, suggests he reach for the crown that rests so uneasily on incompetent Henry's head. Although she suspects that her husband will reject her suggestion, the Duchess hopes to convince him of her support. In her opening speech, a mock conversation with Gloucester, she counters his excuse that his hand is too short to reach the golden "diadem" and offers to "lengthen it" with hers (I.ii.12). Gloucester rebukes her, first in tones of affection:

> O Nell, sweet Nell, if thou dost love thy lord,
> Banish the canker of ambitious thoughts!
> (I.ii.17–18)

Treating her as he would a child, he hopes to dissuade her. When she persists, he next assumes a more authoritarian tone. No longer is he arguing with an equal but directing a subordinate: "Nay, Eleanor, then must I chide outright" (41). The chiding includes such terms as "Presumptuous dame" and "ill-nurtur'd Eleanor" (42). Reminding her of her honors, he then defines the problem that faces both her and Margaret— the meaning of power for a woman of her position:

> Art thou not second woman in the realm?
> And the Protector's wife, belov'd of him?
> (43–44)

Is this enough for a woman? On the one hand, she is expected to listen and sympathize while her husband confides his problems; on the other, she is denied rational exercise of her opinions. She must sit at the executive dining table, entertain, be charming, exercise her wit, intelligence, and tact; she must encourage, listen, and pretend to be mindless; she must not act on her assumptions. Simone de Beauvoir, although writing of woman's situation today, makes a comment relevant to the relationship between Gloucester and Eleanor:

> In the bosom of the family, woman seems in the eyes of childhood and youth to be clothed in the same social dignity as the adult males. Later on, the young man, desiring and loving, experiences the resistance, the independence of the woman de-

sired and loved; in marriage, he respects woman as wife and
mother, and in the concrete event of conjugal life she stands
there before him as a free being. . . . But when he is in conflict
with her, . . . his theme will be the existing inequality, and he
will even take it as justification for denying abstract equality.¹³

During the exchange between them, Gloucester reveals
a consistent inability to perceive women as people rather than
objects or possessions. To him, women are another breed—
intellectually and emotionally man's inferior. When his wife
suggests that the dropping of the contract will have further
consequences because he has evoked Margaret's hostility,
Gloucester naively protests that he meant no harm to his
nephew "virtuous Henry" (I.ii.20). If Shakespeare wanted us
wholeheartedly to like the Duke, these two scenes question
such a premise. They muddle the portrait complicating our
responses to him, but they do reveal the dramatist's insights
into sexual politics as it functions among those who occupy
positions of power.

Gloucester's myopia leads to the frustration expressed
in Eleanor's soliloquy immediately after his departure. Bitter
and misanthropic, she bewails her fate and muses on the advantages of being a man:

> Were I a man, a duke, and next of blood,
> I would remove these tedious stumbling-blocks,
> And smooth my way upon their headless necks.
> (63–65)

Like Lady Macbeth, Eleanor misunderstands the meaning of
manliness, interpreting it as ruthlessness. In *2 Henry VI* her
voice resembles the Duke of York's, whose soliloquy on climb-
ing to the throne closed the previous scene. Unlike him, however, she lacks political and military power. She can neither
organize troops nor prepare to lead them at the opportune
time. Instead, Eleanor relies on more abstract ethereal aids.
Not solid deeds, but ephemeral magic will breathe reality into
her dreams.

Shakespeare then shifts the focus back to Margaret. Em-
bittered and disillusioned, she seeks to exert power but mis-

reads its limits. Walking with Suffolk, she is confronted by two petitioners with complaints. Mistaking her companion for Gloucester, the men are caught with a complaint against Suffolk. Margaret, finally allowed an opportunity to use her power, takes the petition and tears it up. Since it represents the wishes of a whole township, her action antagonizes the commoners in the play as well as the audience. In an interesting new work on the crown, parliament, and the law, Edna Zwick Boris observes that, in the sixteenth century, an English monarch was expected to be sensitive to the wishes of the people. The author points out that Margaret's action here reflects her attitude as a French woman who substituted the absolutism of the French for the English system.[14]

But Margaret's action, while it builds antagonism toward her, also expresses her frustration and confusion as to her role. Speaking with Suffolk, in a lyrical passage of great beauty, she wonders who she is. As she attempts to define and understand the court, the people, and most of all her own husband, her lines take us back to the last act of *1 Henry VI* when Suffolk promised her a rich and glittering world.

> My Lord of Suffolk, say, is this the guise,
> Is this the fashions in the court of England?
> (I.iii.42–43)

She wonders at the bickering of the lords and at the rudeness of Gloucester. Not waiting for an answer, she enumerates the many disappointments that led to her disenchantment:

> Is this the government of Britain's isle,
> And this the royalty of Albion's king?
> (44–45)

Parallels abound as she continues. Moving from the general to the more and more specific—from England to England's government, to England's King, endowing him with "royalty" and breadth of empire—she wonders:

> What, shall King Henry be a pupil still
> Under the surly Gloucester's governance?
> (46–47)

The adjective "surly" interjected by Margaret may contradict
the general opinion of the multitude that he is "good Duke
Humphrey," but it describes accurately the man who dropped
the marriage agreement and refused to read on. Most important, if Henry is not a king, but only a pupil, then what is she?

> Am I a queen in title and in style,
> And must be made a subject to a duke?
> (48–49)

The request for a specific definition of role evokes mem-
ories of Gloucester's assurance to Eleanor: "Art thou not second woman in the realm? / And the Protector's wife, belov'd
of him?" (ii.43–44). Both times Shakespeare has phrased the
thoughts in the form of questions. And both times, the women
find themselves defined by their husbands' positions. For
Margaret, the unresolved limits of Henry's authority exaggerate the uncertainty of hers.

As her speech rolls on from sharp questions to wistful
recollections, she reveals the young woman who romantically
listened to the King's messenger, confusing him with his master. There follows a lengthy exposition of the qualities of Suffolk, the man who won her heart for Henry. We hear, although
far less clearly defined than in *The Winter's Tale*, intimations of
Perdita's paean to Florizel:

> . . . when in the city Tours
> Thou ran'st a-tilt in honor of my love
>   .   .   .
> I thought King Henry had resembled thee
> In courage, courtship, and proportion.
> (I.iii.50–54)

Disillusioned, disappointed, she finds herself married to a
holy man, not a gallant hero.

Then follows an encounter that emphasizes the ambiguity of a woman's role and the antagonisms that divide
women. Accompanied by Eleanor, Henry and the men of his
court enter bickering among themselves over political policy
in personal power plays. Margaret interrupts them, attempting

to claim for the King, and through him for herself, the right to make his own decisions. But Gloucester, asserting his belief in male superiority, crosses her:

> Madam, the King is old enough himself
> To give his censure. These are no women's matters.
>
> (I.iii.116–17)

So intensely does she feel his scorn that she later concentrates all her political anger against him, overlooking her many enemies waiting quietly on the side. Millett observes: "Whatever the 'real' differences between the sexes may be, we are not likely to know them until the sexes are treated differently, that is alike." [15] Although the Queen is a woman of "wit and pollicie," the necessity to fight the stigma of incompetence based on sex blinds her to the greater dangers. In the breach between the Queen and Gloucester, York will build his nest. Unaware of this, she retorts:

> If he be old enough, what needs your Grace
> To be Protector of his Excellence?
>
> (118–19)

Having unsuccessfully challenged Gloucester at this time, Margaret then turns to his wife. Earlier in the scene, when alone with Suffolk, the Queen had enumerated the characteristics of those she disliked at court—the ambitious, imperious churchman, the grumbling York, and the "haughty Protector." Her greatest contempt, however, was reserved for the woman now facing her—"that proud dame, the Lord Protector's wife." Objecting to the way Eleanor swept through the court, Margaret had jealously commented:

> She bears a duke's revenues on her back,
> And in her heart she scorns our poverty.
>
> (I.iii.80–81)

Ironically, in attempting to understand the limits of her own power, Margaret fails to note any resemblance between herself and Eleanor. Instead, the Queen is guilty of adopting

the prejudices of the ruling group—the men—and the psychological characteristics of the powerless—the women. Frequently, when a woman achieves success, she rejects her
identification as a woman and scorns other women. She believes that success erases the differences between herself and
the men with whom she moves, but creates a great gap between herself and other women. Various explanations for this
behavior exist. Kate Millett thinks that women internalize and
accept the values of the patriarchal system and therefore dis-
dain other women. Dorothy Dinnerstein, the contemporary
psychologist, believes that the antagonism of women toward
other women grows out of the early mother-child relationship.[16] She theorizes that because girls, like boys, are most
helpless during infancy when in the care of a woman, they
find that the most threatening power figure is female rather
than male. Whatever the origin of the antagonism, Shakespeare recognized its reality and gave it life in these plays.
Here a close connection appears between Gloucester's assertion, "These are no women's matters," and Margaret's open
hostility toward the Duchess of Gloucester.

Like a square dance, moving from one couple to the
next, the scene then repeats the actions of the beginning of
the play. The entrance of the Duchess of Gloucester signals the
music to begin. This time the caller is Margaret, not Gloucester; this time, a fan, not a marriage contract, is dropped; and
this time the Duchess of Gloucester, not Margaret, must dance
in the center of the circle. The scores are being evened. Insisting that Eleanor pick up the fan, Margaret "gives the Duchess
a box on the ear." Answering too swiftly, the Duchess pledges:
"She shall not strike Dame Eleanor unreveng'd" (147). Both
women are misjudging the meaning of power, thinking they
are manipulating a situation when, in reality, they are exhibiting the frustrations of powerlessness. The men are in command.

The extensiveness of power and its elusiveness for
women are poignantly illustrated over and over again in these
plays. Margaret, hoping to prove her power, plots against
Gloucester and meets defeat. Eleanor, hoping to avenge herself, turns to magic, grasping at a will-o-the-wisp. Perhaps
like the many people who read their horoscopes in the daily

newspapers today, Eleanor found her most substantial promise of greatness in those smoke-filled dreams. She too fails. While listening to predictions that she will be Queen and Humphrey King, she is caught. Ironically, Eleanor, although powerless to deal with the political situation, knows that she is being used as a pawn. She knows that her husband's enemies have trapped her. Despite her foolish involvement with witchcraft, she realistically answers York's accusations when he breaks in on the seance and arrests her. She protests that her actions are "Not half so bad as thine to England's King, / Injurious duke, that threatest where's no cause" (I.iv.47–48). But no one listens, least of all her husband.

Hearing of her involvement with witchcraft, Gloucester thinks first of himself and of his relationship with Henry. Addressing the Queen, present when news of Eleanor's fall arrives, the Duke assures her majesty:

> Madam, for myself, to heaven I do appeal,
> How I have lov'd my king and commonweal;
> And for my wife, I know not how it stands.
> (II.i.186–88)

If she is guilty, Gloucester promises not that he will be loyal to her and attempt to help her clear her name, but:

> I banish her my bed and company,
> And give her as a prey to law and shame,
> That hath dishonored Gloucester's honest name.
> (193–95)

Gloucester's concern for the kingdom takes precedence over all others. Although unable to respect his wife or take her warnings seriously, he is an honest and not guileful man. When he first hears of Eleanor's arrest, he shows great unhappiness despite his concern for his "honest name." But he does expect a kind of absolute behavior from her and allows no room for any wavering. One recent critic, Robert B. Pierce, believes that Gloucester's behavior illustrates *An Homily Against Disobedience and Wilful Rebellion*, a work well known in Shakespeare's time, which dictates that the "wife should be obedient unto her husband, the children unto the parents, the servants unto their masters." [17] Pierce then observes in this 1971 work:

> Gloucester can no more control his wife's ambition than he can maintain order and degree in the commonwealth. Her usurpation of *manly* concerns shows in little what is happening in the kingdom. She and the other *ambitious* and *mannish* women of these plays show that in a collapsing social order women cannot *fulfill their natural and traditional functions.* [18] (italics mine)

Although the critic is writing about Shakespeare's history plays, attitudes toward the role of women in society color his interpretation. Were these dramas as rooted in their time as is here suggested, they would no longer be enjoyed. As Moody Prior, a distinguished Shakespearean scholar, observes in a 1973 book warning against any narrow interpretation of the histories, "the variety and diversity of the political situations" in the plays and the astuteness and compassion with which the characters are depicted "required something more than the view of man in history that Shakespeare found in the most doctrinaire statements of his sources." [19]

Shakespeare's portrait of Gloucester is of a very human man whose aberrant vision prevents him from recognizing his wife's perceptiveness. Comparing the subsequent scenes between him and Eleanor with their equivalent in the eighteenth-century version by Ambrose Philips, *Humfrey, Duke of Gloucester* (1723), one realizes the unromantic picture Shakespeare presents and the paradox of power for a woman that he dramatizes. He creates two scenes: the third and fourth in Act II. In the first of these, Eleanor is found guilty and is sentenced. In the second, wearing a white sheet and carrying a taper in her hand, she walks barefoot through the public streets. Gloucester, present at her hearing, assures her: "I cannot justify whom the law condemns" (II.iii.16). When, after her exit, he admits: "Mine eyes are full of tears, my heart of grief" (17), he follows this with distress over his own reputation:

> Ah, Humphrey, this dishonor in thine age
> Will bring thy head with sorrow to the ground!
> (II.iii.18–19)

Nevertheless, as we discover in the following scene, he does feel genuine pity for his wife. Philips omits the sorcery scene, substituting for it a scene in prison where Eleanor bewails her fate, asserting, "By false Accusers,—by invented Crimes,— / My Enemies have triumphed." Gloucester enters protesting against her doing public penance: "No,—Eleanor: / Sooner, would I submit to the Indignity!" Vehemently, he continues, "For thy lov'd sake, it shall not:—Come,—what may! / Audacious Prelates!—Ministers of Rome!" Gloucester offers to defend her, calling her "injur'd Innocence." Only because she insists on being the long-suffering wife who, through her submission to penance, will help preserve England's quiet, does Gloucester acquiesce, agreeing to remain silent. Unlike Shakespeare's Gloucester, Philips' character acknowledges, "O, Eleanor!—In Vertue finish'd;—Wise / Beyond thy Sex!—Well doest Thou caution me."[20] But Shakespeare knew better. He understood where gallantry of the type found in romantic tales and sentimental tragedy ends and where reality begins. He understood that a man of Humphrey's character, although labeled "good," had weaknesses which made him vulnerable to the attacks and plots of his enemies. For Gloucester's private self and public self were two separate beings. His insistence on this dichotomy allowed no room for a wife who would venture into the public arena except as decoration.

In the second scene between them—Eleanor's march through the public streets as penitent—Shakespeare again compares the man's perception of living in two separate worlds with the woman's belief that such a separation cannot validly exist. Awaiting her arrival, Gloucester expresses his private grief in a lament. When, however, Eleanor appears and the servant offers to "take her from the sheriff" (II.iv.17), Gloucester orders, "stir not" (18). The scene is hers; the lines are hers. A woman whose private self and public self are commingled, she finds it impossible to accept his "Be patient, gentle Nell, forget this grief" (26).

In her long speech describing her role, Eleanor, like Margaret earlier, lists her claims to power:

> . . . thy married wife,
> And thou a prince, Protector of this land,
> . . . . .

Sometime I'll say, I am Duke Humphrey's wife,

$\cdot$ $\cdot$ $\cdot$

. . . he stood by, whilest I, his forlorn duchess,
Was made a . . . pointing-stock.

(28–46)

Seeing the angry crowd staring at her husband, she warns him
of his enemies at court—Suffolk, York, Beauford—men who
"have all lim'd bushes to betray thy wings" (54). Unlike the
Humfrey of the eighteenth-century version, Shakespeare's
character refuses to accept his wife's evaluation of his enemies.
Nor does he believe that the accusations against her are really
directed at him. He has difficulty respecting the opinions of
women.

Margaret's power, too, is defined by her role as wife.
Like Eleanor, she confuses marital alliance with political
power. Forgetting her husband's arbitrariness in giving and
retracting power, specifically when he chose her as his bride,
Margaret exults at Gloucester's fall. When Henry finally denies
his uncle the role of Lord Protector, she joyously proclaims
"Why, now is Henry king, and Margaret queen" (II.iii.39). But
she fails to understand her role. Like a child suddenly loosed
in a room full of toys, she grabs and grabs. The supply seems
limitless. Unschooled in the intricacies of the political intrigue
surrounding Henry, she reacts with hatred to her most obvious enemy, Gloucester. She supports and encourages Suffolk's accusation that Gloucester is a traitor. Worse still, she
helps plot his murder.

Margaret exemplifies the thesis that women imitate men
because theirs seems like the most direct path to success, but
she also illustrates the human drive that Simone de Beauvoir
calls the desire for transcendence. This the writer defines by
comparing it with immanence, or stagnation:

Every subject . . . achieves liberty only through a continual
reaching out toward other liberties. . . . Every time transcendence falls back into immanence, stagnation, there is a degradation of existence into the *"en-soi"*—the brutish life of
subjection to given conditions. . . . This . . . spells frustration
and oppression. . . . Every individual concerned to justify his

existence feels that his existence involves an undefined need to transcend himself, to engage in freely chosen projects.

De Beauvoir then observes that woman, because of her position in relation to man, is condemned to a life of immanence since her transcendence is "overshadowed and forever transcended by another ego *(conscience)* which is . . . sovereign."[21] Margaret seeks transcendence; but she also relies on political models from among the men. Unfortunately, she has seen few worth imitating.

The "good" Duke Humphrey who might have opened new vistas for her chooses instead to reject her and to denigrate women generally. Even in their last encounter, he misreads her: "And you, my sovereign lady, with the rest, / Causeless have laid disgraces on my head" (III.i.161–62). But the causes are real for her, having begun when she first arrived in England and continuing later with his reprimand: "these are no women's matters." Nor does her husband offer a model. The chronicle describes him as modest and "meke," a man "governed of them whom he should have ruled, and brideled of suche, whom he sharpely should have spurred."[22] Shakespeare presents a more confused and arbitrary ruler who declines to act when the choices are difficult.

Margaret therefore must stumble along, following Suffolk's advice. Thinking her action politically astute and her position secure, she endorses Gloucester's murder. Unaware of the pressure of the patriarchal system on her decisions, she inclines to Suffolk, misreads York, and is deaf to the sentiment against her in the land. Although a queen, she allows an ambitious man to guide her.

The greatest scene in the play—the discovery of the murder of Gloucester (III.ii.)—belongs to Margaret. Her arrogance, wiliness, self-confidence, dissimulation, quick-wittedness, and tenderness all appear here. Her reaction to the King's response to news of Gloucester's death is a remarkable inversion of values—a transposition of priorities. Her rhetoric is magnificent. Reprimanding her husband for his swooning at the news of Gloucester's death, she speaks of her unhappiness and the suspicion that will fall on her—the slanderous tongues that will now try to accuse her of Gloucester's death because she did not like him. She bemoans her decision to come to England, enumerating the terrors of her trip across the sea to England, she speaks of the murderous weather, reminding him of how she threw the diamond necklace into the sea, hoping to abate the terror of the storm.

Margaret verbosely protests his actions:

> What, dost thou turn away and hide thy face?
> I am no loathsome leper, look on me.
> What? art thou like the adder waxen deaf?
> Be poisonous too, and kill thy forlorn queen.
> Is all thy comfort shut in Gloucester's tomb?
> Why then Dame Margaret was ne'er thy joy.
> (III.ii.74–79)

Then Shakespeare sets himself the challenge of evoking multiple conflicting responses from his audience by creating a woman whom it must abhor, because of her duplicity in the early part of the scene, and pity at its close. The sudden return to reality, the touch with life and its terrors, strikes the audience as it witnesses the humanity of the character who has just been involved in murder. King Henry condemns Suffolk to banishment:

> And therefore by His majesty I swear,
> Whose far-unworthy deputy I am,
> He shall not breathe infection in this air
> But three days longer, on the pain of death.
> (285–88)

We listen to Margaret's real terror. The staccato-like statements, one on top of another, and the reference to herself in third person as "Dame Margaret" disappear. What remains is the simple human one-to-one relationship, expressed in a single line: "O Henry, let me plead for gentle Suffolk!" (289). How sparse the language, how well chosen: "Henry," not England's King or Albion's monarch, words that had studded her earlier lines; "me," not Dame Margaret; and then the two words "plead" and "gentle," words that Henry immediately picks up in his response beginning, "Ungentle queen" (290). Shakespeare's character definition of Margaret as she slides

from the heights of rhetoric to that single, eloquent line is a
dramatic coup, reminding us of her powerlessness.

According to Shakespeare's major source for these
plays, Suffolk was "the Quenes dearlynge" whom Henry had
planned to exile for only five years, permitting Suffolk's return
when the commons were pacified. Then Henry would "revo-
cate him into his olde estate, as the Quenes chefe frende and
counsailer."²³ In Shakespeare's play, however, Henry neither
limits the term nor indicates any revocation of the exile. Instead, he rather emphasizes its eternal character by stating
explicitly to Margaret: "Had I but said, I would have kept my
word; / But when I swear, it is irrevocable" (III.ii.293–94). Her
helplessness is emphasized.

At the King's departure, after announcing the edict of
banishment for Suffolk, Margaret, in an act of powerlessness,
curses her husband. Her speech builds in anger and intensity
until for the third time we hear the word "gentle." A word of
many meanings, including "noble born," warm, and compas-
sionate, it springs from Suffolk. "Cease, gentle Queen"
(III.ii.305), he counsels. Ironically she castigates him for womanliness: "Fie, coward woman and soft-hearted wretch! / Hast
thou not spirit to curse thine enemy?" (307–8). Like Lady Macbeth, and so many women seeking the road to power, Margaret believes it lies in scorn of her own sex. Suffolk reacts
instantly to this derisive label, spitting out a string of curses.
A male, he need not strive to be "unsexed." In rational terms,
he can suggest the futility of words. "Wherefore should I curse
them?" (309) he asks, knowing that curses do not kill.

In the last scene between them, she promises to exert
her influence on his behalf, knowing she will be a powerless
supplicant. "I will repeal thee, or, be well assur'd, / Adventure
to be banished myself" (349–50), she pledges, allowing the
audience to know their relationship. His lines complement
hers:

> . . . where thou art, there is the world itself,
>
> .   .   .
>
> And where thou art not, desolation.
>
> (362–64)

Suffolk, despite the closing lines of *1 Henry VI* has, in his relationship with Margaret, adhered more closely to his earlier intent: to bring Margaret to England for his own happiness rather than solely for his political advancement.

> Away! . . .
> .   .   .
> And take my heart with thee
> (403,408)

she counsels. It is a heart she will never regain. The scene establishes their relationship as lovers—unacceptable in a queen although acceptable in a king. Members of Shakespeare's audience must have recollected Mary of Scots, the murder of Darnley, and her marriage to Bothwell. They knew the fate of Mary.[24]

Margaret is a woman alone. Her plaint to Suffolk which keynotes part 2—"I thought King Henry had resembled thee / In courage, courtship, and proportion" (I.iii.53–54)—indicates her dilemma. Her first challenge in her drive for personal survival occurred when she was Suffolk's prisoner in *1 Henry VI*. Now, with Suffolk's banishment, she once again faces challenges forcing her to find new solutions. Henry's decisive act makes her realize his power, his courage, and his political domination of her life. Her solution to finding someone who had "resembled thee" led her, like Desdemona, to choose the man himself. Now, alone, she must begin to deal with her "aloneness."

Her adventures with Gloucester and Suffolk establish the reality of her position as wife of a monarch. Will her world disintegrate? Will she retreat to a private world? A gory scene visually accosts us when Margaret next appears: "Enter the King with a supplication, and the Queen with Suffolk's head, the Duke of Buckingham and the Lord Say." In the public halls of state, not the privacy of her chamber, she has been given the murdered Suffolk's bodiless head.

> Oft have I heard that grief softens the mind,
> And makes it fearful and degenerate.
> (IV.iv.1–2)

She wonders how and if she will survive this awful experience and vows revenge as an antidote to collapse. Her actions, however, contradict the confidence of her words.

> Here may his head lie on my throbbing breast;
> But where's the body that I should embrace?
>   (5–6)

Although the stage direction in some modern editions indicates that this is spoken as an "aside," the action must be obvious to Henry and the others. Her lament alternates in stichomythic pattern with the cold plans for military action by the men. Finally, the King can stand it no longer: "How now, madam?" (21) he asks. Aware of her gestures, if not her words, he challenges with an air of jocularity and self-confidence:

> Still lamenting and mourning for Suffolk's death?
> I fear me, love, if that I had been dead,
> Thou wouldst not have mourn'd so much for me.
>   (22–24)

Margaret's remarkable resilience, the quality that led her to speculate when a prisoner, "Tush, women have been captivate ere now," sustains her here: "No, my love, I should not mourn, but die for thee" (25). Robert Ornstein, the contemporary critic who has written at length on the histories, observes that "Margaret's evolution during the tetralogy from romantic stereotype to pitiless Fury is a remarkable achievement for an apprentice playwright, because the pathological warping of her character is acutely and convincingly portrayed. Not born the she-devil the Chronicles describe, Margaret becomes one as frustration and vindictive rage coarsen her passionate nature."[25] That Margaret develops into a bitter woman of rage and passion during the tetralogy is true, but to label her a "she-devil" suggests that Shakespeare has failed to create a convincing portrait. Exposed to brutality in this scene, where she holds the bodiless head of Suffolk, she survives. Her experience resembles that of men who are trained for war and acquire a callousness so that they may then participate in war's violence. Margaret, too, will fight in battle. But she will also retain a sense of herself as a woman. In the next play, we watch the conflict between her stereotyped perceptions of the roles of women and men and her belief that she must function as a man.

In the broad panorama of Shakespeare's canvas, reminding us of a Brueghel painting, Margaret's story in 2 *Henry VI* is only one of many. The intensity of the study of this character in one section of the painting merely enhances the whole. It must not be mistaken for the broad vista. The play includes the Cade Rebellion, the machinations of York, and the flight of Henry and Margaret to London. Interwoven in the plot are Margaret's reaction to Suffolk's death, her responses to the rebellious York, and her stability in moments of defeat.

When next seen, she is dealing with a new problem, her role as a mother. Because children are theoretically the concern of mothers, a play that deals with inheritance and progeny as does 3 *Henry VI*, should involve women. It does. 2 *Henry VI* dramatized a husband's control of his wife's right to exercise power. 3 *Henry VI* dramatizes a woman's new role as parent. Margaret learned that as wife she must subordinate herself to her husband, the ultimate source of power. As a mother, however, she discovers new power, also new motivation for action —the protection of her child. Again the fact that the mother is a queen and the child an heir apparent intensifies the portrait. Nevertheless, one may perceive the conflict that faces all women in the conflict that faces Margaret.

"Is this a husband?" she had asked Suffolk in part 2. In part 3 another riddle faces her. "Is this a father?" she must wonder. Once again, as in the earlier play, Shakespeare stresses her powerlessness before a husband who gives and retracts power; who disclaims any wish for power and then in broad, decisive gestures exercises it. (Shakespeare, in later plays—*As You Like It, The Tempest*, and *King Lear*—was to explore the right of a man in power to abdicate his responsibility without giving up the power as well. Here the dramatist places such a ruler in relationship to his wife.) Margaret had expected a strong, gallant husband; instead she got Henry. She had assumed that Henry would act the normal role of father; instead he shocks and surprises her, forfeiting his son's right to the crown. What must a woman do, married to such a man?

In Hall we find the following definition of her activities:

> And although she joyned her husbande with hir in name, for a countenaunce, yet she did all, she saied all, and she bare the whole swynge, as the strong oxe doth when he is yoked in the plough with a pore silly asse.[26]

Shakespeare does not accept this portrait. He poses more difficult problems for her. Although historically Henry went mad and Margaret for a time was ruler, Shakespeare never allows her this option—a solution that would eliminate the constant frustration and blind responses she must give to a man who slips in and out of a role.

When *3 Henry VI* opens, Henry is on the defensive against a victorious York. The latter has chosen to occupy the throne moments before Henry enters. A political and military dilemma confronts him. As a solution, he decides to name York his heir. This means that upon Henry's death the title of King would automatically go to York and then to his heirs rather than to Henry's own son. Amazed at his actions, the Queen derides the foolishness of naming his enemy his successor: "Such safety finds / The trembling lamb environed with wolves" (I.i.241–42). But she also challenges his actions as those of a father: "Hath he deserv'd to lose his birthright thus?" (219) she asks. Then with maternal concern, she continues:

> Hadst thou but lov'd him half so well as I,
> Or felt that pain which I did for him once,
> Or nourish'd him as I did with my blood,
> Thou wouldst have left thy dearest heart-blood there
> Rather than have made that savage duke thine heir,
> And disinherited thine only son.
>
> (I.i.220–25)

Her speech, intense in its expression of a mother's feeling for her child, details the relationship of the mother to the unborn fetus and to the child she bore. The chronicle tells us of her love for her son; Shakespeare dramatizes it in *3 Henry VI* where Margaret acts the warrior to regain the title for her son.

Forced by her desire to save her son's inheritance, she actively takes charge of the army. Nevertheless, she retains her stereotyped attitude toward herself as a woman, believing that strength and the qualities of tenderness usually associated with a woman are not coexistent. As a result, she is vulnerable to attacks on her womanliness. The first hint of this vulnerability occurs when York, taken prisoner by Margaret, aims his attack at her lack of femininity. Her role as mother supports her. Later, however, when Edward, York's son, blames her for all the evils befalling the country, she reveals how trapped she is by the stereotypes.

Margaret Fuller, noting the problems facing strong women, wrote:

> . . . early I perceived that men never, in any extreme of despair, wished to be women. . . . When they admired any woman, they were inclined to speak of her as "above her sex." Silently I observed this, and feared it argued a rooted scepticism, which for ages had been fastening on the heart, and which only an age of miracles could eradicate.[27]

Speaking through the persona of a character, early trained in "self-reliance," Fuller explains, "And were all women as sure of their wants as I was," they would naturally develop self-respect.[28] Few women, unfortunately, are in this position.

Stereotyped attitudes toward women as naturally inferior to men permeate the plays, affecting the perspective of male as well as female characters. Only very occasionally do these attitudes advance a woman's cause. Such a moment occurs when Richard, York's son, hearing that the Queen is besieging them with twenty thousand men, jeeringly retorts: "A woman's general: what should we fear?" (I.ii.68). Reality, rather than the sex of the leader, determines the success of her venture. Margaret triumphs; York falls. He becomes her prisoner. Then follows the famous confrontation between them in which he attacks her as "she-wolf of France."

Unfortunately, as I have shown, Margaret has assimilated patriarchal values. Kate Millett labels one of the areas where this interior colonization has occurred as temperament, defining it as:

> the formation of human personality along stereotyped lines of sex category ("masculine" and "feminine"), based on the needs and values of the dominant group and dictated by what its members cherish in themselves and find convenient in subordinates: aggression, intelligence, force, and efficacy in the male; passivity, ignorance, docility, "virtue," and ineffectuality in the female.[29]

Doomed to die, unless by some miracle he can verbally overwhelm Margaret, York begins his attack. Psychologically he aims at the Margaret he knows, the Margaret he saw being made Queen, the Margaret with whom he conspired about the death of Gloucester, the Margaret who was lover of Suffolk, the Margaret who later insisted on York's allegiance to Henry, the Margaret he once defeated in battle. This is the Margaret he faces now, hoping to defeat her with words that will strike at her innermost being, hoping to save his own life.

Throughout his lengthy defense, York charges his language with attacks on her as a woman. Is this where she is most vulnerable? Obviously he thinks so:

> How ill-beseeming is it in thy sex
> To triumph like an Amazonian trull.
> (I.iv.113–14)

After a reference to her strength and military leadership, he returns to the subject of her womanliness:

> But that thy face is vizard-like, unchanging,
>   .   .   .
> I would assay, proud queen, to make thee blush.
> (116,118)

Here he attacks her appearance. Next come references to her lineage and her heritage, more usual among enemies. For York, however, they but mark a pause. Quickly, he returns to her characteristics as a woman:

> 'Tis beauty that doth oft make women proud,
> But God he knows thy share thereof is small.
>   (128–29)

York himself had been present at her first entering England as
Queen. Did he mean all this? Had she changed so much? From
beauty it is but a short step to virtue. Again he assaults her
lack of womanliness:

> 'Tis virtue that doth make them most admir'd,
> The contrary doth make thee wond'red at.
>   (130–31)

Thus York hammers away at her divergence from the expected
norms of her sex.

But who is York? What murders has he committed,
what insurrections led? Deceitful, plotting dissimulator, he
killed the elder Clifford; he broke his vow of allegiance to
Henry; and he caused the murder of Suffolk.

> O tiger's heart wrapp'd in a woman's hide!
> How couldst thou drain the life-blood of the child,
>   (137–38)

he moans upon seeing the handkerchief stained with his
young son Rutland's blood. Although Clifford, not she, had
killed Rutland, York concentrates his attack on Margaret. She,
in return, ignoring all of his words, assails only his presump-
tion to the crown, his attempt to deprive her son of rightful
succession: "What, was it you that would be England's King?"
(70). If he will speak of sons she too will speak of sons—hers
and his. She progresses from her defense of her own son to an
examination of his. The intimacy of the references, the demy-
thologizing of the Yorks, seethes through every line:

> Where are your mess of sons to back you now,
> The wanton Edward, and the lusty George?
> And where's that valiant crook-back prodigy,
> Dicky, your boy, that with his grumbling voice
> Was wont to cheer his dad in mutinies?
>   (73–77)

To her, they seem like a fairly unattractive progeny—wanton, lusty, mutinous, hardly worthy of kingship. Later we hear Henry commenting on the father killing his son and the son killing his father. In contrast with that scene is this one where Shakespeare is showing us a mother evaluating the offspring of another. One is distant, stilted, philosophical; the other passionate, intimate, intense.

After crowning York with a paper crown, she reveals her deepest antagonism: "this is he that took King Henry's chair, / And this is he was his adopted heir" (I.iv.97–98). For his part, York continues his own line of attack, needling her for her lack of womanliness, "women are soft, mild, pitiful, and flexible" (141). York perceives women as objects; Margaret, a woman driven to act by the intensity of her feelings as a mother, knows that women are human beings.

York continues to drag out the stereotypes. His words have a built-in irony: "Thou stern, obdurate, flinty, rough, remorseless" (142). Of all the epithets thrown at Margaret by York, this last series would be most easy for her to accept. For she sees herself as flinty and obdurate, necessary qualities for a leader, qualities that her husband lacks. Andrew Cairncross, the editor of the recent modern edition of this play, writes that Shakespeare follows conventions for "a formal rhetorical invective on Margaret's parentage, personal appearance, character, conduct, and nationality, with appropriate comparisons, and general introduction." [30] Rhetorical conventions may govern the overall pattern of the speech, but York's emphasis on Margaret's sex, his choice of the words "Amazonian trull," "she-wolf," "ruthless queen," and then the contrasting "beauty" are not "appropriate comparisons" such as one might make between Margaret and another woman who was a commander in the field, or between Margaret and other women whose children have been disinherited. They are comparisons limited to the stereotype for "woman."

Although York is unsuccessful in saving himself from death—from Margaret's indignation at his usurping her son's rightful place—he correctly discerned her weakness. The bludgeoning of Margaret for her unwomanliness finally succeeds later in the play when York's son, Edward, repeats his father's approach. This time on the military defensive after the murder of York, Margaret finds herself unsupported by her weak husband. Again her battle—this time with York's heirs—is verbal. Again Margaret's weaknesses are listed. Edward, pretender to the crown, attempting to separate husband and wife, accuses her:

> Hadst thou been meek, our title still had slept,
> And we, in pity of the gentle king,
> Had slipp'd our claim until another age.
> (II.ii.160–62)

A psychological trick, it works. For, moments later, when Edward, stalking off stage, orders "Let our bloody colors wave! / And either victory, or else a grave" (173–74), Margaret gently begs, "Stay, Edward" (175). But the young, handsome Edward, already determined to win the crown, sneeringly turns: "No, wrangling woman, we'll no longer stay, / These words will cost ten thousand lives this day" (176–77).

Shakespeare insists that we recognize the guile of Edward's attack on Margaret by creating a parallel situation later in the play in which Edward uses a similar verbal technique. Claiming he has no intention of taking the crown, Edward, already once King, stands at the gates of York asking only his rights as heir to the dukedom. After entering the gates, however, he accepts the acclamation "Edward the Fourth" (IV.vii.71) and successfully defeats Henry's forces. This same kind of dishonesty motivates his words to Margaret, for they are part of the characterization of the man.

A critic who tends to accept either York's description of her or Edward's is overlooking the dramatic context in which the speeches occur, and forgetting that these speeches reinforce the earlier portraits of father and son: York is a master rhetorician, guileful, convincing, and dishonest, and Edward is a young man who follows in his father's footsteps. Nor should Margaret accept these evaluations. As Fuller observed:

> . . . men do *not* look at both sides, and women must leave off asking them and being influenced by them, but retire within themselves, and explore the ground-work of being till they find their peculiar secret.[31]

But the Queen, although confident of herself as a mother, is far less confident of herself as a woman.

In a recent article, the eminent Shakespearean scholar, Eugene Waith, writes of his surprise at discovering Margaret as one of the *Nine . . . Most Worthy Women of the World* in a work written in 1640, some time after Shakespeare's plays first appeared. Comments Waith, "To find this tiger's heart, wrapped in a woman's hide, held up as exemplary, rather than cautionary, is initially breathtaking." Waith then analyzes the text to understand what led the author, Thomas Heywood, to choose Margaret as one of the three Christian worthies and concludes that "Heywood is perhaps closest to the primitive heroic tradition which values greatness above moral goodness, or assumes that *virtus* is the greatest virtue." The word "virtu" was applied during the Renaissance to those qualities that distinguished the hero, and includes such ideas as bravery, the heroic spirit, military prowess, and magnanimity. "Sheer will and energy command Heywood's respect," observes Waith, and cites particularly Margaret's "defiance of King Edward even when she is in his power."[32] Although many of the qualities of "virtu" distinguish Margaret, she herself becomes confused by the demands on her as a woman, having internalized the values of the patriarchal society. As for the critics, the majority adopt York's point of view.

In this multifaceted gallery of women of power, Shakespeare next introduces Lady Elizabeth Grey. Less heroic than Margaret, she evokes less admiration but also less intense hostility. Like Margaret, she is offered a crown, and like Margaret, she has little choice but to accept. In this complicated plot sequence, Elizabeth first enters the tetralogy as a petitioner to King Edward IV after he has temporarily deposed Henry as ruling monarch. A widow, she asks for the return of her slain husband's lands. In response, Edward—"the wanton Edward" of Margaret's speech to York—fancies Elizabeth for his own, whether as mistress or, if necessary, as wife. Then follows an exchange in Act III, scene 2, reminiscent of Margaret's first scene with Suffolk when she was a captive princess.

Again Shakespeare employs the aside to illuminate the conflicting readings of the same words by men and women. An antiphonal chorus of voices speaks in aside during the

Lady Elizabeth Grey appeals to King Edward in *3 Henry VI* while Clarence and Richard whisper in asides, a moment captured in this mid-nineteenth-century illustration by John Masey Wright. FOLGER SHAKESPEARE LIBRARY

exchange between King and supplicant. Standing slightly apart from them, Richard and George, Edward's brothers, exchange slurring comments about their brother before he himself privately divulges his intention to the audience. They leave no doubt as to Edward's aim. "I see the lady hath a thing to grant, / Before the King will grant her humble suit" (III.ii.12–13), Richard observes to George while Elizabeth is asking King Edward publicly, "May it please your Highness to resolve me now, / And what your pleasure is shall satisfy me" (19–20). Again Richard confides to his brother: "And if what please him shall pleasure you. / Fight closer or, good faith, you'll catch a blow" (22–23). To Richard and Clarence, Edward's intentions are clear. To Elizabeth they are completely masked.

As Edward and Elizabeth repartee, she continues to misunderstand his meaning. Even when he asks her to "love a king" (III.ii.53), she can respond with ease, "That's soon perform'd, because I am a subject" (54). Only when she thanks him and indicates "I take my leave with many thousand thanks" (56), does he clearly state: "But stay thee, 'tis the fruits of love I mean" (58). Even then Lady Grey refuses to understand him: "My love till death, my humble thanks, my prayers— / That love which virtue begs and virtue grants" (62–63). When she finally understands, her answer resembles Isabella's in *Measure for Measure*. "My mind will never grant what I perceive / Your Highness aims at, if I aim aright" (67–68), Elizabeth asserts.

Some critics suggest that the forwardness of this proposal in contrast with Suffolk's indicates the moral breakdown of the realm, because Suffolk spoke to Margaret with some tact, some measure of hesitancy. I believe that the dramatist was realistically presenting the typical attitude of a man toward a widow. Today one might include divorced women in this category. We see, in the play, that men still perceive women as sexual objects rather than as persons. Women's status as formerly married persons simply means that the men need express themselves with less tact. "To tell thee plain, I aim to lie with thee" (69), Edward announces. Lady Grey moves from the fancy language of royalty to the simple language of a subject, "To tell you plain, I had rather lie in prison" (70). As Edward seeks to pursue the argument, Lady Grey attempts to end the encounter.

> But, mighty lord, this merry inclination
> Accords not with the sadness of my suit.
> Please you dismiss me, either with ay or no.
> (III.ii.76–78)

Then he, like Suffolk, speaks in aside: "One way or other, she is for a king, / And she shall be my love or else my queen.—" (87–88). Turning to her, he continues; "Say that King Edward take thee for his queen?" (89). Again, like Margaret, Elizabeth dismisses the proposal, its utter irrationality obvious to her:

> I am a subject fit to jest withal,
> But far unfit to be a sovereign.
> .   .   .
> I know I am too mean to be your queen,
> And yet too good to be your concubine.
> (91–98)

Children, mentioned earlier by Edward as additional motivation for her complying with his request, are now introduced as a subject by Elizabeth. " 'Twill grieve your Grace my sons should call you father" (100), she says. "No more than when my daughters call thee mother" (101), he responds. The exchange between them becomes more intense, concluding with his assertion: "thou shalt be my queen" (106).

Like the men who surrounded Henry, those who surround Edward are hostile to the new Queen. But unlike Margaret who responded to Gloucester's slight with a desire for revenge, Elizabeth seeks a reconciliation with her brothers-in-law, "So your dislikes, to whom I would be pleasing, / Doth cloud my joys with danger and with sorrow" (IV.i.73–74). However neither Elizabeth's conciliatory attitude, nor Margaret's independence, self-reliance, or "manliness" makes any difference. Although their methods differ and their personalities are unalike, neither woman is accepted by those closest to her husband. To the men, they are lesser creatures. In the patriarchal structure, they have no right to think for themselves, to act on their own initiative, or to institute new actions.

As power alternates between the forces of Henry and Edward, Shakespeare continues to concentrate on the subject of progeny. The women, whether as mothers or daughters, play a role, but hardly as persons in their own right. Elizabeth, pregnant with Edward's offspring, must seek refuge. Margaret, hoping to defend her son, seeks help from France. An English lord, Warwick, shifting allegiance from Edward to Henry, pledges his daughter in marriage to Henry's son. Finally, in the last scenes, progeny invades. Margaret's son, Edward, is murdered by York's sons—Edward, Richard, and George. Her agony resembles York's when told of Rutland's death. The coldness of the murderers is comparable to that earlier coldness.

No one weeps for Margaret. Unlike Northumberland, who pitied York, no one in the play pities Margaret, whose loss of an only child is surely as great, if not greater, than York's travail. The sympathy felt for York because of his long harangue is not felt for Margaret; she had defied the conventions of role. York, in his murders, rebellions, and oath-breaking, had conformed to the stereotypes of the strong man. He could arouse sympathy, even from an enemy, another man. When a man weeps, all pity him; when a woman weeps, she merely plays her expected role.

Some critics have compared Margaret with Richard because of her ruthlessness in the scene of the death of York. Others have compared her with Warwick, the instigator of revolt. But Margaret can only be fully understood as an adjunct to power, and, for a brief moment, a wielder of power. The background she brings to her role differs from that of any of the men in the plays. It is rooted in her stereotypical experiences as a woman—whether in the way she is wooed, in her powerlessness to defend her lover although herself a queen, or in her drive to protect her son.

By the close of *3 Henry VI* the women's roles have shifted. Margaret, widowed and now childless, is a person of little hope. Elizabeth, although previously widowed, is wife, queen, and mother of new life. Wives of kings, the women hold their power through marriage and through the goodwill, the sufferance, the whims of their husbands.

In *Richard III*, four widows walk the stage: Margaret, Elizabeth, the Duchess of York, and Anne. If women are confused by the meaning of power when they are young, being wooed or acting as wives to men of power, they realistically discover its meaning when they become widows. They learn that their husbands were not only the source of their power, but worse still, of their identity. How does a woman cope with this discovery, this becoming a nonperson? Shakespeare offers four versions in *Richard III*, from the simple acceptance of her status by the Duchess of York to the anxious search for new patterns by Elizabeth, who first entered this tetralogy when, as a widow suing for rights to her husband's lands, she discovered her powerlessness for the first time. Saved by her wit and beauty, she then moved from powerlessness to power. Like Margaret earlier, she became a queen and the mother of princes. When, in *Richard III*, the pattern repeats itself, Elizabeth seeks more substantial answers.

Her experience continues to mirror Margaret's despite deviations. Elizabeth's husband, instead of being murdered by Richard, dies, his illness aggravated by Richard's histrionics. Instead of losing one son and heir to the throne, she loses two. Instead of being childless at the end of the play, she remains a mother with surviving children. Instead of being a widow of a defeated monarch, she is widow of a man who was in power. But it little matters. Like Margaret, Elizabeth too loses power, discovering the strength of the patriarchal system. Finally, near the play's close, she seeks alternatives. Shakespeare offers a tentative glimpse at women supporting women, women relying on women, women bonding—even if in bitterness—with women.

To do this, the dramatist alters history and creates one of the most interesting studies in the play—he retains Margaret. Historically, she never returned to England after the deaths of her son and husband. Moreover, she died before the time of the action of this play. According to the chronicles, she roamed the French court, a woman in mourning for the rest of her life:

And where in the beginning of her tyme, she lyved like a Quene, in the middel she ruled like an empresse, toward thende she was vexed with troble, never quyet nor in peace, & in her very extreme age she passed her dayes in Fraunce, more lyke a death then a lyfe, languishyng and mornyng in continuall sorowe, not so much for her selfe and her husbande, whose ages were almost consumed and worne, but for the losse of prince Edward her sonne (whome she and her husband thought to leve, both overlyver of their progeny, and also of their kyngdome) to whome in this lyfe nothyng coulde be either more displeasant or grevous.[33]

Shakespeare not only brings her back to England but gives her an important role in the play. She acts as narrative voice; she is seer and sibyl, predicting the doom of those responsible for the deaths of her son and husband; but she is also a dynamic woman, an anomalous character, roaming the palace of a rival monarch, expressing her opinions in positive language, sneering at York's unattractive progeny who now control power. Having lost all, she fears no one.

Margaret, who weaves in and out of this tetralogy, the only woman character whose growth we observe from youth to old age, may also have challenged Shakespeare as a creative artist. Knowing that she walked through the court in France, a person in constant mourning, he might have wanted to project this image on the stage. Would such a woman have learned anything? Would she have grown? How might she have handled life, alone, in a hostile environment? Finally, has she made any breakthrough in self-knowledge; did she learn anything about herself as a woman?

Before she enters, Shakespeare introduces her principal antagonist, Richard, the title character. He defines the power and powerlessness of women in the first scene of *Richard III*. Introduced in soliloquy, he confides his plans to reach the throne despite the mass of relatives standing between him and his objective. "I am determined to prove a villain" (I.i.30), he proclaims, baring his plot to frame his brother Clarence. When the latter enters, en route to prison, Richard immediately blames a woman for Clarence's present fate. "Why, this it is, when men are rul'd by women" (62), Richard asserts, implying Queen Elizabeth's evil influence on Edward. Misogyny runs wild, for Clarence easily agrees, adding Mistress Shore's name to those who "rule" the King. Before the scene closes, a third woman is mentioned. Richard, again in soliloquy, admits,

> . . . I'll marry Warwick's youngest daughter.
> What though I kill'd her husband and her father?
> The readiest way to make the wench amends
> Is to become her husband and her father.
>
> (I.i.153–56)

Moments later Anne, the play's third widow, walks on following the coffin of King Henry, her father-in-law, and taking it to burial. Asking the pall bearers to "set down" their "honorable load" (I.ii.i), Anne delivers a long set speech of mourning explicitly cursing the murderer, Richard. She then orders the pallbearers to resume the trek to the place of burial. Richard, unobserved, interferes, countermanding her order. "Stay, you that bear the corse, and set it down" (33). At their attempt to continue, Richard threatens with his sword. They obey. Graphically, this scene illustrates Richard's power and Anne's powerlessness. Helpless to challenge him physically, she attempts to disarm him with words. She seeks to force her will. Scorn, hatred, vehemence, curses: all fall from her lips. Little anticipating the aim of his confrontation, she is astonished and completely bewildered when Richard offers marriage.

Historically, Richard pursued Anne for two years before winning her. Shakespeare compresses this into one scene, choosing a moment when she is most confused and emotionally most unstable. In a long protracted courtship, their debates—her responses to his persistent claims—would have to be developed so that the many variables in personality could influence the decision. When compressed into a single scene, his duplicity and her confusion must be apparent at once. Some critics believe that the scene offers an opportunity to prove Richard's extraordinary ability.[34] More recently critics have become aware of the psychological vulnerability of a person at a time of emotional crisis such as the loss of a husband and a father-in-law.[35]

First Richard tries flattery, but Anne resists, assuring him that she would scratch her beauty with her nails (I.ii.126) if she thought it were the cause of the death of her husband or father-in-law. Then Richard, the consummate actor, offers her his sword and "lays his breast open" for her to kill him. He challenges her in a style that she cannot fathom. Untrained in the use of the sword, unwilling to take a human life, Anne reacts as a normal human being might, especially someone who has not been initiated into the games of war and murder. Although Richard continues "Nay, do not pause: for I did kill King Henry— / But 'twas thy beauty that provoked me" (179–80), she drops the sword. But Richard's words are really superfluous. All of her training as a woman assures him success. Men are trained to kill. Women are not. Here, against a defenseless person, in a time of uncertain peace, to kill the brother of the King would be insanity as well as suicide.

Richard then poses a false dichotomy for her: "Take up the sword again, or take up me" (I.ii.183). He leaves her no option; she must either kill him or accept him as her husband. Caught between suspicion and her training as a woman, Anne can do no more than say, "Arise, dissembler! Though I wish thy death, / I will not be thy executioner" (184–85). Still she does not acquiesce to marriage. The key interchange between them occurs moments later when Richard offers "Then bid me kill myself" (186) but refuses to accept her words, "I have already" (187). Instead, he then questions the honesty of her original intention. "That was in thy rage. / Speak it again" (187–88) he challenges, promising to kill himself for love. Anne's agonized words, "I would I knew thy heart" (192) are spoken by many of the characters throughout the play. No one knows Richard's "heart"—his intention—until it is too late. For a woman being wooed, however, the price is particularly high—not friendship or allegiance, but marriage.

Although Richard congratulates himself on his success —"To take her in her heart's extremest hate, / With curses in her mouth, tears in her eyes" (I.ii.231–32)—Shakespeare here creates a situation in which a manipulative liar has the best chance of success, a moment when his prey is most confused. Richard's timing, audacity, overwhelming flattery, and histrionics with the sword are beyond Anne's ability to cope. She belongs with such characters as Ophelia, who is conforming, obedient, docile, "feminine." Historically, having resisted Richard for two years, she may have had more of the strength

of a Margaret or an Elizabeth. She may also have had as few
options as they did, being sought by the persistent brother of
the King. But rather than repeat a pattern already twice told,
Shakespeare creates another type of woman, caught in a different situation, and reacting on a level not yet dramatized in
this tetralogy. The man she must confront is the man who
boasted in the previous play:

> Why, I can smile, and murther whiles I smile,
>
> .   .   .
>
> Deceive more slily than Ulysses could,
>
> .   .   .
>
> Change shapes with Proteus for advantages,
>
> .   .   .
>
> Can I do this, and cannot get a crown?
> Tut, were it farther off, I'll pluck it down.
>   (*3 Henry VI*, III.ii.182–95)

Richard applies his abilities, skills, and techniques to convince
Anne.

    Critics have been harsh in their evaluation of her. Au-
gust W. Von Schlegel, the nineteenth-century German scholar,
writes that "Anne disappears without our learning anything
further respecting her: in marrying the murderer of her husband she had shown a weakness almost incredible." [36] William
Richardson, in the eighteenth century, concludes that "She is
represented by Shakespeare of a mind altogether frivolous;
incapable of deep affection; guided by no steady principles of
virtue . . . ; the prey of vanity, which is her ruling passion."
As Richardson continues, he not only says that Richard understands her perfectly but that she is a character of "no rational
or steady virtue, and consequently of no consistency of character." He even suggests that it is "resentment, rather than
grief, which she expresses." [37] Georg Gervinus, the nineteenth-century German literary historian, offers a more balanced appraisal, however, when he writes, "We must take into
account the extraordinary degree of dissimulation, which de-
ceives even experienced men," noting also how stereotypical
a portrait Shakespeare creates in Anne by having her delight
in saving "such a penitent." [38]

Anne appears in only one other scene, and that without Richard. Now married, she hopes to visit her nephews—the heirs apparent—held in the tower by her husband. Unlike her historical prototype, she admits:

> Lo, ere I can repeat this curse again,
> Within so small a time, my woman's heart
> Grossly grew captive to his honey words,
> And prov'd the subject of mine own soul's curse.
>
> (IV.i.77–80)

She is self-deprecating, and blames herself for her fate. Her conventionality is perhaps best testified to by the fact that she survives in all versions of the play. In Colley Cibber's version, Richard even tries to tempt her to commit suicide.[39] In a recent production at the Cort Theatre starring Al Pacino, she appears so cold, self-righteous, and vindictive that audiences applaud Richard's success.[40] There, although the text that remains is Shakespeare's, the cuts are reminiscent of Cibber's popular eighteenth-century work.

On the other hand, the one woman who most frequently disappears from productions is the one who challenges Richard, the least conventional woman—Margaret. Cibber set the pattern in 1700 when he eliminated her from his text. Since then, his version with its heavy emphasis on the male "star" role has seldom left the stage. But even when Shakespeare's text is used, Margaret frequently disappears or loses most of her lines. For example, in a Phelps 1845 promptbook, she no longer functions as an individual, cursing the many members of the court, but acts rather as a choral voice of doom.[41] Very similar cutting appears in a 1964 typescript of the play.[42] She is also absent from Laurence Olivier's film version and from the Pacino 1979 production.[43] Comparing the Cibber version with Shakespeare's play, Arthur Colby Sprague writes that:

> the more obviously memorable episodes . . . have survived.
> . . . But Margaret is gone and Clarence and Hastings and Edward: the price paid for compactness was high. It is a version . . . which does best when it keeps to surfaces and shallows; an opportunist version, cunning, prosaic and vulgar.[44]

Many productions of *Richard III*, like Olivier's and Pacino's mentioned above, follow Shakespeare's text but also take their cues for cutting from Cibber. It is perhaps difficult for audiences to realize how deeply eighteenth-century changes—perhaps because they reflect attitudes toward women that still exist—continue to intrude on, shape, and gently distort the text.

Margaret's absence necessarily affects the total impact of the play; her entrance, in Act I, scene iii, offers a welcome antidote to Richard's swaggering triumph with Anne. Listening to Queen Elizabeth and Richard arguing, Margaret, once again, as she did so long ago in *1 Henry VI* speaks in asides. This time, however, her asides are not the questions of a young virgin but the bitter comments of an old woman. She listens to the conversation of those in power. To Elizabeth's "Small joy have I in being England's Queen" (109), Margaret mutters to herself:

> And less'ned by that small, God I beseech him!
> Thy honor, state, and seat is due to me.
> (I.iii.110–11)

At once we are reminded that Margaret is a deposed queen. We wonder at her presence in this court. Commenting on Richard's words, but still speaking in aside, she exclaims:

> Hie thee to hell for shame, and leave this world,
> Thou cacodemon, there thy kingdom is.
> (142–43)

Only the audience hears her; nevertheless, her lines establish her strange position. What is she doing at the court, this woman, so unafraid of Richard who, in asides, tells us of the murder of Henry in the tower and the killing of her son Edward? When she speaks aloud, Margaret pierces the false veneer of Richard, but also reveals antagonism for the woman who has made her a shadow, a nonbeing, the woman who is Queen. Although Richard reminds Margaret that she is "banished on pain of death" (166), she dismisses the threat, challenging him to enforce it. "I do find more pain in banishment

H.Singleton del: C.Taylor excudit.

QUEEN MARGARET.

Live each of You the subject of his hate,

And he to yours, and all of You to Gods'!

The sweep of her arm and the sharp twist of her neck in this
illustration by Henry Singleton for Boydell's Gallery reinforce the
sense of Margaret's frustration when she curses the members of the
court in Act I of *Richard III*. FOLGER SHAKESPEARE LIBRARY

/ Than death can yield me here by my abode" (167–68). He
then pursues another direction. Always aware of his audience,
the people around him on the stage, he attacks Margaret for
the murders of York and Rutland. As a result the squabbling
members of the court unite against her. Aware of Richard's
technique, she taunts:

> What? were you snarling all before I came,
>
>   · · · ·
>
> And turn you all your hatred now on me?
>
> (187–89)

She then curses each of them. Still wrestling with the
patriarchal values she has absorbed, she first curses the
Queen, her alter ego in this strange arrangement where kings
are murdered to make way for kings but queens in number are
permitted to survive. Listing the parallels between them, Margaret wishes the other woman a fate like her own:

> Though not by war, by surfeit die your king,
> As ours by murther, to make him a king!
> Edward thy son, that now is Prince of Wales,
> For Edward our son, that was Prince of Wales,
> Die in his youth by like untimely violence!
>
> (I.iii.196–200)

She keeps returning to her role of mother.

> Long mayst thou live to wail thy children's death,
> And see another, as I see thee now,
> Deck'd in thy rights as thou art stall'd in mine!
>
> (203–5)

Finally, she condemns Elizabeth to a fate too familiar to
women.

> Long die thy happy days before thy death,
> And after many length'ned hours of grief,
> Die neither mother, wife, nor England's queen!
>
> (206–8)

In this long passage, Margaret details her own life as queen. Unlike the curses one might choose for a man, those chosen for Elizabeth have a different emphasis—not death but life continued after joy has passed.

When the bitter woman fails to stop her cursing, Richard interrupts. In verbal battle, she responds, wishing him a fate more heinous than the others. Her curse concludes with "Thou detested———." Never one to refuse a challenge, Richard quickly interjects the word "Margaret." But she is not to be deflected from her purpose. Her sentence continues, ending with "Richard!" Elizabeth, although she bears no love for Richard, is still a victim of that minority status psychology that mandates she express her deepest contempt for another woman. "Thus have you breath'd your curse against yourself" (239), she mocks. Her words are hardly worth including in this exchange except to remind us of the difference between the two women—the sibyl-like, intense, passionate Margaret, and the more pedestrian, rational Elizabeth.

Finally, Cassandra-like, Margaret warns the one person exempt from her vengeance to beware of Richard:

> Have not to do with him, beware of him;
> Sin, death, and hell have set their marks on him,
> And all their ministers attend on him.
>   (I.iii.291–93)

But Buckingham rejects her warning. Nevertheless, he shudders at her curses. Ironically, she is attacked as being a witch and a lunatic although her listeners recognize the core of truth in her words. During this scene Dorset, the new young lord who is Elizabeth's son, warns "Dispute not with her, she is lunatic" (253). Buckingham expresses the impact of the curses for all of them, "My hair doth stand an end to hear her curses" (303).

When her curses come true, she believes her mission is completed. But Shakespeare suggests that one possibility lies ahead—women extending their hands to each other in support—creating bonds with each other, rather than living in separate isolated worlds, connected only with the men whom they have wed. Entering in Act IV, scene iv, Margaret, in soliloquy, mutters "So now prosperity begins to mellow" (IV.iv.1). Still bitter, overflowing with anger and hatred, she plans to go to France, hoping the lives of those who robbed her of son and husband will prove "bitter, black, and tragical" (7). She is a figure from the revenge tragedy of the period, asking right for right and Plantagenet for Plantagenet. It is only after the Duchess of York exclaims

> O Harry's wife, triumph not in my woes!
> God witness with me, I have wept for thine
> (IV.iv.59–60)

that Margaret explains herself to them: "I am hungry for revenge" (61). She prays for Richard's end. Aware of her anomic position, Margaret returns to the theme of displacedness— "Thou didst usurp my place"—and to the role of childlessness and widowhood. She cannot establish a bond with any woman—not lend support, or seek help, or accept friendship.

"Vain flourish of my fortune" (IV.iv.82), she had called Elizabeth. Detailing its meaning, the displaced Queen recognizes the role she played, "One heav'd a-high, to be hurl'd down below" (86). She knows now that she was merely

> The flattering index of a direful pageant;
>
> .   .   .
>
> .   .   . a bubble;
> A queen in jest, only to fill the scene.
> (85–91)

She then enumerates the functions of a queen, listing the bending peers and thronging troops that followed her and Elizabeth when each was Queen. This speech, by the dramatist who later was to list the many roles of man as he progressed from infancy to old age, vibrates with the emptiness of a woman's roles. "Vain flourish of my fortune," Margaret had repeated. It is a line that many older women might speak, watching young women seeking success in the world and misreading their husbands' glories for their own.

Although Margaret's words are full of venom, hatred, and disappointment, Elizabeth seeks to create some bond,

RICHARD III.

In this small picture, Louis Boulanger dramatically interprets the sense of urgency and despair of the three women who turn to one another for help near the close of the play. FOLGER SHAKESPEARE LIBRARY

some tenuous connection, with this other woman. The scene marks a shift in attitude and is the first in which these women finally speak to each other as equals. Frequently referred to as the scene of the wailing women, it is also the beginning of mutual supportiveness. "My words are dull, O, quicken them with thine!" (124), Elizabeth begs, asking Margaret for instruction in cursing.

> Think that thy babes were sweeter than they were,
> And he that slew them fouler than he is.
> (IV.iv.120–21)

The older woman offers a basic premise that provides strength for Elizabeth's next encounter.

Clues to a sometimes ambiguous exchange between characters frequently appear in the sequential arrangement of Shakespeare's scenes. Moments after Margaret's advice to Elizabeth, Richard enters and asks for Elizabeth's daughter's hand in marriage. Uncle Richard, murderer of the young woman's brothers, now King, anticipates success. In the debate between them, Elizabeth has her first opportunity to apply her newly learned lesson. Questions rather than answers characterize most of her replies. "Shall I be tempted of the devil thus?" (418), she asks. "Ay, if the devil tempt you to do good" (419), Richard sanctimoniously replies. "Shall I forget myself to be myself" (420), she continues. "Ay, if yourself's remembrance wrong yourself" (421), he answers. When she seems to equivocate, Richard simply carries on as best he can, picking up what he thinks are hints of affirmation. Even Elizabeth's "Yet thou didst kill my children" (422) fails to daunt him. He offers what he considers a perfectly logical response:

> But in your daughter's womb I bury them;
> Where in that nest of spicery they will breed
> Selves of themselves, to your recomforture.
> (IV.iv.423–25)

This speech, so ugly in its lasciviousness, reflecting the character of the man who is speaking, must be answered without disgust by a mother. Again Elizabeth resorts to a question, rather than an answer. "Shall I go win my daughter to thy will?" (426). Has she finally fooled Richard? Immediately after her departure, he gloats, "Relenting fool, and shallow, changing woman" (431).

She should not fool us. We have heard her scene with Margaret. We have listened to her first words to Richard in this encounter—"For my daughters, Richard, / They shall be praying nuns, not weeping queens" (201–2)—and we have seen her pity for Anne. The choice of a convent for her daughters grows not from religious conviction—we have not heard any deep expressions of religious faith from Elizabeth—but from the wish to give her daughters control over their own bodies. Elizabeth has expressed herself on this subject from the time of her first appearance in *3 Henry VI*.

When one compares Anne's response to Richard with Elizabeth's series of rhetorical questions topped by the instruction: "Write to me very shortly, / And you shall understand from me her mind" (428–29), one realizes Shakespeare's artistry. Richard, thinking that he is repeating an earlier wooing scene, assumes a repetition of that success—this time with far less effort than in his encounter with Anne. Because of his misogyny, he fails to hear the nuances that separate the responses of the women. He forgets the differences between them: one a young, unwordly heiress, the other a mature woman who has lived a varied existence. Finally, he has figured without understanding the impact of the death of one's child on a parent. The superb manipulator of people, Richard fails to read a woman accurately, because he fails to understand her feelings toward herself and her children.

To an extent, then, Elizabeth has triumphed. She has begun to understand the meaning of power and the necessity for choosing one's language with care, for restraining one's words, refraining from cursing. She has learned that she must function alone, leading, not leaning. In this her first test after her encounter with Margaret and her awareness of the role of queen as shadow, she has begun to understand the limits of power for a woman. She succeeds in fooling Richard, but had he not lost his life in battle, she probably would have been powerless against him. Her daughter, instead of becoming a nun, marries Richard's victorious adversary: Richmond, later

Henry VII. Thus, she too becomes a queen, wearing the borrowed robes of power.

The women in these plays, queens and duchesses, wives of men of political strength, seek to exert power but discover its elusiveness. Margaret Fuller writes: "A profound thinker has said 'No married woman can represent the female world, for she belongs to her husband. The idea of Woman must be represented by a virgin.' " Perhaps the Queen in Shakespeare's audience believed this. The women in these plays, however, demonstrate the powerlessness of women whether virgins, wives, or widows. Fuller herself countered the argument by blaming marriage and "the present relation between the sexes, that the woman *does* belong to the man, instead of forming a whole with him."[45]

This chapter opened with references to power and to women's powerlessness in a society where sexual politics is so pervasive that women have internalized the message. Shakespeare illustrates this by revealing the minority psychology of the women. They scorn other women, attempt to imitate men, and tend to believe in their own inferiority. The men too believe the women inferior to them, whether the women are self-confident and challenge male power, or whether they acquiesce, seeking to appease male anger. The stereotypes do not exist solely among the characters in the plays, but appear also in the world outside the plays—in the criticism and productions. We read of Margaret's unwomanly strength, and of Richard's womanly guile. A recent critic describes the character's histrionic talents and sensitivity to people and atmosphere: "His awareness of other people has, in the best Hitlerian manner, an almost *feminine* subtlety. The list of roles he assumes is endless"[46] (italics mine). On the basis of evidence within the plays, one might have expected a different conclusion. For—as well as Richard—York, Edward, Buckingham, and Warwick have been the supreme manipulators, men of guile, organizing behind the scenes and plotting insurrection. Misogyny persists.

Optimistically, Fuller recommends that women not be influenced by men because they fail to see the entire picture. She instructs women to look within themselves to find their own "peculiar secret." This means rejecting the stereotypes and accepting their own strengths. Margaret, struggling with the concept that strength is "masculine," is vulnerable to the attack of "unwomanliness." Elizabeth, perhaps discovering her own "peculiar secret," tries to establish a bond of friendship or support with the woman she had scorned. But learning to curse is hardly a start on the path to understanding that the stereotypes (for "maleness" strength, courage, and initiative; and for "femaleness" docility, passivity, and weakness) must be denied if women are to gain power, not over the lives of others, but over their own lives. Shakespeare dramatizes the reality that women cannot do this alone. These plays reveal the limited world that exists as long as people believe that power belongs to men and powerlessness to women, refusing to recognize "the benefits . . . the world would gain by ceasing to make sex a disqualification for privileges and a badge of subjection."[47]

No resonances of Egypt may be found in this mid-nineteenth-century interpretation of Cleopatra wearing elaborate decorations in her hair and a Victorian gown while she delicately applies the asp to her breast. The painting is by J. Rogers. FOLGER SHAKESPEARE LIBRARY

CHAPTER EIGHT

Union of Roles

ANTONY AND CLEOPATRA

"Give me my robe, put on my crown,

. . . Husband, I come!"

(V.ii.280,287)

*I*n *Antony and Cleopatra*, Shakespeare suggests that a woman of power has the unusual opportunity of combining her sexual and political selves. She commands others and is sovereign over herself. Because she lives in a patriarchal society, however, she may still be limited by the stereotypes for female behavior and subject to the rules established by the dominant group. To illuminate the problems even a woman who is queen may face, the dramatist creates male characters who express the views of society: they derisively challenge her right to self-sovereignty, suggesting that she thereby dominates a man, and minimize or forget her role as a political person. "Nay, but this dotage of our general's / O'erflows the measure" (I.i.1–2), exclaims Philo, a friend of Antony's in the play's opening lines. Preceding the entrance of the two principals, Philo describes Cleopatra in terms of her impact on Antony. She is a "strumpet" and a "gipsy"; he "a strumpet's fool," "a bellows," and a "fan" "to cool a gipsy's lust" (13,9–10). Although reference to Antony as "Mars" as well as "general" occurs, Cleopatra is seldom dignified by the title of queen.

When, however, she and Antony sweep onto the stage, the close interweaving of her roles as sexual being and political person becomes immediately apparent. "If it be love indeed, tell me how much" (I.i.14), she insists, seeming to illustrate Philo's observation. But talk of love quickly gives way to discussions of political strategy when a messenger from Rome enters with news. Compared with Antony's wish for a brief summary of the message, Cleopatra repeatedly insists "Nay, hear them, Antony" (19), "Call in the messengers" (29), and again later pleads with him to attend to them. Although she refers to those back in Rome with mockery—Antony's wife, Fulvia, and his fellow Triumvir, Caesar—Cleopatra reveals a sensitivity to the angry feelings of a neglected wife and the ambitions of a young man seeking full control of power. With remarkable insight, she anticipates the scene that will occur in Rome:

> . . . who knows
> If the scarce-bearded Caesar have not sent
> His pow'rful mandate to you: "Do this, or this;
> Take in that kingdom, and enfranchise that;
> Perform't, or else we damn thee."
>
> (I.i.20–24)

Gliding quickly back and forth between pragmatic political advice and subjective personal response, Cleopatra chides, "Fulvia perchance is angry" (20). Wondering if his wife is summoning him back to Rome, the Queen teases:

> As I am Egypt's queen,
> Thou blushest, Antony, and that blood of thine
> Is Caesar's homager; else so thy cheek pays shame
> When shrill-tongu'd Fulvia scolds.
>
> (29–32)

The speech is interesting for its contrast between Cleopatra's self-image as "Egypt's queen," and her derisive portrait of Fulvia as a "shrill-tongu'd" wife. Throughout, Cleopatra's advice that he listen to the messenger beats a refrain.

Always, in answer, Antony speaks only to her as a woman.

> Let Rome in Tiber melt, and the wide arch
> Of the rang'd empire fall! Here is my space,
> Kingdoms are clay; our dungy earth alike
> Feeds beast as man; the nobleness of life
> Is to do thus—when such a mutual pair
> And such a twain can do't.
>
> (33–38)

One of the great speeches of the play, it nevertheless follows Cleopatra's advice that Antony listen to the messengers from Rome. This hyperbole to love seems to have been prompted by his desire to silence her request. He will counter any rational arguments with what appears primary—the love between two people. But Cleopatra is not to be deterred. Again she returns to the subject of Rome.

Does he wish to speak of a "mutual pair"? Then why not speak of his wife? Is she not the person with whom he is paired?

> Excellent falsehood!
> Why did he marry Fulvia, and not love her?
> (I.i.40–41)

Cleopatra asks, rebutting his reference to a "twain," a pair of lovers. Thematically, the concept of the direct relationship between love and marriage weaves through the text, illuminating one aspect of Cleopatra's personality. Unsurprisingly, in the play's last moments when she speaks of meeting Antony in death, she does not say "Beloved, I come," but, reinforcing her earliest comment, "Husband, I come" (V.ii.287).

Although brief, that early reference to Fulvia has resonances throughout the drama as Cleopatra keeps questioning Antony's ideas about the meaning of a "mutual pair" and wondering at his perception of marriage. An artist at the height of his power, Shakespeare, one must assume, knew what he was doing when he wrote this drama with only two major characters—one of whom, Cleopatra, spans the entire work. He would not have given her lines that contradict the portrait or seem inconsistent with the whole. Addressing an audience already familiar with the story, an audience bringing its own prejudices toward the pair to the theater, an audience also familiar with the rule of a queen—Shakespeare probably sought to develop a believable, if extraordinarily complex woman.[1] Strangely, however, some critics have had difficulty accepting Cleopatra as one of Shakespeare's more finely wrought, fully realized portraits. Others have theorized that she changes at midpoint in the drama.[2] A recent article by an astute Shakespeare critic, Leeds Barroll, offers one possible explanation. Barroll writes about the danger of ascribing to the dramatist the ideas expressed by one of the characters and warns against calling a character "choric" unless designated as "chorus" by Shakespeare. And yet this has occurred in interpretations of *Antony and Cleopatra*. Comments Barroll:

> Approving of the statements of a specific character whom we then choose as the "choric figure," we are simply using our own approval as guide to what we "deem" the ethical orientation of the play itself.[3]

In *Antony and Cleopatra*, the ethical orientation coincides with the point of view of Antony's most trusted adviser, Enobarbus, frequently dubbed the "choric figure." Like Philo, he too denigrates Cleopatra, particularly as a person of power. Because he praises her "infinite variety" as a woman, we believe him an objective commentator. But Enobarbus misdirects us if we identify with his point of view rather than listen to the characters themselves. As another critic suggests in a warning against accepting Philo's words, "May not Shakespeare's play be, after all, intended to persuade Philo to revise his accepted ideas?"[4]

In Cleopatra, Shakespeare portrays a woman whose self-sovereignty saves her from self-denigration. She likes herself and moves with confidence. Although she makes mistakes, she has a clear sense of herself as a woman and a ruler —as a sexual being and person of power. In contrast with the women of the histories, she refuses to separate her political from her sexual self. She sees no need to "unsex" herself in order to prove her role as political person. But the men in the play, representing the attitudes of the patriarchal society, find it difficult to accept such a woman who is sexually alive and politically aware of her role as ruler.

Karen Horney writes of the power struggle between the sexes:

> At any given time, the more powerful side will create an ideology suitable to help maintain its position and to make this position acceptable to the weaker one. In this ideology the differentness of the weaker one will be interpreted as inferiority, and it will be proven that these differences are unchangeable, basic, or God's will. It is the function of such an ideology to deny or conceal the existence of a struggle.[5]

We may apply this theory to *Antony and Cleopatra*. The more powerful side, the male side, creates an ideology that does not permit a woman to combine the two qualities that can be observed in Cleopatra: political power and sexual independence. Although Cleopatra's "differentness" consists merely in the fact that she is a woman, she may not behave as would her male counterpart, a king, without eliciting societal condemnation. The ideology of our society mandates marriage for a woman as the stamp of approval for a sexual alliance with a man, no matter how permanent, how faithful, the union.

Unfortunately, the rules of our society also establish a hierarchy of power within marriage. Therefore a woman who wishes to live as a sexually fulfilled being must, if she is to retain the sanction of society, marry. If she is a queen with real powers, she sacrifices a great deal for societal approval. The people of Shakespeare's time had wrestled with the problem of what to do when a woman monarch chose to remain a virgin queen rather than relinquish power by marrying. Surely an artist, living under such a ruler, would have incorporated this experience into his portrait of Cleopatra.

Perhaps he speculated with an ideal, wondering what might result if the concept of marriage were not hierarchical but more equal. What if the kind of relationship envisioned meant mutual respect between two equals, people of power and self-respect, who also loved one another? As Mill suggests, we might then have a richer society because one half of it would not be limiting the role of the other half.[6]

In the play's first scene, this possible equality is still an uncertainty. While Cleopatra has the confidence and independence required of a woman monarch, Antony perceives her primarily as a sexual being. Pursuing their debate, Antony lyrically chides: "Now for the love of Love, and her soft hours, / Let's not confound the time with conference harsh" (I.i.44–45). "Hear the ambassadors" (48), she succinctly answers. If he is a strumpet's fool, a "bellows" and "a fan" to cool a gypsy's lust, this first scene fails to illustrate her strumpetlike qualities. We do not hear a lusting Cleopatra. Rather Shakespeare presents a woman with a range of interests and a man who thinks only of love-making even when in the last moments before they exit he calls her Queen. "Fie, wrangling queen!" (48), he asserts before leading her off stage and dismissing the messengers. He, not she, commands the situation, but she has the potential for equality because of her self-sovereignty.

The men standing on the sidelines see only what they wish to see. "Is Caesar with Antonius priz'd so slight?" (I.i.56), challenges Philo's companion. The narrator assures his listener that such shortcomings may be observed only when Antony is not himself. The men have failed to see Cleopatra in any role but seductress although Shakespeare has presented her as a woman with political as well as personal interests.

In the following scene, still another of Antony's men, Enobarbus, offers his perceptions of Cleopatra. A light scene at the start, it opens with Cleopatra's women entreating a soothsayer to tell them their fortunes. It closes with Antony resolved to leave Egypt and break the "Egyptian fetters" (I.ii.116) in which he believes himself enslaved. Enobarbus links the two groups, appearing first with Cleopatra's court, and later alone with Antony. The scene, frequently transposed, partially cut, or moved to another section of the play, offers a first clue to this supposedly objective "choric figure." [7] Joking with the group surrounding the soothsayer, Enobarbus suddenly warns, "Hush, here comes Antony" (I.ii.79). In quick response, Charmian, one of Cleopatra's women, corrects him, "Not he, the Queen" (79). To emphasize the irony of Enobarbus' remark, Shakespeare has Cleopatra ask the whereabouts of Antony, "Saw you my lord?" Enobarbus replies,

A seductive-looking, fair-skinned Charmian asks the soothsayer her
fortune. FOLGER SHAKESPEARE LIBRARY

"No, lady" (80). The stage directions in these speeches assure the reader that Antony is nowhere visible. Enobarbus' reference to Cleopatra as "Antony" therefore reflects his own critical attitude toward this woman whose strength, self-confidence, and individuality continually assault and confuse him. Frequently, those attending a production, however, never hear this exchange. Occasionally they, like the audience at the 1909 Winthrop Ames production, may even see Antony enter after Enobarbus' announcement, the irony of the comment completely lost.[8]

Not only Cleopatra, but all women are seen through this lens by Enobarbus. When Antony, hearing of Fulvia's death, suddenly reminds himself of her virtues, Enobarbus, the pragmatist, offers no conventional comfort to the widower, only congratulations for the happy accident of being able to replace an "old smock" with a "new petticoat." He assures Antony, "If there were no more women but Fulvia, then had you indeed a cut, and the case to be lamented . . . your old smock brings forth a new petticoat" (I.ii.165–69). Once again this revealing aspect of Enobarbus' character tends to disappear in the theater. The references to "smock" and "petticoat" are altered for the sake of audience sensibilities.[9]

Anticipating Cleopatra's response to the unwelcome news of Antony's departure for Rome, Enobarbus observes, "Cleopatra, catching but the least noise of this, dies instantly; I have seen her die twenty times upon far poorer moment" (140–42). Elizabethan audiences would have heard the sexual inferences in the word "die." Later audiences still recognize the hostility and condescension in Enobarbus' comment. John Stuart Mill offers the background of such an attitude:

> Think what it is to a boy, to grow up to manhood in the belief that without any merit or any exertion of his own, though he may be the most frivolous and empty or the most ignorant and stolid of mankind, by the mere fact of being born a male he is by right the superior of all and every one of an entire half of the human race: including probably some whose real superiority to himself he has daily or hourly occasion to feel.[10]

This sense of superiority to women pervades Enobarbus' speeches. He perceives Cleopatra only as a sexual being, never

This 1759 drawing by Benjamin West satirizes Mrs. Yates and
David Garrick as Cleopatra and Antony. FOLGER SHAKESPEARE
LIBRARY

as a politically aware person. He speaks of her magic powers, renaming her "sighs" and "tears" as "greater storms and tempests than almanacs can report" (I.ii.148–49). He protests Antony's decision to leave Egypt. But his most telling comment follows Antony's despairing "Would I had never seen her!" (152). Swiftly Enobarbus exclaims, "you had then left unseen a wonderful piece of work" (153–54). The sexual connotations of his remark are obvious. Enobarbus presents a male attitude toward Cleopatra, perceiving her always as "Other."

In these early scenes, Antony himself appears confused as to who the Queen is and what role she plays in his life. He oscillates between extremes: dismissing the messengers in favor of nights of love, then swearing "I must be gone" (136), "She is cunning past man's thought" (145), "Would I had never seen her" (152). Although protesting her power over him, Antony dominates in the early scenes. At the close of scene two, he asserts

> I shall break
> The cause of our expedience to the Queen,
> And get her leave to part.
>
> (I.ii.177–79)

As we discover in the next scene, however, his expression, "get her leave to part," is a mere formality. Determined to go, whether she willingly consents or not, he offers her no option. In these first scenes then, not Cleopatra, but Antony wields the power. Nevertheless, Cleopatra, because of her role as Egypt's Queen and her sense of confidence in herself, retains her composure. Because of this, too, she arouses male hostility.

"What holds women back," according to the psychologist, Florence Denmark, who recently completed a study of antagonism to women in the job market, "is something not quite so amenable to change as a woman's personality: the very fact that she is female."[11] Although Denmark's findings appeared in 1979, they confirm what Shakespeare knew and illustrated in this play. The general hostility expressed by Enobarbus, Philo, and even Antony in the second scene—the perception of woman as "Other," and as seducer of men—

supports Denmark's thesis. To succeed, therefore, a woman must bring all of her strengths, her knowledge, and her ability to any endeavor. For Cleopatra these strengths derive, as do Antony's, from a combination of learned patterns of behavior and native inner resources—of nurture and nature. The fact that she is sovereign over herself gives her greater leverage than most women have. Nevertheless, to present a well-rounded character, Shakespeare must exhibit her learned behavioral characteristics as well as those qualities nurtured by her unusual position as queen.

She exhibits this learned behavior in scene three. Hoping to keep Antony in Eygpt and realistically aware of the power of Roman life to separate him from her, Cleopatra directs her servant:

> See where he is, who's with him, what he does.
> I did not send you. If you find him sad,
> Say I am dancing; in in mirth, report
> That I am sudden sick. Quick and return.
> (I.iii.2–5)

Although her woman, Charmian, considers this a poor device for retaining a man's affection, believing that a better method exists—"In each thing give him way, cross him in nothing" (9)—Cleopatra scorns such acquiescent behavior: "Thou teachest like a fool: the way to lose him" (10). Here Cleopatra applies some of the learned behavior patterns for a woman—patterns noted and decried by Wollstonecraft. Antony in Rome will also rely on learned behavior patterns.

Later in the scene when they confront one another, Cleopatra, angry at the news of his intended departure, returns to the theme introduced in the first scene:

> What, says the married woman you may go?
> Would she had never given you leave to come!
> (I.iii.20–21)

Questioning the permanence of his vows, Cleopatra again refers to Fulvia. "Why should I think you can be mine, and true / . . . Who have been false to Fulvia?" (27–29). Finally, when

Antony announces Fulvia's death, assuring Cleopatra that she should feel safe about his leaving, the Queen poses the question: "Where be the sacred vials thou shouldst fill / With sorrowful water?" (63–64). She also proposes a parallel between herself and his late wife:

> I prithee turn aside, and weep for her,
> Then bid adieu to me, and say the tears
> Belong to Egypt.
>
> (76–78)

Accusing him of dishonesty in his dealings with her, Cleopatra understands what Antony fails, at this early point in the play, to recognize—that their union is more than one of sexual attraction, that it represents, as Ruth Nevo, the contemporary critic, observes, the best type of love between a man and a woman, "a consonance of the imagination and the senses"; that it is a love that includes companionship.[12] Furness, writing much earlier than Nevo, considers many of the qualities she describes in the relationship between a man and a woman as characteristics of a good marriage.[13] In this the *Variorum* editor was challenging the generally prevailing critical opinion that Cleopatra was primarily a sensual, seductive woman—a point of view reinforced by stage productions. A good example is the treatment of this scene recorded in a late nineteenth-century promptbook. The lines beginning "I prithee turn aside, and weep for her"—Cleopatra's admonition to Antony that he not confuse his tears for his late wife with those for the Egyptian Queen—are accompanied by the stage direction: "Cleopatra shields her face with veil but joyfully says, 'O most false love.' "[14] The promptbook offers valuable evidence of the persistence of a point of view. Dated in the late 1880s, it reconstructs an 1874 production in which Jean Davenport Lander played Cleopatra and James H. Taylor played Antony. Undoubtedly, the promptbook was then used, or read, by those who would later produce the play. Thus this hypocritical Cleopatra was assured survival on the stage.

Along with questions about marriage and love, those first scenes also stress Cleopatra's awareness of herself as a political person, another theme that weaves throughout the play. As if to stress the naturalness of these two major interests in a ruler, Shakespeare, during the scene of Antony's leave-taking, gives him lines where they alternate. Like Cleopatra, Antony shifts back and forth between presenting himself as a sexual being and presenting himself as a political person. Explaining the reasons for his return to Rome, he begins, "Our Italy / Shines o'er with civil swords" (I.iii.44–45), then addresses the woman:

> Quarrel no more, but be prepar'd to know
> The purposes I bear; which are, or cease,

16   ANTONY AND CLEOPATRA.   [ACT 1.

And that which most with you should safe my going, —
  Is Fulvia's death.
CLEOP. Though age, from folly could not give me freedom,
  It does from childishness :—Can Fulvia die?
ANTONY. She's dead, my queen :
  Look here, and at thy sovereign leisure read
  The garboils she awaked; at the last, best
  See when and where she died. *(offering letters)*
CLEOP. O most false love! *(takes them and returns them
        sneeringly)*
  Where be the scattered vials thou should'st fill
  With sorrowful water? Now I see, I see,
  In Fulvia's death, how mine received shall be.
ANTONY. (L. C.) Quarrel no more, but be prepar'd to know
  The purposes I bear; which are, or cease,
  As you shall give the advice. Now, by the fire
  That quickens Nilus' slime, I go from hence
  Thy soldier, servant; making peace, or war,
  As thou affect'st.
CLEOP. Cut my lace, Charmian, come ;—
          (ATTENDANTS hurry to CLEOPATRA)
  But let it be *(they retire up, R. C.)* I am quickly ill,
  and well :
  So Antony loves.
ANTONY.   My precious queen, forbear;
  And give true evidence to his love, which stands
  An honourable trial.
CLEOP.   So Fulvia told me.
  I pr'ythee, turn aside, and weep for her;
  Then bid adieu to me, and say the tears
  Belong to Egypt :— Good now, play one scene
  Of excellent dissembling; and let it look
  Like perfect honour.
ANTONY. Now, by my sword,— You'll heat my blood ; no more.
CLEOP. You can do better yet; but this is meetly.
ANTONY. Now, by my sword,— *(crosses,)*
CLEOP. And target. Still he mends;
  But this is not the best. Look, pr'ythee, Charmian,
  How this Herculean Roman does become
  The carriage of his chafe.
ANTONY.   I'll leave you, lady. *(going, L.)*

Stage directions on interleave page of this promptbook indicate hypocrisy expected of Cleopatra in her reaction to the death of Fulvia. FOLGER SHAKESPEARE LIBRARY

As you shall give th' advice. By the fire
That quickens Nilus' slime, I go from hence
Thy soldier, servant, making peace or war
As thou affects.

(66–71)

This natural combination of political and sexual being, acceptable in a man, is unusual in a woman. Nevertheless, recognizing the inevitability of his departure, Cleopatra, too,
interweaves the roles. Gallantly she acknowledges the validity
of his reasons:

Sir, you and I must part, but that's not it;
Sir, you and I have lov'd, but there's not it.
            .   .   .
. . . Your honor calls you hence,
Therefore be deaf to my unpitied folly,
And all the gods go with you!

(87–99)

Moments later, Shakespeare presents a scene that can only
remind us of Cleopatra the political person rather than the
sexual being. We are transported to Rome and listening to the
"scarce-bearded Caesar" damning Antony. Caesar's words so
closely approximate Cleopatra's description that Shakespeare's
intention of creating a woman of political wisdom appears
clear. Addressing Lepidus, the third member of the triumvir-
ate, Caesar assures his colleague:

It is not Caesar's natural vice to hate
Our great competitor.

(I.iv.2–3)

Nevertheless, Caesar manages to catalogue, in detail and with
embellishment, Antony's faults.

Let's grant it is not
Amiss to tumble on the bed of Ptolomy,
To give a kingdom for a mirth, to sit
And keep the turn of tippling with a slave

(16–19)

He mentions adultery and whoring, implying that these are pardonable if they do not interfere with responsibility to one's work. The young Roman general also accuses Antony of familiarity with bums on the street—"and stand the buffet / With knaves that smells of sweat" (20–21). Despite Lepidus' protests, "I must not think there are / Evils enow to darken all his goodness" (10–11), Caesar, the superb politician, continues until Lepidus finally admits, " 'Tis pity of him" (71). As Cleopatra had predicted, the ambitious young Caesar finds Antony "th' abstract of all faults / That all men follow" (9–10).

Promptbooks of *Antony and Cleopatra* frequently omit the beginning of this scene where Caesar emerges as a manipulative, unscrupulous partner. The strong language describing the carousing in Egypt disappears. Instead of a conniving Caesar, a politically motivated head of state is presented, someone difficult for the audience to hate since he faults Antony only for political and military irresponsibilities.

Stage productions can also affect our impression of Cleopatra waiting in Egypt for Antony's return. Shakespeare creates two separate scenes of longing and loneliness for her. Between them, he wafts his audience to Rome to observe the far less lonely Antony. When the scenes in Egypt are grouped together and their order shifted a less sympathetic Cleopatra emerges, the contrast with Antony diminished.

In her first scene alone, Act I, scene v, she reminisces about their days together and thinks only of "sleeping out" the great gap of time while he is gone. She muses on his greatness, "The demi-Atlas of this earth, the arm / And burgonet of men" (23–24). Imagining him longing for her as she does for him, she is less perceptive as a lover than as a politician. "He's speaking now, / Or murmuring 'Where's my serpent of old Nile?' " (24–25), she assures her women. In Rome, however, Antony is feeling very unattached to her as she discovers when news of his marriage interrupts her second scene, one act later.

Shakespeare contrasts her loyalty with Antony's although critics tend to accuse her of deception and attribute to Antony the desire to reestablish himself in the Roman world. Heinrich Heine, the nineteenth-century German poet and critic, for example, writes:

Cleopatra is a woman. She loves and betrays at the same time. We err in thinking that women cease to love us when they betray us. They do but follow their nature.[15]

One might ask, "What then is the nature of men, as illustrated by Antony's actions here?" Horney's observation that the power struggle between the sexes is masked by generalizations about the basic, unchangeable difference between men and women would seem to apply here. Actually, the juxtaposition of scenes heightens the contrast between the loyalty of the lovers.

In Rome, vulnerable to attacks on his "manhood," Antony rejoins the male clique that looks on women as inferior beings. Reacting with almost knee jerk response to Caesar's insinuation that Cleopatra controls him, Antony contracts to marry Caesar's widowed sister, Octavia. Manipulating language, Caesar adroitly reprimands one of his men who suggests the marriage:

> Say not so, Agrippa;
> If Cleopatra heard you, your reproof
> Were well deserv'd of rashness.
> (II.ii.120–22)

The wording of Caesar's comment reminds us of Leontes' reproach to Antigonus for permitting a woman to determine his actions. Playing the stereotypically approved male role, Antony immediately responds, "I am not married, Caesar" (122). He has grabbed the bait.

Continuing to act according to learned patterns of behavior for his sex, he next adopts the classic suitor role while Octavia, in turn, follows the correct pattern of a woman being wooed. To his apology that he may at times be absent from her, she merely says that she will pray to the gods for him when he is away. He then asks her tolerance for his past weaknesses:

> My Octavia,
> Read not my blemishes in the world's report.
> I have not kept my square, but that to come
> Shall all be done by th' rule. Good night,
> dear lady.
> (II.iii.4–7)

Moments later, following the soothsayer's advice to return to Egypt, Antony becomes totally immersed in his role of the typical male, one that conflicts with Cleopatra's ideas on the meaning of allegiance between a man and a woman. He soliloquizes:

> . . . I make this marriage for my peace,
> I' th' East my pleasure lies.
>
> (40–41)

He has divided women into two categories—wives, and women to satisfy men's pleasures. The mutual pair joined in love that Cleopatra believed should also be joined in marriage is an ideal he rejects. Instead, he accepts the traditional male view, perceives women as lesser beings, and commits himself to an inevitably tragic path.[16] Antony has failed to understand the soothsayer's advice, translating it to its most limited meaning:

> Thy daemon, that thy spirit which keeps thee, is
> Noble, courageous, high unmatchable,
> Where Caesar's is not; but near him, thy angel
> Becomes a fear, as being o'erpow'r'd.
>
> (20–23)

In contemporary terms, one may read this as the wisdom of the adviser who counsels departure from a life whose values conflict with one's own and espousal of the life where one's "unmatchable" spirit may flourish. In such a world, Cleopatra, far from inhibiting Antony's greatness, nourishes it.

Back in Egypt, Cleopatra, laughing with her women, remains the completely unconventional person. Happy with herself—an independent woman—she listens while Charmian recollects a trick Cleopatra played on Antony:

> 'Twas merry when
> You wager'd on your angling; when your diver
> Did hang a salt-fish on his hook, which he
> With fervency drew up.
>
> (II.v.15–18)

But laughter quickly gives way to shock, disappointment, and the beginning of her own tragedy. Because while she can look at herself as a total person, the male world in which she moves refuses to accept her. She hears that Antony is married to Octavia. Reacting with rage and anger, Cleopatra strikes the messenger and even draws a knife on him. By the scene's close, however, she says: "Pity me, Charmian, / But do not speak to me" (118–19).

Flashing back to Rome, Shakespeare presents the prototypical, acceptable woman: Octavia. But he editorializes on the portrait. Plutarch tells us that Antony and Octavia were married for many years and that they had children. He also tells us that Antony sought to rid himself of Octavia as a wife. Finally acquiescing to Cleopatra's demand, Antony commanded Octavia to leave his home. Shakespeare omits this information, compresses time, eliminates the children, and offers little hint of any intimacy between Antony and Octavia.[17] The dramatist instead presents an Octavia whose allegiance to her brother equals her loyalty to her husband— suggesting, perhaps, an incestuous bond between brother and sister. Thus, Shakespeare minimizes audience sympathy for Octavia and implies a seemingly sexless, short-lived marriage.

Alternating scenes between her and Cleopatra, he contrasts their allegiance, self-confidence, and conformity. In Act III, Octavia's first two scenes frame Cleopatra's; her last precedes Cleopatra's affirmation of her role as political person. Obvious in the first is Octavia's divided loyalty between brother whom she loves and husband to whom convention binds her. Parting from Caesar, she hesitantly begins, "Sir, look well to my husband's house; and—" (III.ii.44). But she can speak no further. "What, / Octavia?" (45–46), asks the loving brother who has married her off for political reasons. "I'll tell you in your ear" (46), she confides. What a remarkable bit of character definition, particularly since later Cleopatra, although defeated in battle, refuses the request of Caesar's ambassador for a private audience. Insisting that "none but friends" are present, she conducts the interview publicly. Here, Octavia, amidst friends, in a social situation, chooses to whisper to her brother.

The illusion of time standing still, the almost dizzying superimposition of one picture on another, seeming to anticipate modern film technique, returns us to Egypt and the messenger threatened by Cleopatra. In an amusing interlude she quizzes him for details of Octavia's appearance. Seeking specifics of voice, height, carriage, and hair color, the Egyptian Queen finally satisfies herself that Antony will return to her, for she concludes that his wife is "dull of tongue," and "dwarfish" (III.iii.16), "she creeps" (18), and her face is "long and round" (29).

A pure invention of Shakespeare's, the scene has sometimes been cited as an example of Cleopatra's pettiness. Recent scholarship, however, has uncovered parallels with reports of Queen Elizabeth's behavior.[18] If Shakespeare's audience knew of these incidents—a possibility since, at the time of this play's production, Elizabeth was no longer alive—the scene would have strengthened the impression that the dramatist was accurately describing a real queen, a woman of power. The successful woman ruler had been a reality. She had governed for forty-six years, had survived far beyond her "salad days," had never relinquished complete control of power (although in her late years the people complained of her relying on favorites) and, in her seventieth year, still proclaimed that she was "Prince" of her kingdom.[19] Through analogy, the dramatist would have been reinforcing the known portrait of a woman monarch.

The next scene, in Athens, sharpens the contrast between wife and Queen. Octavia, troubled and uncertain, divided by news of a conflict between husband and brother, bewails her position:

> A more unhappy lady,
> If this division chance, ne'er stood between,
> Praying for both parts.
> .　　.　　.
> Husband win, win brother,
> Prays, and destroys the prayer.
> (III.iv.12–19)

Compared with Cleopatra's overwhelming loyalty to Antony, Octavia's divided loyalty reflects her uncertain sense of self. She would conform to role of wife. Antony, too, adopts a properly conventional posture. Chiding her first, he then asks that she strive to be fair, but warns of the difficulty:

> . . . our faults
> Can never be so equal that your love
> Can equally move with them.
>   (34–36)

Nowhere does one sense the mutuality that Cleopatra affirmed was a vital part of marriage.

Octavia's last scene stresses the usual, familiar pattern that governs the behavior of women of power. Like the women of the early histories, the Roman matron derives her identity from her relationship with husband and brother.[20] Returning to her brother's home and expecting to act the mediator between Caesar and Antony, she finds herself berated instead for improper behavior:

> Why have you stol'n upon us thus? You come not
> Like Caesar's sister. The wife of Antony
> Should have an army for an usher, and
> The neighs of horse to tell of her approach.
>   (III.vi.42–45)

She is told exactly how she should be traveling, then is given a report of Antony's return to Egypt, told of his adulterous life and his "abominations" and, lastly, offered the standard palliative for women, "Pray you / Be ever known to patience" (97–98). The portrait seems intentionally designed to enhance the individuality of Cleopatra through contrast, for Plutarch's Octavia was a woman of more initiative than Shakespeare's.

"I will be even with thee, doubt it not" (III.vii.1) explodes Cleopatra to Enobarbus a moment later, catapulting us back to Egypt. "But why, why, why?" (2), repeats Enobarbus. If time stood still between earlier scenes in Egypt and those in Rome, now it spurts ahead. The contention between Antony and Caesar that Octavia had planned to mediate has burst into war. And Cleopatra, as "president" of her kingdom, intends to be present at the battle:

CLEOPATRA: Thou has forspoke my being in these wars,
              And say'st it is not fit.
ENOBARBUS: Well; is it, is it?

CLEOPATRA: If not denounc'd against us, why should not we
            Be there in person?

                                        (III.vii.3–6)

The swift shift of scenes contrasts the two women—the uncertain, compliant sister, torn between husband and brother, and the spurned Cleopatra, now asserting her rights as head of her kingdom. Unfortunately, the Octavia scenes, whole or in part, frequently disappear from the stage either because of excision or because someone else's version of Shakespeare's play replaces the original.[21] This occurred during the Restoration and eighteenth century when Dryden's *All for Love* became the popular stage favorite and Shakespeare's work remained in the study.[22] A different Octavia emerges. The mother of Antony's children, she brings them with her to Egypt to plead with him to return home. In Shakespeare's drama, not Octavia, but Cleopatra is the mother of Antony's children. Dryden's Antony, torn between the women, chooses to sacrifice "all"—home, family, empire—for love. No such contrast exists for Shakespeare's Antony. Nor are the women equally strong. Rather, as we see here, Octavia's uncertainty dramatizes Cleopatra's sense of independence.

In the above scene with Enobarbus, she asks a logical question. Although perhaps motivated, as some critics suggest, by the fear that Antony will join with Caesar, she may also wish to exercise her role as queen. Political power means the right to function as more than decoration. It means the right to make wrong decisions and have them obeyed. It means the right to command the actions of a nation. If her decision proves wrong, not female wiles but poor judgment should be the accusation; but it is not. Antony attributes his defeat to her action—a foolish retreat that he unthinkingly follows because, he claims, of his love for her.

During these moments before the battle, Shakespeare gives Cleopatra lines that emphasize her position as monarch. Again, he may have hoped that his audience would hear echoes of the words of their late Queen. Enobarbus explains that Cleopatra should withdraw because of rumors in Rome that Photinus, "an eunuch," and her maids "Manage this war." The Queen rationally replies,

> A charge we bear i' th' war,
> And as the president of my kingdom will
> Appear there for a man.
>
> (III.vii.16–18)

The audience may well have been reminded of Elizabeth's "Golden Speech" to her parliament of 1601. There she defined her role as defender of her kingdom.

> . . . from peril, dishonour, tyranny and oppression.
>
> There will never Queen sit in my seat with
> more zeal to my country, care for my subjects,
> and that will sooner with willingness venture
> her life for your good and safety, than myself.[23]

Some scholars believe that Shakespeare may have waited to write his play until after Elizabeth's death because of such parallels.[24]

No resemblance, however, existed between the sexual lives of the two Queens. Did this mean that Elizabeth would have been less openly attacked for womanliness? Perhaps. Enobarbus, having failed to convince Cleopatra through argumentation, finally relies on a more expected answer—one still being used three hundred years later to exclude women from participation in the public activities of society:

> Well, I could reply:
> If we should serve with horse and mares together,
> The horse were merely lost; the mares would bear
> A soldier and his horse.
>
> (III.vii.6–9)

The speech reinforces the portrait of Enobarbus already begun in the first act. But it also intensifies that portrait of Cleopatra, adding fine lines of shading, particularly if one rejects the stage direction added by Samuel Johnson: an "[Aside]" preceding the speech.

Together, lines and stage direction project an attitude at once protective and disparaging of women because they assume that Cleopatra did not hear Enobarbus and would rage had she heard him. She responds with the question, "What is't you say?" Such a conclusion, however, denigrates Cleopatra's talents as a political being, one who is realistically aware of her position. She understood the limits of her power well enough to announce that without Antony's support she could not wield the same extensive control. As a woman, she understood herself well enough to exclaim, "Pity me, Charmian, / But do not speak to me" (II.v.118–19). She had accepted Antony back at her court despite her disappointment and disillusionment. Historically, she had no choice. May she not also have had little choice in the type of comments Antony's trusted companion would make to her? Her words—"What is't you say?"—would then indicate the self-possession and regal manner of a political figure who had already learned to adjust to disappointment.

Although Enobarbus' speech frequently disappears from the stage, probably because it so clearly defines his point of view toward women, the argument he presents persists into the twentieth century. Virginia Woolf quotes a 1936 "Report of the Archbishops' Commission on the Ministry of Women." Offering several reasons for excluding women from the ministry, the report notes:

> We believe . . . that it would be impossible for the male members of the average Anglican congregation to be present at a service at which a woman ministered without becoming unduly conscious of her sex.

Woolf comments:

> In the opinion of the Commissioners, therefore, Christian women are more spiritually minded than Christian men—a remarkable, but no doubt adequate, reason for excluding them from the priesthood.[25]

To adapt Woolf's observation to Cleopatra's experience, women at war are more single minded than men. Apparently Cleopatra was. Although she fled the battle, she had not expected Antony to follow her. She had acted as a political person whose poor military judgment dictated flight. He had reacted to her as a woman, not as a head of state. When she answers his query: "O, whither hast thou led me, Egypt?" (III.xi.51), she is expressing an honest response to his behavior:

> O my lord, my lord,
> Forgive my fearful sails! I little thought
> You would have followed.
>
> (54–56)

His departure for Rome, his marriage to Octavia, his too easy separation of wife and mistress all fail to prepare her for this dramatic shift in Antony's behavior. Nor can the audience easily accept his claim:

> Egypt, thou knew'st too well
> My heart was to thy rudder tied by th' strings,
> And thou shouldst tow me after.
>
> (56–58)

She, not he, should evoke our pity.

Despite his complaint, he has dominated her rather than she him. Until this moment in the drama, his words have determined events, whether something as slight as the dismissal of the messengers, or as important as the decision to return to Rome. Nor has the relationship of equals existed between them, despite his claim that they were a "mutual pair." In his actions he has committed himself to the idea that mutuality cannot exist between a man and a woman. By marrying Octavia, but determining to return to Egypt for his pleasure, he has opted against mutuality. In this scene, when he suddenly asserts that she is responsible for his behavior, he again rejects mutuality—a concept that means mutual respect as well as love between a man and a woman. As the scene draws to a close, Cleopatra, pitying his anguish, adopts the female role only, taking sole responsibility for the defeat by repeating, chorus-like, the word "pardon."

But Cleopatra's self image mandates that she question rationally the areas of human responsibility. A political person, she too suffers a great loss. After Antony leaves, she wonders: "Is Antony or we in fault for this?" (III.xiii.2). Enobarbus confirms her own belief. "Antony only" (3), but this friend of Antony then continues: "that would make his will / Lord of his reason" (3–4). Hoping for military or political analysis, she receives an answer based only on her sexual identification. That she is Queen, monarch of a kingdom to be captured by Caesar, does not affect Enobarbus' perception of her. Nor does she receive political advice to her earlier question, "What shall we do, Enobarbus?" He responds with a purely personal, defeatist answer, "Think, and die" (1). His answer is inadequate.

Political realities face her immediately. She must use all of her talents—learned traits and native strengths—to confuse her enemy. Ironically, Caesar, the victor, although he would take her as a political trophy, also thinks of her only as a woman—a person of lesser intelligence and greater vanity than men. He instructs his messenger, Thidias, to promise her anything, explaining:

> . . . Women are not
> In their best fortunes strong, but want will perjure
> The ne'er-touch'd vestal.
>
> (III.xii.29–31)

This expectation that women can be easily bought, this sense of the superiority of men—that Mill observes begins when men are boys—persists. Quick to discern this weakness in Thidias' opening words, Cleopatra responds with equal guile. For Thidias assures her that Caesar "knows that you embrace not Antony / As you did love, but as you fear'd him" (III.xiii.56–57). "O!" exclaims Cleopatra in astonishment. Aware that she is being wooed as a political person, she allows him to continue:

> The scars upon your honor, therefore, he
> Does pity, as constrained blemishes,
> Not as deserved.
>
> (58–60)

The humor of this suggestion, the implied insult to Cleopatra's intelligence and political wisdom, leads her to answer: "Mine

honor was not yielded, / But conquer'd merely" (61–62). Playing with words, she would match his wit and cordiality. But
neither he nor Enobarbus, who is listening, understands her.
    Believing she is betraying Antony, Enobarbus in solil-
oquy muses:

> Sir, sir thou art so leaky
> That we must leave thee to thy sinking, for
> Thy dearest quit thee.
>   (III.xiii.63–65)

Eventually he, not she, deserts. Because of his misogyny, observed in his earliest references to Cleopatra as "Antony," in
his comments on her as "a wonderful piece of work," "a new
petticoat," and, obliquely, as a "mare," Enobarbus has little
difficulty misreading her political maneuverings. This is the
man critics have mistaken for the voice of the dramatist because of his extensive description of her coming to meet Antony at Cydnus, and the famous lines, "Age cannot wither her,
nor custom stale / Her infinite variety" (II.ii.234–35). Norman
Holland, for example, writes that Shakespeare, the man,

> was probably . . . a sort of Enobarbus, a man's man, aggres-
> sive, competitive, at home in the world of men, the kind of
> man one thinks of as rather puzzled by and a little afraid of
> women whom he tends to see either as ideal figures (in God-
> home-and-mother terms) or as mere amusements put on earth
> for a man's convenience.[26]

I believe, however, that the confusion in values that leads
Enobarbus to desert Antony and then regret his actions is part
of a larger portrait, not of the dramatist, but of a male whose
inability to understand women as human beings leads him to
other aberrations. Enobarbus is, as Holland suggests, "a man's
man," but not a self-portrait of the dramatist. Nor does this
character represent attitudes that are specifically Roman. Unfortunately, they tend to be universal.
    Cleopatra, contending with such attitudes, uses her in-
telligence and skill. Continuing her interview with Thidias,
she sends conciliatory messages back to Caesar:

I kiss his conqu'ring hand.
.   .   .
Tell him, from his all-obeying breath I hear
The doom of Egypt.
(III.xiii.75–78)

Aware of defeat, she acts as she does later on when, Antony dead, she bows to Caesar. Perhaps because men tend to perceive women as easily blinded by flattery, Thidias approvingly comments: " 'Tis your noblest course. / Wisdom and fortune combating together" (78–79). They are engaged in a verbal game that reminds us of the first play discussed, *Love's Labour's Lost*.

Storming in on this interview at the moment when Cleopatra has extended her hand to be kissed by Thidias, Antony rages, "Moon and stars! / Whip him . . ." and then, turning to the Egyptian Queen, he speaks of her in third person, "So saucy with the hand of she here—what's her name, / Since she was Cleopatra?" (III.xiii.95–99). In a long series of expletives and descriptive phrases, he calls her whore: "You were half blasted ere I knew you" (105), "boggler" (110), "a morsel, cold upon / Dead Caesar's trencher" (116–17), "a fragment / Of Cneius Pompey's" (117–18). Again, promptbooks tend to omit these lines, erasing Antony's violent name-calling and lack of self-control toward Cleopatra.

Patiently, she waits. "Not know me yet?" (157), she asks, wondering, presumably, if he ever will. Oscillating between extremes of temperament—tenderness, warmth, and faith combating jealousy, suspicion, and accusations of betrayal—Antony has great problems "knowing" Cleopatra.[27] When, in this scene, he finally accepts her answer, he confides new plans for battle and for redeeming his reputation:

If from the field I shall return once more
To kiss these lips, I will appear in blood;
I and my sword will earn our chronicle.
(III.xiii.173–75)

Assuring him of her confidence and acting the supportive female role, she exclaims, "That's my brave lord" (176).

Believing he wants the woman only, she becomes just that, suppressing her political self when with him. But they are engaging in an impossible game; neither can erase from consciousness her role as queen. The irony mounts when, buckling on his armor, she listens to him boast:

> O love,
> That thou couldst see my wars to-day . . .
> . . . thou shouldst see
> A workman in't.
>
> (IV.iv.15–18)

Would he really like her to "see" his wars? The rhetoric masks the truth. Nevertheless, Cleopatra acts Woolf's magic mirror, encouraging him and buoying his self-confidence. Only after he departs does she reveal her deep skepticism based on her political wisdom, confiding to Charmian:

> He goes forth gallantly. That he and Caesar might
> Determine this great war in single fight!
> Then, Antony—but now—Well, on.
>
> (36–38)

She knows, even as he heads for battle, that he has little chance of success. This broken last line with its pause contrasts what might have been with what will inevitably occur. Its hesitation reflects Cleopatra's less than confident belief that Antony can win. But he does.

Then follows a brief interlude in which Shakespeare emphasizes Antony's inability to accept Cleopatra as an astute political person, someone who had to match Thidias' duplicity in the earlier scene. "Not know me yet?" she had then asked. In this later scene, following Antony's temporary victory, he resembles the men in the *Henry VI* plays.

Sending word to the woman—"Run one before, / And let the Queen know of our gests" (IV.viii.1–2)—he would have her bestow the gift of a queen. The right to kiss her hand is the reward he would offer one of his men for great feats in battle that day. With defeat, his confusion returns. Raging against her when he discovers that the fleet has defected, Antony again reveals extremes of temperament before arriving at some truce, some temporary knowledge. He lacks confidence in Cleopatra's loyalty. Because she owns herself and is not dependent except when she herself wills a dependency, Antony has great difficulty trusting her. Perhaps he imposes his own earlier, pragmatic approach to political alliance on her actions. Or perhaps he fails to overcome cultural biases that often lead men to view strong women with suspicion.[28]

Once again Shakespeare relies on contrast to illuminate relationships. News of Enobarbus' desertion precedes Antony's final defeat as a result of the defection of the fleet. Blaming himself for the first, Antony exclaims, "O, my fortunes have / Corrupted honest men!" (IV.v.16–17). Enobarbus' treasures are sent after him. No such generosity extends to Cleopatra. "This foul Egyptian hath betrayed me" (IV.xii.10), Antony rages, believing her disloyal, then vows, "The witch shall die" (47). Nor can he accept responsibility for his fate: "I made these wars for Egypt, and the Queen, / Whose heart I thought I had, for she had mine" (IV.xiv.15–16), he dishonestly asserts, determined to remain the hero. In reality, he made the wars because of a political error, his marriage to Octavia, a marriage presented here as cold, passionless, and sexless. But Antony refuses to confront the question rationally. Furiously, he accuses Cleopatra of entering an alliance with Caesar and being responsible for the action of the fleet.

Exhausted by this man of extremes and frightened by his threats, Cleopatra takes Charmian's advice: "To th' monument! / There lock yourself, and send him word you are dead" (IV.xiii.3–4). Earlier, when more confident, Cleopatra had dismissed another of Charmian's suggestions with the comment: "Thou teachest like a fool" (I.iii.10). At this point in the action, however, the distraught Queen accepts her woman's advice. By transferring the major responsibility for this deception from Cleopatra to Charmian, Shakespeare retains sympathy for Cleopatra, the character who is to dominate the last act.

During the scenes following the defeat at Actium, Shakespeare also offers glimpses of the Antony Cleopatra loved. One such moment occurs shortly before Antony receives false news of Cleopatra's death. Calm, and accepting defeat, he muses on the dreams we all have, the fleeting visions that transform our everyday lives:

H.g ravelot in Vol: 7. P. 83.   G. V.ᵈ gucht Sculp

In this eighteenth-century illustration for the scene of the wounded Antony waiting to be lifted to the tomb by Cleopatra and her women, Hubert Gravelot combines a pyramid and sphinx in the background—symbols of Egypt—with a contemporary, curved balcony and heavy drape in the foreground. FOLGER SHAKESPEARE LIBRARY

> Sometime we see a cloud that's dragonish,
> A vapor sometime like a bear or lion,
> A tower'd citadel, a pendant rock,
> A forked mountain, or blue promontory
> . . . that nod unto the world,
> And mock our eyes with air.
>
>   (IV.xiv.2–7)

We hear in his poetry the wonderfully imaginative and creative qualities that distinguish him. The man behind the armor of convention emerges: the man the soothsayer directed to return to Egypt where his greatness might flourish. And when news of Cleopatra's death leads him to choose suicide, we also discover a fresh analogy for marriage. Earlier, shortly before preparing for the battle he expected to lose, he used the word "married" to describe the relationship between himself and his men:

>   Mine honest friends,
> I turn you not away, but like a master
> Married to your good service, stay till death.
> Tend me to-night two hours, I ask no more,
> And the gods yield you for't!
>
>   (IV.ii.29–33)

Among the cruxes of the play, these lines have been variously read depending on the shift of punctuation. Either reading retains the concept of a master-servant relationship surrounding the word "married." Only at his death does Antony alter his perception of marriage to include love. Finally, he accepts Cleopatra's ideal, enunciated at the play's opening, of the bond between love and marriage. About to run on his sword, Antony says:

>   . . . but I will be
> A bridegroom in my death, and run into't
> As to a lover's bed.
>
>   (IV.xiv.99–101)

Until this point in the drama, the bridegroom had not been a lover, but a cold, calculating politician. We have already witnessed Antony as bridegroom and listened to the successive statements:

> My Octavia,
> . . .
> I have not kept my square, but that to come
> Shall all be done by th' rule
>
> (II.iii.4–7)

followed by, "I make this marriage for my peace, / I' th' East my pleasure lies" (40–41). Although after Fulvia's death Antony could speak generously of her virtues, Enobarbus assured us that little love existed between them when she was alive. If Antony's words shortly before his death express his true feelings, then he has finally come to some new understanding of marriage.

Again Shakespeare uses dramatic situation as well as language to convey ideas and define character. When Antony bungles his suicide attempt, he survives long enough to meet with Cleopatra one last time. The text tells us that she is "aloft" in the monument, hoping to protect herself from Caesar. Rather than permitting Antony to die on the bare stage before us, Shakespeare insists that the dying lover be hoisted to the upper platform where Cleopatra has barricaded herself.[29] Refusing to come below, and insisting that her women help lift him, she reveals her independence and political awareness:

> I dare not, dear—
> Dear my lord, pardon—I dare not,
> Lest I be taken.
>
> (IV.xv.21–23)

The same conjunction of references then occurs as were mentioned at the beginning of the play: love, politics, Caesar, wife. "O sun, / Burn the great sphere thou mov'st in!" (9–10), Cleopatra exclaims at the sight of the dying Antony. Then, aware that she will be exhibited by Caesar, she speaks of killing herself. Next, even at this moment of closeness, she mentions Antony's wife:

Your wife Octavia, with her modest eyes
And still conclusion, shall acquire no honor
Demuring upon me.

(27–29)

Finally, she offers to lift him up to the monument: "Help me, my women—we must draw thee up" (30). If we think back to the history plays, we realize that never did a woman there function as these women do, alone but together. Nor did a queen rely on women's help as Cleopatra does here.

Once aloft, Antony, too, finally acknowledges the duality of her roles—political person and woman he loves. "One word, sweet queen: / Of Caesar seek your honor, with your safety. O!" (IV.xv.45–46). But Cleopatra answers knowledgeably, "They do not go together" (47). When Antony then tells her whom to trust, she replies, "My resolution and my hands I'll trust, / None about Caesar" (49–50).

Moments later, Antony dies. Cleopatra swoons and exclaims:

No more but e'en a woman, and commanded
By such poor passion as the maid that milks
And does the meanest chares.

(IV.xv.73–75)

Identifying with other women, even the most modest, who suffer emotionally at the death of a beloved, Cleopatra then continues, linking her personal with her public self:

It were for me
To throw my scepter at the injurious gods,
To tell them that this world did equal theirs
Till they had stol'n our jewel.

(75–78)

Some critics have suggested that the earlier lines indicate a sudden awakening of a new Cleopatra. Harold C. Goddard, for example, writes:

It is as if she must compensate for having been queen by being not merely a woman, but the humblest of women, a menial, a servant.[30]

Cleopatra swoons at the death of Antony. In this 1826 illustration by William Hilton, a meager attempt is made to capture the feeling of Egypt by having a sphinx-like carving as a decoration for the leg of the bed. FOLGER SHAKESPEARE LIBRARY

But the later lines remind us of her awareness of role—an awareness that will dictate many of her actions in the last act. Despite the passion of her outburst, she also reveals a sense of responsibility to Antony's men. She comforts them, promising a proper burial for their general:

> Good sirs, take heart,
> We'll bury him; and then, what's brave, what's noble,
> Let's do't after the high Roman fashion.
>
> (85–87)

The strength and independence that led her to challenge Enobarbus and to question Antony's honesty when speaking of Fulvia sustain Cleopatra here. Shakespeare's portrait is consistent, but the environment has shifted. Whereas earlier her self-dependence led her to disagree with allies, now it saves her from being a cripple when confronting an opponent. Fuller suggests that self-dependence must "unfold" from within, but that women frequently have rules of behavior imposed on them from without. "This is the fault of Man, who is still vain, and wishes to be more important to Woman than, by right, he should be."[31] Cleopatra is censured for her independent behavior during the early scenes, leading some critics to find two different women in her—or one who had radically changed. But skill in performing the job of monarch does not occur suddenly at the moment when necessity demands independence of action. It evolves slowly and derives from self-confidence as well as knowledge of contemporary affairs. When the character is well developed, the actions seem to grow naturally from the earlier outlines. Shakespeare's Cleopatra is well prepared when, in the last act with neither Antony nor Enobarbus any longer alive to censure, direct, inhibit, or motivate her immediate behavior, she must confront her problems alone.

She must evaluate the honesty of each of Caesar's ambassadors as well as that of Caesar himself. She must attempt to understand each man's attitude toward women in general as well as to her as Queen. Ultimately, she must outwit the conqueror who plans to take her back to Rome as hostage. Caesar asserts to his men:

> Go and say
> We purpose her no shame. Give her what comforts
> The quality of her passion shall require.
> (V.i.61–63)

Concluding, he reveals his aim, "for her life in Rome / Would
be eternal in our triumph" (65–66). The political contest she
must enter is immediately apparent, demanding the guile and
verbal dexterity of its participants. In the first encounter, she
loses, tricked by Proculeius, a man whom Antony had told her
to trust. To him she reveals her true aim, to die.

> Shall they hoist me up,
> And show me to the shouting varlotry
> Of censuring Rome?
> (V.ii.55–57)

she challenges, after Proculeius has thwarted her first suicide
attempt. Even worse, however, is the thought of being "chas-
tis'd with the sober eye / Of dull Octavia" (54–55), Antony's
second wife. Dishonestly, Proculeius assures her that Caesar
will treat her with kindness.

When Dolabella, the next of Caesar's men, takes command, Cleopatra, with no previous instruction from Antony,
must judge the messenger by his words. Unlike his predeces-
sor who, upon entering, proclaimed:

> Caesar sends greeting to the Queen of Egypt,
> And bids thee study on what fair demands
> Thou mean'st to have him grant thee.
> (V.ii.9–11)

Dolabella introduces himself tentatively with a question:
"Most noble Empress, you have heard of me?" (71). Her answers, evasive, tell us little: "I cannot tell" and then "No matter, sir, what I have heard or known" (72–73). Cleopatra then
paints the portrait of the man she loved—an Antony we have
hardly seen—a man recollected in a dream:

> O, such another sleep, that I might see
> But such another man!
> .   .   .

His face was as the heav'ns, and therein stuck
A sun and moon, which kept their course, and lighted
The little O, th' earth.

(77–81)

As she continues to describe in hyperbole this man whose
greatness was past the size of dreaming, she reveals her own
poetic imagination, the soaring images drawn from the vast
range of nature. Has she, indeed, heard of Dolabella? Or is
she, in her despair, recollecting another time—another world?
Her grief, her poetry, her loss capture her hearer's sympathy.
"Think you there was . . . such a man?" (93), she asks. Her
listener assuringly answers, no. Then Cleopatra, the political
person, asks a more mundane question, the same one she
asked Proculeius: "Know you what Caesar means to do with
me?" (106). This time she receives a more honest answer. She
will be led in triumph in Rome.

Certain now of her fate Cleopatra, when she meets Caesar, bows low, hailing him with the words, "Sole sir o' th'
world" (V.ii.120). Listening to his false promises of gentleness
and kindness, she matches dishonesty with dishonesty. She
speaks of her wish to bring "lady trifles" to Rome as gifts for
Octavia and Caesar's wife that they might mediate on her behalf. She speaks of her womanly frailties—frailties she knows
Caesar believes belong exclusively to the weaker sex. She rages
at her treasurer when he accuses her of deceit. This permits
Caesar to act the magnanimous male role. Intent on dying, she
knows she must convince Caesar of her great desire to live if
he is to be open and careless about guarding her.

"He words me, girls, he words me, that I should not /
Be noble to myself" (V.ii.191–92), she confides to her women
the moment they are alone. She then describes the life they
may anticipate:

> Mechanic slaves
> With greasy aprons, rules, and hammers shall
> Uplift us to the view.
>
> (209–11)

Some critics have objected to Cleopatra's logical wish to know
her fate, believing that she should have chosen suicide for love

without thought of what would happen in Rome. Eugene Waith offers a well-reasoned defense of her actions:

> If she pauses to find out what would happen to her in Rome, she is no more disloyal to Antony than he is to her when he speaks to Eros about the shame of a Roman triumph after he has already vowed to follow Cleopatra.[32]

During her last moments, Cleopatra knows her direction. Perceptive, uncompromising, she achieves her goal. A political person as well as a woman of genius, she has no difficulty convincing the guard to allow the Clown with the basket of figs—and the asp—to enter. She suggests the potential for women if they could have self-sovereignty and function as complete people, not in a sexless world or a world where, like Queen Elizabeth, they must choose between marriage and career, but in a world where true mutuality might exist between men and women.

The conjunction of roles that marked her from the start illuminates her poetry at her death:

> Give me my robe, put on my crown, I have
> Immortal longings in me.
>   (V.ii.280–81)

The political person, the Queen, speaks of her office. She would join Antony, a god, and also immortal. The interweaving continues:

>   Methinks I hear
> Antony call . . .
> . . . I hear him mock
> The luck of Caesar, which the gods give men
> To excuse their after wrath.
>   (V.ii.283–87)

Echoes of the soothsayer's lines comparing Caesar and Antony take on a new cast, for now luck becomes a paltry, momentary thing. Then she thinks of her personal self, mentioning the role she has longed for, "Husband, I come! / Now to that name my courage prove my title!" (287–88).[33] Although in some of the analogues Antony and Cleopatra marry, Shakespeare retains the concept as an ideal. Perhaps he thought that the mutuality she believed must characterize marriage was unattainable. "Why did he marry Fulvia, and not love her?" Cleopatra had asked in the first scene. Now she suggests that a different kind of mutuality exists, one of courage.

Shakespeare dramatizes the question of the meaning of power in a relationship between a man and a woman by creating two rulers who love one another. He presents the conflicts between them, conflicts frequently born of the struggle for mastery of one human being over another. He stresses the concept of mutuality nourishing the complete development of each of them.

By insisting that Antony die in the fourth act and Cleopatra have the last act alone, Shakespeare forces us to observe her as the one character who spans the entire drama. Capable, politically astute, imaginative, she hardly seems to be a character who should lose her identity in a hierarchical arrangement because she is a woman. Fittingly, Shakespeare continues to intertwine her two selves—lover and political person—at her dying moment: "The stroke of death is as a lover's pinch, / Which hurts, and is desir'd" (V.ii.295–96), she declares, then, to the asp at her breast:

> O, couldst thou speak,
> That I might hear thee call great Caesar ass
> Unpolicied!
>
> (306–8)

I·AM·DYING·EGYPT

ACT·IV·SCENE·XV

Pen and ink drawing by John Byam Lister Shaw
for this Chiswick edition of Shakespeare, 1900.
FOLGER SHAKESPEARE LIBRARY

CHAPTER NINE

Emerging from the Shadows

Women as "Individual as those in Life itself"
—Alexander Pope in his
"Preface," to *The Works of Mr. William Shakespear*

A focus on the major women characters, on their validity
as fully realized and developed portraits, reveals new
meanings in Shakespeare's plays. The women's actions grow
from particularized, specific experiences, presented against
the background of a patriarchal society. In that world, women
must think of themselves as "Other" and man as primary or
"Subject"; banish ideas of self-sovereignty; rely on economic
independence to assure freedom; and forgo challenging societal patterns. Into that world, the dramatist thrusts women of
intelligence and intellectual vigor—women whose individuality mimics life.

Unfortunately, this individuality seldom emerges when
criticism concentrates on the male character and only tangen-
tially on the female, perceiving her as subordinate. Then generalizations about women are a substitute for close scrutiny of
the text. The character's singularity disappears, replaced by a
stereotype or convenient label, or by esoteric theories more
applicable to the male than the female character.

Strong, attractive women trouble critics, just as they
trouble clinicians defining the roles for healthy adults in our
society, as the Brovermans' study on sex-role stereotypes indicates. Nevertheless, such women appear in Shakespeare's
plays, often delighting his audiences and readers just as they

enhance and enrich the world around us. Although originally the conventions of the Elizabethan stage dictated that boys act women's roles, the sex of the performer does not seem to have affected the validity of the portrait. For when, in the late seventeenth century, actresses took over the roles, the characters continued to have vitality, individuality, and power. And when the plays are read in the study, the women offer further testimony to the dramatist's insight—they are remarkable, yet prototypical women.

Because these characters transcend stereotypes, such convenient labels should be eschewed, clues to more comprehensive portraits should be sought in the text, and old familiar conclusions should be questioned. Shakespeare's ironic art masks motives and actions of women as well as men. If, then, Kate is not a woman "tamed," but a woman of wit and intelligence finally discovering that men are not all alike, a reevaluation of Petruchio must occur. And if Cleopatra, who spans an entire play, is not a divided, confusing character but a unified, explicable one, the male characters must be reexamined and new interpretations of the whole reached. Other plays too could profit from this shift in perspective: *A Midsummer Night's Dream* from a focus on Hermia and Helena, for example, and *Troilus and Cressida* from a greater concentration on Cressida in positive terms.

Ideas about sexuality also interfere with a clear understanding of the women. The continence of Petruchio on his wedding night may seem a small matter. But for a woman violently protesting any marriage, such abstinence does not indicate a deprivation of her rights but a respect for her physical independence, her sense of herself as a person with choices. Cleopatra's loyalty to Antony, Margaret's concern about Suffolk, Elizabeth's indignation at Edward's proposition, Antigonus' uncertainty of Hermione's faithfulness—all these should affect the critic's response to the text. Frequently, however, these actions of the women and reactions of the men win scant attention; innuendoes based on sexuality, their implications in character definition are lost.

A woman's right to control her own body becomes an issue for many of Shakespeare's characters. Juliet, Desdemona, and Bianca of *The Taming of the Shrew* refuse to accept their parents' choice of husband. Kate would prefer not to be married at all. The Princess of France and her women reject their suitors, at least temporarily. And Cleopatra chooses to live with Antony, married or not. Margaret attempts to reassure herself when captured by Suffolk, indicating her awareness of self as a sexual being vulnerable to male power. In *Measure for Measure*, Shakespeare again raises the question of woman's personal autonomy—her right to control her body. The complex background of Isabella, who refuses to exchange her virginity for the life of her condemned brother, and the dominance of sexuality and its curbs as thematic core of the play underlie problems facing critics. Isabella variously evokes praise for her virtue or condemnation for her coldness, depending on societal attitudes toward women and chastity. Blocking development of criticism beyond this seesawing is an inability to understand a woman's sense of herself as an individual. An interpretation focusing on her and the multiple pressures that influence her decisions can open the texts to greater understanding of the whole.

Such a focus does not mean overlooking the man although it may shift the central axis of the play. One need not argue the comparative importance of Romeo and Juliet, for example, but one should recognize that here is the tragedy of a young woman—a very young woman, but not a simple, dumb creature—who has the sensitivity and potential of an Anne Frank, perhaps, to cite a parallel from our own time. Nor should emphasis on the women characters be misread as a return to nineteenth-century criticism where the characters were given a life outside the play. This emphasis involves acceptance of the idea that Shakespeare's women are well-integrated, thoughtful portraits that have their base in reality and are integral to the plays in which they appear.

Concentration on the women illuminates the conflict between the ideals and perspectives that women and men bring to marriage. The inherent tragedy in this division is a theme that runs through *Othello*. John Stuart Mill writes of the destructiveness of marriage because it mandates the subservience of one human being to another. Desdemona, a courageous woman who thinks she determines her own life, learns otherwise: the ideal of wife conflicts with the sense of self as vital. Emilia, long married, illustrates the ultimate demoralization that can occur when one abdicates, or loses, control of one's life. Although the role of Iago in fomenting hate, suspicion, and doubt cannot be underestimated, the play reveals the destructiveness of self-abnegation and adherence to conventions.

In a more light-hearted way, Shakespeare examines the contrast between those who follow accepted social forms and those who challenge them in *Much Ado About Nothing*. Offering us another of his outspoken, independent, delightfully alert women—Beatrice—the dramatist not only compares her with her conformist cousin, Hero, but then pairs each of them with an equivalent man. In Beatrice and Benedick, who eschew convention, sex-linked differences of intellect and originality appear nonexistent. A high level of communication exists between them. "Thou and I are too wise to woo peaceably" (V.ii.72), he astutely observes. In Hero and Claudio, their opposites, communication is minimal and understanding nonexistent. As a result, he can jump from thinking his bride a "jewel," to accusing her of unfaithfulness. This work suggests that accepted social formulas may need rethinking.

The play is sometimes called a "love game" comedy, a title implying that forthrightness is merely a game for women and that all dissension disappears between the wooers when wed.[1] Shakespeare questions this by creating descendants of Beatrice in other plays: outspoken, older, married women, like Paulina of *The Winter's Tale*, for example. But such women are far less acceptable as wives than as brides, evoking pejoratives like "shrew" and "witch." After all, power is not meant to belong to women, although it may be lent them temporarily. Nevertheless, such strong women survive in Shakespeare's plays, including *Antony and Cleopatra*, where the theme of the importance of woman's self-sovereignty, her power over herself, is reiterated.

Misconceptions about women's understanding of the meaning of power provide still other obstacles to criticism of the plays. Focusing on the women, one learns how complex power is and how elusive for them. The *Henry VI–Richard III* tetralogy illustrates the difficulty women have in distinguishing between their real and imagined power, discovering, often too late, that all power resides with their husbands. Margaret of Anjou exhibits this struggle. Her independence of mind and spirit equip her for rule. Nevertheless, the illusoriness of her power as queen leads her to misread "manliness" for power. This same confusion appears in the character of Lady Macbeth. She is often considered the prime perpetrator of evil, the perfect illustration of a woman of power. One critic, writing of *Macbeth*, comes close to understanding her when observing that at the drama's core lies a misconception of the meaning of manhood. "The nature of manliness," writes D. W. Harding, "is a question running all through the play, manliness as lived by the man and manliness seen in the distorting fantasy of the woman."[2] Is "manliness" a fantasy of women, or the creation of a patriarchal society? This critic fails to realize that women perceive "manliness" as synonymous with power because it is this special distinction between men and women—power versus powerlessness—that appears sex-linked. "Unsex me here" (I.v.41), asserts Lady Macbeth in one of the great ironic gestures in the play. Seeking power, she swears to abjure her sexuality so as to perform more perfectly the sex-defined role of wife—magic mirror and support for her husband. Nor does she ever wield power independent of him. Rather, she illustrates Kate Millett's comment that powerlessness leads a woman to self-denigration.

The Glen Byam Shaw 1955 Olivier promptbook of *Macbeth* illustrates how the confusion about women and power extends to the stage. Comments accompanying the text are intended to help the actor understand the role:

> Lady Macbeth. 36 [years old]. Vivien Leigh. She has an excessively passionate nature and an extraordinary intensity of purpose. She adores her husband. . . . She is the only person who has any real power over Macbeth and she knows it. She thinks that she understands him well, and she does, to a very considerable degree, but the strange, *imaginative, Celtic side of his nature she doesn't understand.*[3] (italics mine)

Developed at length in the promptbook, the italicized words become important keys to Macbeth's nature. But for Lady Macbeth the cues are more confusing. Reviews indicate that Vivien Leigh's performance was disastrous. Surely the director's interpretation contributed to this. His portrait of Lady Macbeth lacks inherent unity, shifting to accommodate his romanticized ideas about Macbeth.

Revisions, excisions, scene shifts, and stage directions make promptbooks a fruitful source of comparison with the original. They allow scrutiny of the nuances in Shakespeare's definitions of women. Changes in text may be obvious, such as Kate's approvingly listening to Petruchio's lecture on the duties of a wife, or Margaret's disappearing from productions of *Richard III*; or they may be subtle, such as reducing the confrontation between Desdemona and her father, or omitting Enobarbus' sardonic comments about Cleopatra. But their effect is dramatic, altering the dynamics of the interaction between characters and therefore changing the meaning of the play.

We read that when Samuel Phelps brought Margaret back in his 1845 production of *Richard III*, she "dominated the whole play" although even there her role was abbreviated. Summarizing the criticism of the time, Shirley Allen notes: "Her bitter curses, delivered with unforgettable emphasis, seemed to hover over the action of the play as her prophecies were gradually realized. She gave the impression of having more than human significance—'a mystery and a symbol, embodying the spirit of the fearful strife.' "[4] Nevertheless, when the actress playing the role left the company, Richard reemerged; Margaret sank back into the written text. "No qualified actress available," was the excuse. Or was it rather that since the producers were men, such emphasis on the woman's role seemed unnecessary?

Frequently, for the sake of clarity, directors eliminate textual ambiguities or seemingly irrelevant scenes. Kenneth Muir recently observed that this prevents the ideas from fighting themselves out in the minds of the audience.[5] Succinctness and clarity may result; but inferences may be lost. Recalling his production of *Romeo and Juliet*, Michael Langham, for example, regrets having eliminated the long scene of the families at the tomb at the play's close. In retrospect, he believes his cuts weakened the sense of parental responsibility for the fate of children. Sharpening attention on the lovers, he reduced the emphasis on their extreme youthfulness and lost, particularly in the case of Juliet, those additional reverberations of meaning—the ideas that might fight themselves out in the minds of the audience.

The individuality and lifelikeness of Shakespeare's major women characters are a testimony to his artistry. When Alexander Pope wrote, "His Characters are . . . as . . . Individual as those in Life itself," the editor did not distinguish between the men and the women.[6] But that kind of individuality in the women has seldom intrigued critics. Although women function in a patriarchal world and frequently tend to think of themselves as primary, they are not undifferentiated. Generalizations will not do, for against the constants of their environment are the individual backgrounds, endowments, abilities, dreams, and disappointments that give them uniqueness and specificity. Shakespeare captures this combination in his varied, multi-faceted portraits of women. Their beauty, variety, strength, and intelligence, as well as their errors of judgment and tragic flaws, should offer us insights into our own world.

Notes

1. Introduction: Their Infinite Variety

1. Hugh Richmond, *Shakespeare's Sexual Comedy*, p. 71.
2. Samuel Johnson, *Johnson on Shakespeare*, 7:287.
3. J. W. Lever, ed. *Measure for Measure*, p. lxxviii.
4. Ellen Terry, *Four Lectures on Shakespeare*, pp. 95–96.
5. Muriel C. Bradbrook, "Shakespeare and the Multiple Theatres," p. 102.
6. David Wheeler, dir. *Richard III*.
7. Simone de Beauvoir, *The Second Sex*, p. 314.
8. Virginia Woolf, *A Room of One's Own*, p. 98. The exact text reads: "give her a room of her own and five hundred a year."
9. John Stuart Mill, "The Subjection of Women," in *Essays on Sex Equality*, pp. 176, 236.
10. C. H. Williams, "In Search of the Queen," in S. T. Bindoff et al., eds., *Elizabethan Government and Society*, p. 2.

2. Oath-Taking: *Love's Labour's Lost*

1. John Stuart Mill, "The Subjection of Women," in *Essays on Sex Equality*, p. 189.
2. A notable exception is the excellent book by William C. Carroll, *The Great Feast of Language in "Love's Labour's Lost."*
3. Samuel Taylor Coleridge, *Shakespearean Criticism*, 1:92.
4. Edmund K. Chambers, *William Shakespeare*, 1:331, 338; 2:330–32.
5. *Ibid.*, 1:332, 338.
6. See chapter 6.
7. Folger Prompt LLL 1. See also George Winchester Stone, Jr., "Garrick and an Unknown Operatic Version of *Love's Labour's Lost*," pp. 323–28.
8. Folger Prompt LLL 2.
9. Samuel Johnson, *Johnson on Shakespeare*, 7:287.
10. Virginia Woolf, *A Room of One's Own*, p. 38.

11. Warburton's edition of 1747 retains Pope's cuts. See Irene Dash, "Changing Attitudes Towards Shakespeare as Reflected in Editions and Staged Adaptations of *The Winter's Tale* from 1703 to 1762," chapter 6.

12. Una Stannard, "The Mask of Beauty," in Vivian Gornick and Barbara K. Moran, eds., *Woman in Sexist Society*, p. 193.

13. Alexander Pope reduces IV.i.11–40 and 42–52 to small type at the bottom of the page thus eliminating most of this exchange. *The Works of Mr. William Shakespear*, 2:122–23.

14. Folger Prompt LLL 2, 8, 3, and 6. (According to Charles H. Shattuck, *The Shakespeare Promptbooks*, p. 233, no. 6 is a Daly 1874 book.) See also George C. D. Odell, *Shakespeare from Betterton to Irving* 2:187, 202–3, 222, 278. William Winter, in *Shakespeare on the Stage*, observes, "The comedy was produced in London for the first time in more than 240 years on September 30, 1839, at Covent Garden when Eliza Vestris (Mrs. Charles Mathews) began management of that theatre," with Vestris playing Rosaline and "the beautiful Louisa Nisbett as the Princess," p. 184. But note also that some shift of emphasis must have occurred when Ada Rehan became leading actress of Daly's company because she had the role of the Princess and Edith Crane, who was less famous, played Rosaline, p. 194.

According to Marvin Spevack, *Concordance to the Works of Shakespeare*, Berowne has 15.23 percent of the speeches, 22.09 percent of the lines; Navarre has 11.14 percent of the speeches, 11.20 percent of the lines; the Princess of France has 9.90 percent of the speeches, 10.25 percent of the lines; Rosaline has 6.28 percent of the speeches, 5.97 percent of the lines.

15. Richard David, ed., *Love's Labour's Lost*, p. 62.

16. Horace Howard Furness, ed., *A New Variorum Edition of Shakespeare*, 14:117.

17. Pope, *Works of Shakespear*, 1:ii–iii.

18. Edward Dowden, *Shakespeare: His Mind and Art* (London, 1875), p. 62. Reprinted in Furness, *Variorum Shakespeare*, 14:362.

19. Furness, *Variorum Shakespeare*, 14:xix.

20. David, *Love's Labour's Lost*, p. 110.

21. "Vildly" means "vilely" and "simplicity" is often interpreted as "foolishness."

22. Johnson, *Johnson on Shakespeare*, 7:285.

23. Lawrence Stone, *The Crisis of the Aristocracy 1558–1641*, pp. 610–70 and *passim*.

3. CHALLENGING PATTERNS: *The Taming of the Shrew*

1. Richard Hosley, ed., *The Taming of the Shrew*, p. 14.

2. David Garrick, *Catharine and Petruchio*, p. 17.

3. George Meredith, "On the Idea of Comedy and of the Uses of the Comic Spirit, An Essay on Comedy," pp. 238–39.

4. Anne Bradstreet, "In Honour of that High and Mighty Princess Queen Elizabeth of Happy Memory," in *The Works of Anne Bradstreet*, p. 198.

5. Lawrence Stone, *The Family, Sex and Marriage in England 1500–1800*, p. 182.

6. Ibid., p. 136. Stone quotes Robert Cleaver and J. Dod, *A Godlye Forme of Householde Government* (London, 1614).

7. Irving Ribner, "The Morality of Farce: *The Taming of the Shrew*," p. 166.

8. John Stuart Mill, "The Subjection of Women," in *Essays on Sex Equality*, pp. 159–60.

9. Michael West, "Folk Background of Petruchio's Wooing Dance," p. 70.

10. *Ibid.*, p. 71.

11. Jessie Bernard, "The Paradox of the Happy Marriage," in Vivian Gornick and Barbara K. Moran, eds., *Woman in Sexist Society*, p. 153.

12. Samuel Johnson, *Johnson on Shakespeare*, 7:351.

13. Robert B. Heilman, "The *Taming* Untamed; or The Return of The Shrew," p. 156.

14. I wish to thank John Shawcross for this onomastic reference.

15. G. Blakemore Evans, ed., *Riverside Shakespeare*, p. 107.

16. Samuel and Bella Spewack, *Kiss Me Kate*.

17. In an extended discussion of the musical references in this passage, Tommy Ruth Waldo, in *Musical Terms as Rhetoric*, describes "frets" as the "wooden or metal bars placed on the fingerboard" for playing the lute, pp. 35–36. "Fret" also means "ruffled condition of temper" (OED). "To fret and fume" expresses agitation of the mind, thus Kate's use of "fume" in the last line.

18. Nor was much of this material reintroduced when Daly offered his version in the late nineteenth century, or in 1937 when an abbreviated *Taming of the Shrew* was heard by radio audiences.

19. Gilbert Seldes, *The Taming of the Shrew*. As broadcast in the Columbia Shakespeare Cycle.

20. William J. Martz, *Shakespeare's Universe of Comedy*, p. 50.

21. Joseph Papp, *The Taming of the Shrew*.

22. Larry S. Champion, *The Evolution of Shakespeare's Comedy*, pp. 40–41.

23. Garrick, *Catharine and Petruchio*, pp. 13, 15.

24. T. J. B. Spencer, "Shakespeare and the Noble Woman," p. 62.

25. John Lacy, *The Taming of the Shrew* adapted as *Sauny the Scot*.

26. Susan Brownmiller, *Against Our Will*, p. 381.

27. Mill, "The Subjection of Women," pp. 136–37.

28. Alexander Pope and William Warburton, eds., *The Works of Shakespear* (London, 1747), 2:457–58.

29. Winfried Schleiner, "Deromanticizing the Shrew," p. 84.

30. Garrick, *Catharine and Petruchio*, p. 50.

31. Margaret Loftus Ranald, "The Manning of the Haggard; or The Taming of the Shrew," *Essays in Literature* (Fall 1974), 1(2):149–65.

32. Heilman, "The *Taming* Untamed," pp. 157–58.

33. Jan Harold Brunvand, "The Folktale Origin of *The Taming of the Shrew*," pp. 345–59. After discussing the folktale sources of the Shrew story, many of which are oral, Brunvand concludes: "It is a story which still appeals to people and which still is being disseminated by word of mouth; . . . there is no reason to think that it will be forgotten, any more than Shakespeare's play will, so long as the theme of mastery in a family remains meaningful to people."

34. Virginia Woolf, *A Room of One's Own*, p. 35.

35. Garrick, *Catharine and Petruchio*, pp. 54, 56.

4. Growing Up: *Romeo and Juliet*

1. Kenneth MacMillan, *Romeo and Juliet*.
2. Simone de Beauvoir, *The Second Sex*, p. 314.
3. Ann Jennalie Cook, "The Mode of Marriage in Shakespeare's England," pp. 126–32.
4. Arthur Brooke, "The Tragicall Historye of Romeus and Juliet," in Geoffrey Bullough, ed., *Narrative and Dramatic Sources of Shakespeare*, 1:334, line 1860.
5. Richard Grant White, ed., *The Works of William Shakespeare*, 10:34.
6. Among contemporary historians, Peter Laslett, in *The World We Have Lost* and Lawrence Stone, in *The Family, Sex and Marriage in England 1500–1800* disagree. Laslett observes that "the average age of these Elizabethan and Jacobean brides was something like twenty-four," p. 82. He then suggests that "there is the possibility that Shakespeare was deliberately writing a play about love and marriage amongst boys and girls," p. 84. Stone rejects several of Laslett's ideas, including the observation that "noble bridegrooms were about five years younger than their brides in the first half of the seventeenth century," p. 692n6. Nor is Stone convinced that there are sufficient statistics on the age of menarche before the nineteenth century to provide any conclusions, p. 693n14.
7. Stone, *The Family, Sex and Marriage*, pp. 20, 46. There was also the belief that children of early marriages were likely to be weaklings.
8. de Beauvoir, *The Second Sex*, p. 314.
9. *Ibid.*, p. 262.
10. *Ibid.*
11. Samuel Johnson, *Johnson on Shakespeare*, 7:62.
12. Alexander Pope, ed., *The Works of Mr. William Shakespear*, 6:259.
13. Folger Prompt Rom 39. I want to thank Harry W. Pedicord for generously permitting me to read in manuscript his chapter on *Romeo and Juliet* for the edition of *Garrick's Adaptations of Shakespeare, 1759–1773.*
14. Pope places these lines in small type at the bottom of the page. See chapter 2 for a discussion of Pope's technique.
15. Brooke, "The Tragicall Historye," line 1860.
16. *Ibid.*, line 949.
17. *Ibid.*, lines 1601–7.
18. *Ibid.*, lines 1651–52.
19. Samuel Taylor Coleridge, *Literary Remains*, 2:152.
20. Theophilus Cibber, *Romeo and Juliet*.
21. Folger Prompt Rom 39, p. 27.
22. *Ibid.*, pp. 27–28.
23. Folger Prompt Rom 12.
24. Both Thomas Otway, in *The History and Fall of Caius Marius*, and Theophilus Cibber, in his version of *Romeo and Juliet*, eliminate the Rosaline interest. In Otway's work, Marius Junior (the Romeo character) is smitten with love for Lavinia (the Juliet character) from the beginning of the play and waits in the garden to see her, pp. 17–18. In Cibber's work, old Mountague says to his son at the beginning of the play, "No, Juliet is not for thee—Sighs thou Boy? / At that, unlucky Name, thou changest Colour" (p. 6). Romeo, after accepting the fact that Juliet is a member of a

hated family, nevertheless exclaims, "Oh! Juliet, there is musick in thy Name . . ."
(p. 7). Garrick borrowed from both predecessors. In fact, Cibber accused Garrick of
plagiarism.

25. William Hazlitt, *New Writings: Second Series*, p. 129.

26. de Beauvoir, *The Second Sex*, pp. 262–63.

27. Richard Grant White, in Horace Howard Furness, ed., *A New Variorum Edition of Shakespeare*, 1:81.

28. *Ibid.*, 1:82.

29. Charles Beecher Hogan, *Shakespeare in the Theatre, 1701–1800*, 1:405.

30. Folger Prompt Rom 17.

31. Folger Prompt Rom 39, p. 19.

32. BBC-TV and Time-Life Television co-production, *Romeo and Juliet*.

33. Robert Ornstein, "Bourgeois Morality and Dramatic Convention in *A Woman Killed with Kindness*," p. 130.

34. *Ibid.*

35. de Beauvoir, *The Second Sex*, p. 314.

36. Harry Levin, "Form and Formality in *Romeo and Juliet*," in *Shakespeare and the Revolution of the Times*, and M. M. Mahood, *Shakespeare's Wordplay*. I profited from the excellent analyses of the language in these works.

37. de Beauvoir, *The Second Sex*, p. 314.

38. *Ibid.*

39. Although this is the text of the Second, Third, and Fourth Quartos, the editors of *The Riverside Shakespeare* prefer the Hoppe arrangement which reads "Day, night, work, play, / Alone. . . ." See pp. 1093, 1097 for further discussion. I have adopted the Q2 version, found also in J. A. Bryant, Jr., ed., *Romeo and Juliet* (III.v.178–80).

40. de Beauvoir, *The Second Sex*, p. 262.

41. Levin, "Form and Formality," p. 108.

42. Germaine Greer, *The Female Eunuch*, p. 219.

43. This is the text of the First Quarto. *The Riverside Shakespeare* reads: "Art thou gone so, love, lord, ay, husband, friend!"

44. Harley Granville-Barker, *Prefaces to Shakespeare*, 4:87.

45. Irving Ribner, " 'Then I Denie You Starres': A Reading of *Romeo and Juliet*," p. 276.

46. Marvin Spevack, *A Complete and Systematic Concordance to the Works of Shakespeare*, vol. 3.

47. "Introduction," George Ian Duthie, in John Dover Wilson and George Ian Duthie, eds., *Romeo and Juliet*, pp. xxv, xxvi.

48. Michael Langham, "Director's Preface," p. xxv.

49. Clifford Leech, "The Moral Tragedy of *Romeo and Juliet*," p. 66; Susan Brownmiller, *Against Our Will: Men, Women and Rape, passim*.

50. Philip Edwards, *Shakespeare and the Confines of Art*, p. 77.

5. A WOMAN TAMED: *Othello*

1. Emile Durkheim, *Suicide*, pp. 269–72, 275–76.

2. John Stuart Mill, "Letter of Contract," in *The Letters of John Stuart Mill*, 1:158.

3. Helen Gardner, "The Noble Moor," p. 189.

4. Samuel Taylor Coleridge, *Shakespearean Criticism*, 2:354.

5. Thomas Rymer, *A Short View of Tragedy*, p. 110.

6. Susan Snyder, "*Othello* and the Conventions of Romantic Comedy," pp. 123–42.

7. Folger Prompt Oth 27.

8. Folger Prompt Oth 19.

9. Folger Prompt Oth 2.

10. Folger Prompt Oth Fo 2.

11. Jessie Bernard, "The Paradox of the Happy Marriage," in Vivian Gornick and Barbara K. Moran, eds., *Woman in Sexist Society*, p. 154; Simone de Beauvoir, *The Second Sex*, p. xvi.

12. Virginia Woolf, *A Room of One's Own*, p. 35.

13. Charles Lamb, *The Art of the Stage as set Forth in Lamb's Dramatic Essays*, p. 22.

14. Among recent critics who have written at length on the subject are Bernard Spivack who cites the Vice of the morality play as the major ancestor of Iago, in *Shakespeare and the Allegory of Evil*; Leah Scragg, who contends that the Devil was the prototype, "Iago—Vice or Devil?"; and Joyce H. Sexton, who believes Envy most closely resembles Iago, *The Slandered Woman in Shakespeare*, pp. 50–60.

15. Edmund K. Chambers, *The Medieval Stage*, 2:149–57; A. P. Rossiter, *English Drama from Early Times to the Elizabethans*, pp. 102–9.

16. Alvin Kernan, for example, writes, "Desdemona is balanced by her opposite, Iago; love and concern for others at one end of the scale, hatred and concern for self at the other." Kernan, ed., *Othello*, p. xxiv.

17. After arriving at my conclusions, I found similar observations on the general blandness of the criticism of Desdemona in Carol Thomas Neely's interesting article, "Women and Men in *Othello*," pp. 133–58.

18. Marvin Rosenberg, *The Masks of Othello*, p. 7.

19. Bernard, "Paradox of the Happy Marriage," pp. 154–55.

20. John W. Draper, "Desdemona: A Compound of Two Cultures."

21. Bernard, "Paradox of the Happy Marriage," p. 149.

22. Andrew C. Bradley, *Shakespearean Tragedy*, p. 179.

23. John Stuart Mill, "The Subjection of Women," in *Essays on Sex Equality*, p. 151.

24. Thomas McFarland, *Tragic Meaning in Shakespeare*, p. 88.

25. Derek A. Traversi, *An Approach to Shakespeare*, p. 136.

26. Bernard McElroy, *Shakespeare's Mature Tragedies*, p. 112.

27. Joseph Allen Bryant, Jr., *Hippolyta's View: Some Christian Aspects of Shakespeare's Plays*, pp. 140, 145.

28. Hugh M. Richmond, *Shakespeare's Sexual Comedy*, p. 71; H. A. Mason, *Shakespeare's Tragedies of Love*, p. 142.

29. Helen Gardner, "*Othello*: A Retrospect, 1900–67," p. 5. (Gardner here quotes John Holloway, *The Story of the Night*, p. 37.)

30. Tillie Olsen, *Silences*, p. 258.

6. COURAGEOUS WIVES: *The Winter's Tale*

1. See chapter 2.
2. Lewis Theobald, ed., *The Works of Shakespeare*, 3:105–6.
3. Samuel Johnson, *Johnson on Shakespeare*, 7:299.
4. Anna Jameson, *Shakespeare's Heroines*, pp. 182–83.
5. Joan Hartwig, *Shakespeare's Tragicomic Vision*, p. 105.
6. G. Wilson Knight, *The Crown of Life*, p. 127.
7. Robert Grams Hunter, *Shakespeare and the Comedy of Forgiveness*, pp. 199–200.
8. Northrop Frye, *Anatomy of Criticism*, p. 138. See also the criticism of F. C. Tinkler quoted in an excellent article summarizing tendencies in the first half of the twentieth century, "Shakespeare's Romances: 1900–1957," by Philip Edwards, pp. 7–8; *Historic Doubts on the Life and Reign of King Edward III* in *London Magazine for 1768* (Feb.), 37:86; Edward Dowden, quoted in preface to *The Winter's Tale*, William J. Rolfe, ed. (New York: Harper and Brothers, 1880), pp. 35–36.
9. See my discussion of the different expectations of men and women in chapter 5. Particularly relevant to Desdemona and Othello is the contemporary article, "The Paradox of the Happy Marriage," by Jessie Bernard in Vivian Gornick and Barbara K. Moran, eds., *Woman in Sexist Society*.
10. David Garrick, *Florizel and Perdita*. See Irene Dash, "A Penchant for Perdita on the Eighteenth-Century Stage."
11. See Folger Prompt WT 26, 14, 10 (which cuts many of Leontes' raw lines and Paulina's responses), 7 (many cuts), and 1 (many cuts).
12. Inge K. Broverman, et al., "Sex-Role Stereotypes and Clinical Judgments of Mental Health," p. 1.
13. *Ibid.*, pp. 4–5.
14. Phyllis Chesler, *Women and Madness*, pp. 68–69.
15. Barbara A. Mowat, *The Dramaturgy of Shakespeare's Romances*, p. 1.
16. See Rosalie Colie, *Shakespeare's Living Art*; Anne Righter, *Shakespeare and the Idea of the Play*; and Norman Rabkin, *Shakespeare and the Common Understanding*.
17. Karen Horney, *Feminine Psychology*, pp. 59–61.

7. THE PARADOX OF POWER: The *Henry VI–Richard III* Tetralogy

1. Kate Millett, *Sexual Politics*, p. 25.
2. *Ibid.*, p. 56.
3. Throughout this chapter, the phrase "the women in the tetralogy" refers only to Margaret, Eleanor, Elizabeth, and Anne.
4. Margaret Fuller, *Woman in the Nineteenth Century*, p. 63.
5. Mary Wollstonecraft, *A Vindication of the Rights of Woman*, p. 9.
6. Sir Barry Jackson, "On Producing *Henry VI*," p. 50; see also Homer D. Swander, "The Rediscovery of *Henry VI*."
7. Susan Brownmiller, *Against Our Will: Men, Women and Rape*, p. 32.

8. *Ibid.*, p. 34.

9. Fuller, *Woman in the Nineteenth Century*, p. 43.

10. David Bevington, "The Domineering Female in *I Henry VI*," p. 56.

11. Fuller, *Woman in the Nineteenth Century*, p. 40.

12. Bevington, "The Domineering Female," p. 56.

13. Simone de Beauvoir, *The Second Sex*, p. xxv.

14. Edna Zwick Boris, *Shakespeare's English Kings, the People, and the Law*, pp. 25, 48, 93, *passim*.

15. Millett, *Sexual Politics*, p. 29.

16. Dorothy Dinnerstein, *The Mermaid and the Minotaur*, p. 194.

17. Robert B. Pierce, *Shakespeare's History Plays, the Family and the State*, p. 58.

18. *Ibid.*, p. 64.

19. Moody E. Prior, *The Drama of Power*, p. 33.

20. Ambrose Philips, *Humfrey, Duke of Gloucester*, pp. 11–14.

21. de Beauvoir, *The Second Sex*, p. xxviii.

22. Edward Hall, "The Union of the Two Noble and Illustre Famelies of Lancastre and Yorke," in Geoffrey Bullough, ed., *Narrative and Dramatic Sources of Shakespeare*, 3:105.

23. *Ibid.*, 3:112.

24. John Bennett Black, *The Reign of Elizabeth 1558–1603*, pp. 103–8.

25. Robert Ornstein, *A Kingdom for a Stage*, p. 43.

26. Bullough, *Narrative and Dramatic Sources*, 3:106.

27. Fuller, *Woman in the Nineteenth Century*, p. 41.

28. *Ibid.*, p. 40.

29. Millett, *Sexual Politics*, p. 26.

30. Andrew S. Cairncross, ed., *The Third Part of King Henry VI*, p. 29.

31. Fuller, *Woman in the Nineteenth Century*, p. 121.

32. Eugene M. Waith, "Heywood's Women Worthies," pp. 229–30.

33. Bullough, *Narrative and Dramatic Sources*, 3:206–7.

34. See, for example, Mark Eccles, ed., *Richard III*, p. xxiv.

35. Donald R. Shupe, "The Wooing of Lady Anne," pp. 28–36.

36. August W. Von Schlegel, *Dramatic Art and Literature, Lectures*, tr. J. Black (London, 1815), p. 437. Reprinted in Horace Howard Furness, Jr., *A New Variorum Edition of Shakespeare*, 16:13.

37. William Richardson, *Essays on Shakespeare's Dramatic Characters* (London, 1797), p. 18. Reprinted in Furness, Jr., *Variorum Shakespeare*, 16:43–44.

38. G[eorg] G. Gervinus, *Shakespeare Commentaries*, tr. Fanny Bunnett (London, 1863), 1:377. Reprinted in Furness, Jr., *Variorum Shakespeare*, 16:44–45.

39. Colley Cibber, *The Tragical History of King Richard the Third*.

40. David Wheeler, dir. *Richard III*.

41. [Samuel Phelps, actor and manager], *Richard III*.

42. American Shakespeare Festival, *Richard III*.

43. Laurence Olivier and Alan Dent, *Richard III*.

44. Arthur Colby Sprague, *Shakespeare's Histories: Plays for the Stage*, p. 124.

45. Fuller, *Woman in the Nineteenth Century*, p. 176.

46. A. L. French, "The World of *Richard III*," p. 37.

47. John Stuart Mill, *Essays on Sex Equality*, p. 236.

8. UNION OF ROLES: *Antony and Cleopatra*

1. Madeleine Doran, *Shakespeare's Dramatic Language*, p. 162; see also, S. L. Bethell, *Shakespeare and the Popular Dramatic Tradition*, pp. 25 ff.

2. See review article, J. C. Maxwell, "Shakespeare's Roman Plays: 1900–1956," pp. 1–11; Joseph Allen Bryant, *Hippolyta's View: Some Christian Aspects of Shakespeare's Plays*, pp. 183–86; Reuben A. Brower, *Hero and Saint, Shakespeare and the Graeco-Roman Heroic Tradition*, p. 318; L. T. Fitz, "Egyptian Queens and Male Reviewers: Sexist Attitudes in *Antony and Cleopatra* Criticism," pp. 297–316.

3. J. Leeds Barroll, "Ethical Premises in Shakespearean Criticism," p. 27; see also Peter Bilton, "Shakespeare Criticism and the 'Choric Character,' " p. 257.

4. Maurice Charney, *Shakespeare's Roman Plays*, p. 114.

5. Karen Horney, *Feminine Psychology*, p. 116.

6. John Stuart Mill, *Essays on Sex Equality*, p. 236.

7. See the following promptbooks of *Antony and Cleopatra*: Folger Prompt Ant 3, 8, 9; Charles Calvert, adaptor, *Antony and Cleopatra*; Herbert Beerbohm Tree, adaptor, *Antony and Cleopatra*. See also [David Garrick and Edward Capell], *Antony and Cleopatra* (both London and Dublin editions); John Philip Kemble, *Antony and Cleopatra* (both Folger Library manuscript and London edition).

8. Winthrop Ames, dir. *Antony and Cleopatra*.

9. Folger Prompt Ant 1.

10. Mill, *Essays on Sex Equality*, p. 218.

11. Virginia Adams, "Women Held Back by their Sex, Not Personality, Study Suggests."

12. Ruth Nevo, "The Masque of Greatness," p. 126. See also her *Tragic Form in Shakespeare*. See also Thomas McFarland, *Tragic Meaning in Shakespeare*, p. 68.

13. Furness challenges Coleridge's thesis that this is the "love of passion and appetite opposed to the love of affection and instinct" that we see in *Romeo and Juliet*. Furness notes that the activities of Antony and Cleopatra might be those of a husband and wife. "Where is there a word which, had it been addressed by a husband to a wife, we should not approve? . . . Is wandering through the streets and noting the quality of the people sensual? Is fishing sensual? Is teasing past endurance sensual? Such are the glimpses that we get into the common life of this 'sensual' pair." Horace Howard Furness, ed., *A New Variorum Edition of Shakespeare*, 15:xiv.

14. Folger Prompt Ant 1, interleave facing page 16. See also Charles H. Shattuck, *The Shakespeare Promptbooks*, pp. 35–36 and 3–5.

15. Heinrich Heine, *Heine on Shakespeare. A Translation of his Notes on Shakespeare Heroines*, p. 63; see also G. Wilson Knight, *The Imperial Theme*, who writes, "She is unfair, quite irrational, typically feminine," p. 294.

16. As Maynard Mack observes, "Antony . . . never . . . reflect[s] for our benefit on his betrayal of Cleopatra in marrying Octavia or his betrayal of Octavia and Caesar in returning to Cleopatra." "*Antony and Cleopatra: The Stillness and the Dance*," p. 81.

17. "Plutarch's Lives of the Noble Grecians and Romanes," in Geoffrey Bullough, ed., *Narrative and Dramatic Sources of Shakespeare*, 5:254–321.

18. Helen Morris, "Queen Elizabeth I 'Shadowed' in Cleopatra," pp. 271–78.

19. Jonathan E. Neale, *Elizabeth I and her Parliaments, 1584–1601*, p. 428.

20. See chapter 7 for a full discussion of this concept.

21. Folger Prompt Ant 3, 9, and 1. The sequence of scenes is altered in the stage version of 1937, Herbert Beerbohm Tree, adaptor, *Antony and Cleopatra*.

22. John Dryden's *All for Love* was first performed in 1677. See William Van Lennep et al., eds., *The London Stage*, for its history on the Restoration and eighteenth-century stage. See George C. D. Odell, *Shakespeare from Betterton to Irving*, for an account of the relationship between Dryden's and Shakespeare's works. In the advertisement for the combined version (London: J. Barker, 1813), appears the following comment. Shakespeare's play has

> . . . stood the test of modern times less than many of our great Bard's revived Dramas. . . . Something has been wanting to render it what is termed a Stock Play:—Dryden's Play has been long upon the shelf; nor does it appear suited to the present taste, without much departure from the original; but there is much to be admired in both the Plays. Under these circumstances, an amalgamation of wonderful poetical powers has been considered the best method to be adopted; and it is hoped, that the present arrangement will be found sometimes to have softened the violations of those Unities in Shakespeare, which it cannot easily encrease.

23. Neale, *Elizabeth I*, p. 391.

24. Bullough, *Narrative and Dramatic Sources*, 5:216.

25. Virginia Woolf, *Three Guineas*, p. 161.

26. Norman N. Holland, *Psychoanalysis and Shakespeare*, p. 140.

27. For interesting analyses see: Janet Adelman, *The Common Liar*, and Ernest Schanzer, *The Problem Plays of Shakespeare*.

28. Mill, *Essays on Sex Equality*, pp. 201, 242; Virginia Woolf, *A Room of One's Own*, pp. 27–37.

29. This detail appears in Plutarch (Bullough, *Narrative and Dramatic Sources*, 5:309).

30. Harold C. Goddard, *The Meaning of Shakespeare*, 2:200; see also Bryant, *Hippolyta's View*, p. 185.

31. Margaret Fuller, *Woman in the Nineteenth Century*, p. 40.

32. Eugene M. Waith, *The Herculean Hero*, p. 214.

33. For other interpretations, see J. L. Simmons, *Shakespeare's Pagan World*, p. 162; Derek A. Traversi, *Shakespeare, The Roman Plays*, p. 199; Philip J. Traci, *The Love Play of "Antony and Cleopatra,"* pp. 153–57.

9. EMERGING FROM THE SHADOWS

1. See particularly David Lloyd Stevenson, *The Love-Game Comedy*.

2. D. W. Harding, "Women's Fantasy of Manhood: A Shakespearian Theme," p. 245.

3. Michael Mullin, ed., *"Macbeth" On Stage*, pp. 59–60.

4. Shirley S. Allen, *Samuel Phelps and Sadler's Wells Theatre*, p. 230.

5. Gareth Lloyd Evans, "Kenneth Muir in Conversation with Gareth Lloyd Evans," p. 12.

6. Alexander Pope, *The Works of Mr. William Shakespear*, 1:ii-iii.

Bibliography

CRITICAL SOURCES

Adams, Virginia. "Women Held Back by their Sex, Not Personality, Study Suggests." *New York Times*, July 23, 1979.

Adelman, Janet. *The Common Liar: An Essay on Antony and Cleopatra*. New Haven: Yale University Press, 1973.

Alexander, Peter. "The Original Ending of *The Taming of the Shrew*." *Shakespeare Quarterly* (1969), 20:111–116.

Allen, Shirley S. *Samuel Phelps and Sadler's Wells Theatre*. Middletown, Conn.: Wesleyan University Press, 1971.

Ardinger, Barbara R. "Cleopatra on Stage: An Examination of the Persona of the Queen in English Drama, 1592–1898." Ph.D. dissertation, Southern Illinois University, 1976.

Barroll, J. Leeds. "Ethical Premises in Shakespearean Criticism." *Shakespearean Research Opportunities* (1966), 2:24–37.

—— *Artificial Persons*. Columbia: University of South Carolina Press, 1974.

Bayley, John. *The Characters of Love*. London: Constable, 1960.

Beauvoir, Simone de. *The Second Sex*. Translated and edited by H. M. Parshley. New York: Alfred A. Knopf, 1953. Reprint. Bantam Books, 1961.

Bell, Arthur H. "Time and Convention in *Antony and Cleopatra*." *Shakespeare Quarterly* (1973), 24:253–64.

Bergeron, David M. *English Civic Pageantry 1558–1642*. Columbia: University of South Carolina Press, 1971.

—— "The Play-Within-the-Play in *3 Henry VI*." *Tennessee Studies in Literature* (1977), 22:37–45.

Bernard, Jessie. *American Family Behavior*. New York: Harper, 1942.

Berry, Edward. *Patterns of Decay: Shakespeare's Early Histories*. Charlottesville: University Press of Virginia, 1975.

Berry, Ralph. *Shakespeare's Comedies*. Princeton: Princeton University Press, 1972.

Bethell, S. L. *Shakespeare and the Popular Dramatic Tradition*. Durham, N. C.: Duke University Press, 1944.

Bevington, David. "The Domineering Female in *I Henry VI*." *Shakespeare Studies* (1966), 2:51–58.

Bilton, Peter. "Shakespeare Criticism and the 'Choric Character.' " *English Studies* (1969), 50:254–60.

Bindoff, S. T., J. Hurstfield, C. H. Williams, eds. *Elizabethan Government and Society*. London: Athlone Press, University of London, 1961.

Black, John Bennett. *The Reign of Elizabeth 1558–1603*. Vol. 8 of *Oxford History of England*. 2d ed. London: Oxford University Press, 1959.

Bodkin, Maud. *Archetypal Patterns in Poetry*. London: Oxford University Press, 1934.

Boris, Edna Zwick. *Shakespeare's English Kings, the People, and the Law*. Rutherford, N.J.: Fairleigh Dickinson University Press, 1974.

Bradbrook, Muriel C. *Shakespeare and Elizabethan Poetry*. London: Chatto and Windus, 1951.

—— "Shakespeare and the Multiple Theatres of Jacobean London." In *The Elizabethan Theatre VI*. Papers given at the International Conference on Elizabethan Theatre. July 1975. Waterloo, Ontario: Macmillan of Canada and University of Waterloo, 1977, pp. 88–104. Published in the United States by Shoe String Press, Hamden, Conn., 1978.

Bradley, Andrew C. *Shakespearean Tragedy*. 1904. Reprint. London: Macmillan, 1960.

Bradstreet, Anne. *The Works of Anne Bradstreet*. Edited by Jeannine Hensley. Cambridge: Belknap Press of Harvard University, 1967.

Branam, George C. *Eighteenth-Century Editions of Shakespearean Tragedy*. Berkeley and Los Angeles: University of California Press, 1956.

Brockbank, J. Philip. "The Frame of Disorder in *Henry VI*." In *Early Shakespeare*. Stratford-Upon-Avon Studies, no. 3, edited by John Russell Brown and Bernard Harris. London: Arnold, 1961.

Brodwin, Leonora Leet. *Elizabethan Love Tragedy*. New York: New York University Press, 1971.

Broverman, Inge K., et al. "Sex-Role Stereotypes and Clinical Judgments of Mental Health," *Journal of Consulting and Clinical Psychology* (February 1970), 34:1–7.

Brower, Reuben A. *Hero and Saint, Shakespeare and the Graeco-Roman Heroic Tradition*. New York: Oxford University Press, 1971.

Brown, John Russell. "S. Franco Zeffirelli's *Romeo and Juliet*." *Shakespeare Survey* (1966), 15:147–55.

Brownmiller, Susan. *Against Our Will: Men, Women and Rape*. New York: Simon and Schuster, 1975.

Brunvand, Jan Harold. "The Folktale Origin of *The Taming of the Shrew*." *Shakespeare Quarterly* (1966), 17:345–59.

Bryant, Joseph Allen, Jr. *Hippolyta's View: Some Christian Aspects of Shakespeare's Plays*. Lexington: University of Kentucky Press, 1961.

Bullough, Geoffrey, ed. *Narrative and Dramatic Sources of Shakespeare*. 8 vols. London: Routledge and Kegan Paul, 1957–75.

Burnim, Kalman A. *David Garrick, Director*. Pittsburgh: University of Pittsburgh Press, 1961.

Camden, Carroll. "Iago on Women," *Journal of English and Germanic Philology* (January 1949), 48:57–61.

Campbell, Oscar James. *Shakespeare's Satire*. London: Oxford University Press, 1943.

Carlisle, Carol Jones. *Shakespeare from the Greenroom: Actors' Criticisms of Four Major Tragedies*. Chapel Hill: University of North Carolina Press, 1969.

Carroll, Berenice A., ed. *Liberating Women's History*. Urbana: University of Illinois Press, 1976.

Carroll, William C. *The Great Feast of Language in "Love's Labour's Lost."* Princeton: Princeton University Press, 1976.

Chambers, Edmund K. *The Medieval Stage*. 2 vols. 1903. Reprint. London: Oxford University Press, 1963.

—— *William Shakespeare*. 2 vols. Oxford: Clarendon Press, 1930.

Champion, Larry S. *The Evolution of Shakespeare's Comedy*. Cambridge: Harvard University Press, 1970.

—— " 'Prologue to their Play': Shakespeare's Structural Progress in *2 Henry VI*." *Texas Studies in Language and Literature* (1977), 19:294–312.

Charlton, H. B. *Shakespearean Comedy*. London: Methuen, 1938.

Charney, Maurice. *Shakespeare's Roman Plays*. Cambridge: Harvard University Press, 1961.

Chesler, Phyllis. *Women and Madness*. New York: Doubleday, 1972.

Coleridge, Samuel Taylor. *Literary Remains*. Edited by Henry Nelson Coleridge. 4 vols. London: William Pickering, 1836–39.

—— *Shakespearean Criticism*. Edited by Thomas Middleton Raysor. 2 vols. Cambridge: Harvard University Press, 1930.

Colie, Rosalie. *Shakespeare's Living Art*. Princeton: Princeton University Press, 1974.

Cook, Ann Jennalie. "The Mode of Marriage in Shakespeare's England." *Southern Humanities Review* (1977), 11:126–32.

Craig, E. Gordon. *Henry Irving*. New York: Longmans, Green, 1930.

Dash, Irene. "Changing Attitudes Towards Shakespeare as Reflected in Editions and Staged Adaptations of *The Winter's Tale* from 1703 to 1762." Ph.D. dissertation, Columbia University, 1971.

—— "The Touch of the Poet." *Modern Language Studies* (1974), 4:59–64.

—— "A Penchant for Perdita on the Eighteenth-Century Stage." In *Studies in Eighteenth-Century Culture*, no. 6, edited by R. Rosbottom. Madison: University of Wisconsin Press, 1977, pp. 331–46. Reprinted in *The Woman's Part*, edited by Carolyn Ruth Swift Lenz, Gayle Greene, and Carol Thomas Neely. Urbana: University of Illinois Press, 1980, pp. 271–84.

Dickey, Franklin. *Not Wisely But Too Well*. San Marino, Ca.: Huntington Library, 1957.

Dinnerstein, Dorothy. *The Mermaid and the Minotaur*. New York: Harper & Row, 1977.

Doran, Madeleine, *Shakespeare's Dramatic Language*. Madison: University of Wisconsin Press, 1976.

Dowden, Edward. *Shakespeare, A Critical Study*. London, 1875.

Draper, John W. "Desdemona: A Compound of Two Cultures." *Revue de Littérature Comparée* (1933), 13:337–51.

Durkheim, Emile. *Suicide*. Translated by J. A. Spaulding and George Simpson. New York: Free Press, 1951.

Dusinberre, Juliet. *Shakespeare and the Nature of Women*. New York: Harper & Row, 1975.

Edwards, Philip. "Shakespeare's Romances: 1900–1957." *Shakespeare Survey* (1958), 11:1–18.

—— *Shakespeare and the Confines of Art*. London: Methuen, 1968.

Elliot, John R., Jr. "The Shakespeare Berlioz Saw." *Music and Letters* (1976), 57:292–308.

Evans, Gareth Lloyd. "Kenneth Muir in Conversation with Gareth Lloyd Evans." *Shakespeare Quarterly* (1979), 30:7–14.

Farnham, Willard. *The Medieval Heritage of Elizabethan Tragedy*. Oxford: Basil Blackwell, 1963.

Fiedler, Leslie. *The Stranger in Shakespeare*. New York: Stein & Day, 1972.

Fitz, L. T. "Egyptian Queens and Male Reviewers: Sexist Attitudes in *Antony and Cleopatra* Criticism," *Shakespeare Quarterly* (Summer 1977), 28:297–316.

French, A. L. "The World of *Richard III*." *Shakespeare Studies* (1969), 4:25–39.

Friedan, Betty. *The Feminine Mystique*. New York: W. W. Norton, 1963.

Frye, Northrop. *Anatomy of Criticism*. 1932. Reprint. Princeton: Princeton University Press, 1957.

Fuller, Margaret. *Woman in the Nineteenth Century*. 1845. Reprint. New York: W. W. Norton, 1971.

Garber, Marjorie B. *Dream in Shakespeare*. New Haven: Yale University Press, 1974.

—— "Coming of Age in Shakespeare." *Yale Review* (66:1977), 517–33.

Gardner, Helen. "The Noble Moor." *Proceedings of the British Academy* (1955), 41:189–205.

—— "*Othello:* A Retrospect, 1900–67." *Shakespeare Survey* (1968), 21:1–11.

Gies, Frances and Joseph. *Women in the Middle Ages.* New York: Thomas Y. Crowell, 1978.

Gilman, Charlotte Perkins. *Women and Economics.* Boston: Small, Maynard, 1898.

Goddard, Harold C. *The Meaning of Shakespeare.* 2 vols. Chicago: University of Chicago Press, Phoenix Books, 1951.

Goldman, Michael. *Shakespeare and the Energies of Drama.* Princeton: Princeton University Press, 1972.

Gornick, Vivian, and Barbara K. Moran, eds. *Woman in Sexist Society.* New York: New American Library, 1972.

Granville-Barker, Harley. *Prefaces to Shakespeare.* 4 vols. 1945–46. Reprint. Princeton: Princeton University Press, 1965.

Greer, Germaine. *The Female Eunuch.* New York: McGraw-Hill, 1971.

Hamilton, Donna B. "*Antony and Cleopatra* and the Tradition of Noble Lovers," *Shakespeare Quarterly* (1973), 24:245–51.

Harding, D. W. "Women's Fantasy of Manhood: A Shakespearian Theme," *Shakespeare Quarterly* (1969), 20:245–53.

Hartwig, Joan. *Shakespeare's Tragicomic Vision.* Baton Rouge: Louisiana State University Press, 1972.

Hazlitt, William. *New Writings: Second Series.* Edited by P. P. Howe. London: Martin Secker, 1927.

Heilbrun, Carolyn G. *Toward a Recognition of Androgyny.* New York: Alfred A. Knopf, 1973.

Heilman, Robert B. *Magic in the Web: Action and Language in "Othello."* Lexington: University of Kentucky Press, 1956.

—— "The *Taming* Untamed; or The Return of the Shrew." *Modern Language Quarterly* (1966), 27:147–61.

Heine, Heinrich. *Heine on Shakespeare. A Translation of his Notes on Shakespeare Heroines.* Translated by Ida Benecke. Westminster: Archibald Constable, 1895.

Heywood, Thomas. *The Exemplary Lives and Memorable Acts of Nine the Most Worthy Women of the World.* London, 1640.

Hogan, Charles Beecher. *Shakespeare in the Theatre, 1701–1800.* 2 vols. London: Oxford University Press, 1952–57.

Holland, Norman N. *Psychoanalysis and Shakespeare.* New York: McGraw-Hill, 1964.

Holloway, John. *The Story of the Night.* Lincoln: University of Nebraska Press, 1961.

Horney, Karen. *Feminine Psychology.* 1967. Reprint. New York: W. W. Norton, 1973.

Hunter, Robert Grams. *Shakespeare and the Comedy of Forgiveness.* New York: Columbia University Press, 1965.

Jackson, Sir Barry. "On Producing *Henry VI.*" *Shakespeare Survey* (1953), 6:49–52.

Jameson, Anna. *Shakespeare's Heroines.* London: Saunders and Otley, 1832. Reprint. New York: A. L. Burt Company, n.d.

Johnson, Samuel. *Johnson on Shakespeare.* Edited by Arthur Sherbo. Vols. 7 and 8 of *Works of Samuel Johnson.* New Haven: Yale University Press, 1968.

Jones, Eldred. *The Elizabethan Image of Africa.* Charlottesville: University Press of Virginia, 1971.

—— "Racial Terms for Africans in Elizabethan Usage." *Review of National Literatures* (1972), 3(2):54–89.

Kahn, Coppelia. "*The Taming of the Shrew:* Shakespeare's Mirror of Marriage." *Modern Language Studies* (Spring 1975), 5:88–102.

Kelso, Ruth. *Doctrine for the Lady of the Renaissance.* Urbana: University of Illinois Press, 1956.

Kirsch, Arthur C. "The Integrity of *Measure for Measure.*" *Shakespeare Survey* (1975), 28:89–105.

Knight, G. Wilson. *The Imperial Theme.* 1931. Reprint. London: Methuen, University Paperbacks, 1965.

—— *The Shakespearean Tempest.* 1932. Reprint. London: Methuen, 1971.

—— *The Crown of Life.* 1947. Reprint. New York: Barnes and Noble, 1966.

Kott, Jan. *Shakespeare Our Contemporary.* 1964. Reprint. New York: W. W. Norton, 1974.

Lamb, Charles. *The Art of the Stage as Set Out in Lamb's Dramatic Essays.* Commentary by Percy Fitzgerald. London: Remington, 1885.

Laslett, Peter. *The World We Have Lost.* London: Methuen, 1965.

Lawrence, William Witherle. *Shakespeare's Problem Comedies.* New York: Macmillan, 1931.

Leavis, F. R. *The Common Pursuit.* London: Chatto & Windus, 1952.

Leech, Clifford. "The Moral Tragedy of *Romeo and Juliet.*" In *English Renaissance Drama: Essays in Honor of Madeleine Doran and Mark Eccles,* edited by Standish Henning, Robert Kimbrough, and Richard Knowles. Carbondale: Southern Illinois University Press, 1976.

Leggatt, Alexander. *Shakespeare's Comedy of Love.* London: Methuen, 1974.

Levin, Harry. *Shakespeare and the Revolution of the Times.* New York: Oxford University Press, 1976.

McElroy, Bernard. *Shakespeare's Mature Tragedies.* Princeton: Princeton University Press, 1973.

McFarland, Thomas. *Tragic Meaning in Shakespeare.* New York: Random House, 1968.

Mack, Maynard. "*Antony and Cleopatra:* The Stillness and the Dance." In *Shakespeare's Art,* edited by Milton Crane. Chicago: University of Chicago Press, 1973.

MacKenzie, Agnes Mure. *The Women in Shakespeare's Plays.* New York: William Heinemann, 1924.

Mahood, M. M. *Shakespeare's Wordplay.* London: Methuen, 1957.

Manheim, Michael. *The Weak King Dilemma in Shakespeare.* Syracuse, N.Y.: Syracuse University Press, 1973.

Martz, William J. *Shakespeare's Universe of Comedy.* New York: David Lewis, 1971.

Mason, H. A. *Shakespeare's Tragedies of Love.* London: Chatto and Windus, 1970.

Maxwell, J. C. "Shakespeare's Roman Plays: 1900–1956." *Shakespeare Survey* (1957), 10: 1–11.

Mead, Margaret. *Sex and Temperament in Three Primitive Societies.* New York: William Morrow, 1935.

Meredith, George. "On the Idea of Comedy and the Uses of the Comic Spirit." In *The Idea of Comedy,* edited by W. K. Wimsatt. Englewood Cliffs, N.J.: Prentice-Hall, 1969, pp. 238–83.

Mill, John Stuart. *The Letters of John Stuart Mill.* Edited by Hugh S. R. Elliot. 2 vols. London: Longmans, Green, 1910.

Mill, John Stuart, and Harriet Taylor Mill. *Essays on Sex Equality.* Edited by Alice S. Rossi. Chicago: University of Chicago Press, 1970.

Millett, Kate. *Sexual Politics.* New York: Doubleday, 1970.

Mills, Lauren J. *The Tragedies of Shakespeare's Antony and Cleopatra.* Bloomington: Indiana University Press, 1974.

Morris, Helen. "Queen Elizabeth I 'Shadowed' in Cleopatra." *Huntington Library Quarterly* (1969), 32:271–78.

Mowat, Barbara A. *The Dramaturgy of Shakespeare's Romances.* Athens: University of Georgia Press, 1976.

Neale, Jonathan E. *Elizabeth I and Her Parliaments 1584–1601.* London: Jonathan Cape, 1957.

Neely, Carol Thomas. "Women and Men in *Othello*" *Shakespeare Studies* (1977), 10:133–58.

Nevo, Ruth. "The Masque of Greatness." *Shakespeare Studies* (1967), 3:111–28.

—— *Tragic Form in Shakespeare.* Princeton: Princeton University Press, 1972.

Odell, George C. D. *Shakespeare from Betterton to Irving.* 2 vols. 1920. Reprint. New York: Dover, 1966.

—— *Annals of the New York Stage.* 15 vols. New York: Columbia University Press, 1927–49.

Olsen, Tillie. *Silences.* New York: Delta/Seymour Lawrence, 1978.

Ornstein, Robert. *A Kingdom for a Stage.* Cambridge: Harvard University Press, 1972.

—— "Bourgeois Morality and Dramatic Convention in *A Woman Killed with Kindness.*" In *English Renaissance Drama: Essays in Honor of Madeleine*

Doran and Mark Eccles, edited by Standish Henning, Robert Kimbrough, and Richard Knowles. Carbondale: Southern Illinois University Press, 1976.

Pedicord, Harry W. *The Theatrical Public in the Time of Garrick.* 1954. Reprint. Carbondale: Southern Illinois University Press, 1966.

Pedicord, Harry W. and Frederick L. Bergmann, eds. *Garrick's Adaptations of Shakespeare, 1759–1773.* Vols. 3 and 4 of *The Plays of David Garrick.* Urbana: Southern Illinois University Press, in press.

Pierce, Robert B. *Shakespeare's History Plays, The Family and The State.* Columbus: Ohio State University Press, 1971.

Pratt, Samuel M. "Shakespeare and Humphrey Duke of Gloucester: A Study in Myth." *Shakespeare Quarterly* (1965), 16:201–16.

Prior, Moody E. *The Drama of Power.* Evanston, Illinois: Northwestern University Press, 1973.

Puknat, Elizabeth M. "Romeo Was a Lady: Charlotte Cushman's London Triumph." *The Theatre Annual* (1951), 9:59–69.

Rabkin, Norman. *Shakespeare and the Common Understanding.* New York: Free Press, 1967.

Rabkin, Norman, ed. *Approaches to Shakespeare.* New York: McGraw-Hill, 1964.

—— *Reinterpretations of Elizabethan Drama.* Selected Papers from the English Institute. New York: Columbia University Press, 1969.

Rackin, Phyllis. "Shakespeare's Boy Cleopatra." *PMLA* (1972), 87:201–12.

Ranald, Margaret Loftus. "The Manning of the Haggard; or *The Taming of the Shrew.*" *Essays in Literature* (1974), 1:149–65.

Ribner, Irving. " 'Then I Denie You Starres': A Reading of *Romeo and Juliet.*" *Studies in English Renaissance Drama in Memory of Karl Julius Holzknecht.* Edited by Josephine W. Bennett, Oscar J. Cargill, and Vernon Hall, Jr. New York: New York University Press, 1959.

—— "The Morality of Farce: *The Taming of the Shrew.*" In *Essays in American and English Literature Presented to Bruce Robert McElderry, Jr.,* edited by Max F. Schulz et al. Athens: Ohio University Press, 1968.

Richmond, Hugh M. *Shakespeare's Sexual Comedy.* New York: Bobbs-Merrill, 1971.

Riggs, David. *Shakespeare's Historical Histories: "Henry VI" and Its Literary Tradition.* Cambridge: Harvard University Press, 1971.

Righter, Anne. *Shakespeare and the Idea of the Play.* London: Chatto and Windus, 1962.

Rosenberg, Marvin. *The Masks of Othello.* Berkeley: University of California Press, 1971.

Rossiter, A. P. *English Drama from Early Times to the Elizabethans.* 1950. Reprint. New York: Barnes and Noble, 1967.

Rymer, Thomas. *A Short View of Tragedy.* London, 1693.

Saintsbury, H. A. and Cecil Palmer. *We Saw Him Act: A Symposium on the Art of Sir Henry Irving.* London: Hurst & Blackett, 1939.

Schanzer, Ernest. *The Problem Plays of Shakespeare.* London: Routledge and Kegan Paul, 1963.

Schleiner, Winfried. "Deromanticizing the Shrew: Notes on Teaching Shakespeare in a 'Women in Literature' Course." In *Teaching Shakespeare,* edited by Walter Edens et al. Princeton: Princeton University Press, 1977.

Scragg, Leah. "Iago—Vice or Devil?" *Shakespeare Survey* (1968), 21:53–65.

Sexton, Joyce H. *The Slandered Woman in Shakespeare.* English Literary Studies Monograph Series, no. 12. Victoria, B. C., Canada: University of Victoria, 1978.

Shattuck, Charles H. *The Shakespeare Promptbooks.* Urbana: University of Illinois Press, 1965.

Shupe, Donald R. "The Wooing of Lady Anne," *Shakespeare Quarterly* (1978), 29:28–36.

Simmons, J. L. *Shakespeare's Pagan World.* Charlottesville: University of Virginia Press, 1973.

Snyder, Susan. "*Othello* and the Conventions of Romantic Comedy." *Renaissance Drama* (1972), N.S.5:123–41.

Spencer, T. J. B. "Shakespeare and the Noble Woman." *Shakespeare Jahrbuch* (1966), 49–62.

Spevack, Marvin. *A Complete and Systematic Concordance to the Works of Shakespeare.* 6 vols. Hildesheim, Germany: Georg Olms, 1968–70.

Spivack, Bernard. *Shakespeare and the Allegory of Evil.* New York: Columbia University Press, 1958.

Sprague, Arthur Colby. *Shakespeare's Histories: Plays for the Stage.* London: Society for Theatre Research, 1964.

Stevenson, David Lloyd. *The Love-Game Comedy.* New York: Columbia University Press, 1946.

Stilling, Roger. *Love and Death in Renaissance Tragedy.* Baton Rouge: Louisiana State University Press, 1976.

Stoll, Elmer Edgar. *Shakespeare's Young Lovers.* 1935. Reprint. New York: AMS Press, 1966.

Stone, George Winchester, Jr. "Garrick and an Unknown Operatic Version of *Love's Labour's Lost,*" *Review of English Studies* (1939), 15:323–28.

—— "Garrick's Handling of Shakespeare's Plays and His Influence Upon the Changed Attitude of Shakespearian Criticism During the Eighteenth Century." Ph.D. dissertation, Harvard University, 1940.

Stone, George Winchester, Jr., and George M. Kahrl. *David Garrick: A Critical Biography.* Carbondale: Southern Illinois University Press, 1979.

Stone, Lawrence. *The Crisis of the Aristocracy 1558–1641.* Oxford: Oxford University Press, Clarendon Press, 1965.

—— *The Family, Sex and Marriage in England 1500–1800.* New York: Harper and Row, 1977.

Swander, Homer D. "The Rediscovery of *Henry VI.*" *Shakespeare Quarterly* (1978), 29:146–63.

Swinburne, Algernon Charles. *A Study of Shakespeare.* London: Chatto and Windus, 1880.

Terry, Ellen. *Four Lectures on Shakespeare.* In collaboration with Christopher St. John. London: Martin Hopkinson, 1932.

Tillyard, E. M. W. *Shakespeare's History Plays.* 1944. Reprint. London: Chatto and Windus, 1964.

—— *Shakespeare's Problem Plays.* Toronto: University of Toronto Press, 1949.

—— *The Elizabethan World Picture.* New York: Vintage Books, 1959.

Traci, Philip J. *The Love Play of "Antony and Cleopatra."* The Hague and Paris: Mouton, 1970.

Traversi, Derek A. *An Approach to Shakespeare.* 2d ed., rev. and enl. New York: Doubleday Anchor, 1956.

—— *Shakespeare, The Roman Plays.* Stanford, Ca.: Stanford University Press, 1963.

Trewin, J. C. *Shakespeare on the English Stage 1900–1964.* London: Barrie and Rockliff, 1964.

Turner, Robert Y. "Characterization in Shakespeare's Early History Plays." *Journal of English Literary History* (1964), 31:241–58.

Van Lennep, William, et al., eds. *The London Stage, 1660–1800.* 5 parts in 11 vols. Carbondale: Southern Illinois University Press, 1960–68.

Waith, Eugene M. *The Herculean Hero.* New York: Columbia University Press, 1962.

—— "Heywood's Women Worthies." In *Concepts of the Hero in the Middle Ages and the Renaissance,* edited by Norman T. Burns and Christoper J. Reagan. Albany: State University of New York Press, 1975, pp. 222–39.

Waldo, Tommy Ruth. *Musical Terms as Rhetoric.* Salzburg, Austria: Institut fur Englische Sprache und Literature, 1974.

West, Michael. "Folk Background of Petruchio's Wooing Dance." *Shakespeare Studies* (1974), 7:65–73.

Williams, Gwyn. "Suffolk and Margaret: A Study of Some Sections of Shakespeare's *Henry VI.*" *Shakespeare Quarterly* (1974), 25:310–22.

Wilson, J. Dover. *Shakespeare's Happy Comedies.* London: Faber and Faber, 1962.

Winter, William. *Shakespeare on the Stage.* New York: Moffat, Yard, 1916.

Wollstonecraft, Mary. *A Vindication of the Rights of Woman.* 1792. Reprint. New York: W. W. Norton, 1975.

Woolf, Virginia. *A Room of One's Own.* New York: Harcourt, Brace & World, 1929.

—— *Three Guineas.* New York: Harcourt, Brace & World, 1938.

Zeeveld, W. Gordon. *The Temper of Shakespeare's Thought.* New Haven: Yale University Press, 1974.

Selected List of Promptbooks,* Editions, and Versions of the Plays Consulted

Collected Works of Shakespeare

Bell, John, ed. *Bell's Edition of Shakespeare's Plays.* 9 vols. London: J. Bell, 1774.

Evans, G. Blakemore, ed. *The Riverside Shakespeare.* Boston: Houghton Mifflin, 1974.

Furness, Horace Howard, ed. *A New Variorum Edition of Shakespeare.* 27 vols. Philadelphia: J. B. Lippincott, 1871–1955. (Horace Howard Furness, Jr. edited vols. 16–20.)

Malone, Edmond, ed. *The Plays and Poems of William Shakspeare.* 10 vols. London, 1790.

Pope, Alexander, ed. *The Works of Mr. William Shakespear.* 6 vols. London: J. Tonson, 1723–25.

Pope, Alexander and William Warburton, eds. *The Works of Shakespear.* 8 vols. London: J. & P. Knapton et al., 1747.

Theobald, Lewis, ed. *The Works of Shakespeare.* 7 vols. London, 1733.

White, Richard Grant, ed. *The Works of William Shakespeare.* 12 vols. Boston: Little Brown, 1865.

Antony and Cleopatra

Folger Prompt Ant 1. [London] Thomas Hailes Lacy, n.d. [Princess's Theatre. 1867.] Marked by George Becks, actor (ca. 1888). Reconstructs performance of 1874.

Folger Prompt Ant 2. pp. 344–80 of *Works,* n.d. Isabella Glyn, actress. London (ca. 1855).

Folger Prompt Ant 3. London: J. Tonson, 1734. Marked by Edward Capell (ca. 1758).

---

* In these entries title page information appears first. Then, if known, the person who marked or owned the promptbook, and the performance(s) for which it was used are indicated.

Folger Prompt Ant 8. Title page lacking. Marked by Samuel Phelps. Theatre Royal, Sadler's Wells. London, 1849.

Folger Prompt Ant 9. Israel Gollanz, ed. London: J. M. Dent, 1896.

Ames, Winthrop, dir. *Antony and Cleopatra*. New Theatre, New York, 1909. New York Public Library *NCP .51625; typescript *NCP + 51624B.

Calvert, Charles, adaptor. *Antony and Cleopatra*. Arranged in four acts. Edinburgh: Schenck and M'Farlane, 186–.

Dryden, John. *All for Love*. London, 1678.

[Garrick, David and Edward Capell.] *Antony and Cleopatra* fitted for stage by abridging only. London: Tonson, 1758.

[——] *Antony and Cleopatra*. Dublin: Peter Wilson and Wm. Smith, Jr., 1759.

Kemble, John Philip. *Antony and Cleopatra*. Ms. in Kemble's hand. Believed to be in preparation for the 1813 production. Folger Library S.a. 125.

[——] *Antony and Cleopatra*. With alterations and additions from Dryden. Theatre-Royal, Covent-Garden. London: J. Barker, 1813.

Rolfe, William J., ed. *Antony and Cleopatra*. New York: Duprat, 1891.

Tree, Herbert Beerbohm, adaptor. *Antony and Cleopatra*. Mansfield Theatre. New York, November 1937. New York Public Library *NCP + Shakespeare.

THE THREE PARTS OF *Henry VI*

Cairncross, Andrew S., ed. *The Third Part of King Henry VI*. In Arden Shakespeare Paperbacks. London: Methuen, 1969.

Cibber, Theophilus. *An Historical Tragedy of the Civil Wars In the Reign of King Henry VI. Alter'd from Shakespear*. London, 1720.

Philips, Ambrose. *Humfrey, Duke of Gloucester*. (Alteration of *2 Henry VI*.) London: J. Roberts, 1723.

Wilson, J. Dover, ed. *Henry VI, Part I*. Cambridge: Cambridge University Press, 1952.

Love's Labour's Lost

Folger Prompt LLL 1. London: J. Tonson, 1735. Altered into an opera for David Garrick in 1773 by Edward Thompson.

Folger Prompt LLL 2. [London: George Kearsley, 1806]. Elizabeth Vestris, actress and manager. Theatre Royal, Covent Garden, London, 1839.

Folger Prompt LLL 3. Arranged by Augustin Daly. Fifth Avenue Theatre, New York: J. W. Morrissey, 1874.

Folger Prompt LLL 6. As performed at Theatres Royal, London: G. H. Davidson, [n.d.] (Cumberland ed.) Marked for Augustin Daly's 1874 production.

Folger Prompt LLL 8. Pages 105–98 from Vol. III of a *Works*. n.p. n.d. Samuel Phelps, actor and manager. Theatre Royal, Sadler's Wells. London, 1857.

David, Richard, ed. *Love's Labour's Lost*. In *The Arden Shakespeare*. 1951; Reprint. Arden Shakespeare Paperbacks. London: Methuen, 1968.

Macbeth

Mullin, Michael, ed. *"Macbeth" On Stage: An Annotated Facsimile of Glen Byam Shaw's 1955 Promptbook*. Columbia: University of Missouri Press, 1976.

Measure for Measure

Lever, J. W., ed. *Measure for Measure*. In Arden Shakespeare Paperbacks. New York: Vintage Books, 1965.

Othello

Folger Prompt Oth Fo 1. Typescript. Henry Jewett, producer-director and actor. New York. Broadway Theatre, 1895–96.

Folger Prompt Oth 2. Park Theatre. New York: Samuel French, n.d. Stella Boniface, actress. [1878]

Folger Prompt Oth Fo 2. Typescript. Paul Robeson, actor. London. Savoy Theatre, 1930.

Folger Prompt Oth 5. Revised by John Philip Kemble. Theatres Royal. London: John Miller, 1814. Edwin Forrest. Tremont Theatre, Boston, 1842.

Folger Prompt Oth 11. Revised by John Philip Kemble. Theatre Royal, Covent Garden. London: T. N. Longman and O. Rees, 1804. Charles Kean, actor and manager. Park Theatre, New York, 1830.

Folger Prompt Oth 16. Hinds' English Stage. London: Simpkin, Marshall and Co., 1838. William Charles Macready, actor and manager. Theatre Royal, Drury Lane, 1842.

Folger Prompt Oth 17. Oxberry's edition. Theatres Royal. London: W. Simpkin, and R. Marshall, 1822. Edmund Kean, actor, 1831.

Folger Prompt Oth 18. Revised by John Philip Kemble. Theatre Royal Drury-

Lane. London: T. Rodwell, 1818. Edmund Kean, actor.

Folger Prompt Oth 19. Revised by John Philip Kemble. Theatre Royal, Covent Garden. London: T. N. Longman and O. Rees, 1804. Marked by J. P. Kemble. Covent Garden, 1816.

Folger Prompt Oth 26. Pages from a *Works*. John Moore, actor and stage manager. Edinburgh and New York, 1846–70.

Folger Prompt Oth 27. Theatre Royal, Covent Garden. London: C. Hitch et al., 1761. John Palmer, actor. 1766. [King's and Haymarket theatres.]

[Booth, Edwin and H. L. Hinton.] Title page lacking. [1869.] New York. Booth's Theatre, 1869. New York Public Library *NCP .342993.

Kernan, Alvin, ed. *Othello*. New York: New American Library, 1963.

Richard III

Folger Prompt Rich III 8. Title page lacking. [Adapted by Colley Cibber. *King Richard III*. London: Thomas Hailes Lacy, n. d.] Later used as preparation copy by Henry Irving, n.d.

Folger Prompt Rich III 39. Adapted by Colley Cibber. *King Richard III*. Revised by John Philip Kemble. Theatre Royal, Covent Garden. London, 1810.

American Shakespeare Festival. Typescript. *Richard III*. Production June 1964, Stratford, Connecticut. New York Public Library *NCP + 1964.

Cibber, Colley. *The Tragical History of King Richard the Third*. In *Plays Written by Mr. Cibber*. Vol. 1. London, 1721.

Eccles, Mark, ed. *Richard III*. New York: New American Library, 1964.

Olivier, Laurence and Alan Dent, adaptors. *Richard III*. Great Britain: London Films, 1956.

[Phelps, Samuel, actor and manager.] *Richard III*. Title page lacking [1845]. New York Public Library *NCP .164551.

Wheeler, David, dir. *Richard III*. Al Pacino, actor. Cort Theatre. New York, 1979.

Romeo and Juliet

Folger Prompt Rom 1. Mary Anderson. Lyceum Theatre. London: W. S. Johnson, 1884.

Folger Prompt Rom Fo 1. Typescript. Henry Jewett, producer-director. Boston Opera House, 1915.

Folger Prompt Rom 3. Title page lacking. [Booth-Hinton edition, 1868.] New York, Booth's Theatre.

Folger Prompt Rom 12. No proper title page. [pp. 105–245 of a *Works*.] Henry Irving, actor and manager. London. Lyceum Theatre, 1882.

Folger Prompt Rom 13. Adapted by David Garrick. *Romeo and Juliet*. Revised by John Philip Kemble. Theatre Royal, Covent Garden. London, 1811. Charles Kean, actor and manager. Haymarket Theatre, 1841.

Folger Prompt Rom 17. French's Standard Drama No. XLII. New York: T. H. French; London: Samuel French, n. d. Robert B. Mantell, actor.

Folger Prompt Rom 33. Altered by David Garrick. Theatre-Royal, Drury-Lane. London: W. Lowndes, and S. Bladon, 1793. William B. Wood, actor and manager. Philadelphia. Chestnut Street Theatre, 1804.

Folger Prompt Rom 35. Adapted by David Garrick. *Romeo and Juliet*. Revised by John Philip Kemble. Theatre Royal, Covent Garden. London, 1811. Marked by J. P. Kemble (ca. 1815).

Folger Prompt Rom 39. With alterations, and an additional scene by David Garrick. London: Tonson, 1763. [3d edition].

BBC-TV and Time-Life Television co-production. *Romeo and Juliet*. WNET-Thirteen, March 14, 1979.

Bryant, J. A., Jr., ed. *Romeo and Juliet*. New York: New American Library, 1964.

Cibber, Theophilus. *Romeo and Juliet*. London: C. Corbett, 1748.

Garrick, David. *Romeo and Juliet*. London: Tonson, 1748.

Garrick, David. *Romeo and Juliet*. London: Tonson, 1750. [2d revised edition].

Langham, Michael. "Director's Preface." In *Romeo and Juliet*. Edited by Kenneth Weber. Toronto: Festival Editions of Canada, 1970.

MacMillan, Kenneth, choreographer. *Romeo and Juliet*. Music by Sergei Prokofiev. Filmed by Paul Czinner Productions for Poetic Films, 1966.

Otway, Thomas. *The History and Fall of Caius Marius*. London, 1680.

Wilson, J. Dover and George Ian Duthie, eds. *Romeo and Juliet*. Cambridge: Cambridge University Press, 1955.

Zeffirelli, Franco, dir. *Romeo and Juliet*. Verona Productions. Paramount Pictures, 1968.

The Taming of the Shrew

Folger Prompt Shrew 1. Arranged by Augustin Daly. *Taming of the Shrew . . . in Four Acts*. Daly's Theatre. Privately Printed: New York, 1887.

Folger Prompt Shrew Ad 3. David Garrick. *Katharine and Petruchio*. Revised by John Philip Kemble. Theatre Royal, Covent Garden. London, 1810.

Folger Prompt Shrew Fo 3. Typescript. [1923?] Gift of Julia Marlowe Sothern, actress. ca. 1942.

Folger Prompt Shrew 6. Number 12 of an edition of Shakespeare's plays. London: Rivington [1805]. Samuel Phelps, actor and manager. Theatre Royal, Sadler's Wells. London, 1856.

Folger Prompt Shrew Ad 10. Altered by David Garrick. _The Taming of the Shrew; or Catherine and Petruchio_. London: C. Bathurst, 1786.

Folger Prompt Shrew Ad 11. Alter'd by David Garrick. _Catharine and Petruchio_. Dublin: William Sleater, 1756.

Booth, Edwin and William Winter. _Katharine and Petruchio_. New York: Francis Hart and Co., 1878. Booth's Theatre, 1881. New York Public Library. Prompt Book 8 *NCP.

Daly, Augustin. _Taming of the Shrew . . . in four Acts_. Daly's Theatre. Privately printed: New York, 1887. Ada Rehan, actress. 1904–5. New York Public Library. 8-* NCP.

Garrick, David. _Catharine and Petruchio_. London: J. & R. Tonson, 1756.

Hosley, Richard, ed. _The Taming of the Shrew_. Pelican Shakespeare, 1964; rev. ed. New York: Penguin Books, 1970.

Johnson, Charles. _The Cobler of Preston_. Adaptation of "Induction" of _The Taming of the Shrew_. In _Ten English Farces_, edited by Leo Hughes and A. H. Scouten. Austin: University of Texas Press, 1948, pp. 145–69.

Lacy, John. _The Taming of the Shrew_ adapted as _Sauny the Scot_. London: E. Whitlock, 1698.

Lunt, Alfred and Lynn Fontanne. Typescript. _The Taming of the Shrew_. Theatre Guild, New York, 1935. New York Public Library. *NCP 1935.

Papp, Joseph. _The Taming of the Shrew_. New York Shakespeare Festival. Summer 1978.

Seldes, Gilbert. _The Taming of the Shrew_. Columbia Shakespeare Cycle. Presented over the Columbia Broadcasting System. Monday, August 2, 1937.

Spewack, Samuel and Bella. _Kiss Me Kate_. Screenplay by Dorothy Kingsley. Music and lyrics by Cole Porter. Hollywood Metro Goldwyn Mayer, 1953.

The Winter's Tale

Folger Prompt Wint T 1. Arranged by Frank Vernon. Presented by Viola Allen. Knickerbocker Theatre. New York: McClure, Phillips, 1905.

Folger Prompt Wint T 2. Inchbald edition. Theatre Royal, Drury Lane. London: Longman, Hurst et al. [1808] J. R. Anderson, actor. Theatre Royal, Covent Garden, 1837.

Folger Prompt Wint T 7. Pages from a *Works*. Charles Kean, actor and manager. Princess's Theatre. London, 1856.

Folger Prompt Wint T 10. Accurately printed from the text of Mr. Steevens's last edition, n. d. [Charles Kean?] Marked by George Ellis, stage manager (ca. 1855–56).

Folger Prompt Wint T 11. Pages from a *Works*. Marked by various hands. [1839–87?] Review of Mary Anderson, actress. Lyceum Theatre. London, 1887.

Folger Prompt Wint T 14. [Cumberland ed. 1830's.] Samuel Phelps, actor and manager. Theatre Royal, Sadler's Wells, 1845–62.

Folger Prompt Wint T 15. Oxberry's edition. London: W. Simpkin & R. Marshall, 1823. Thos. H. Lacy, actor. [1841 or 37?]

Folger Prompt Wint T 16. Theatres Royal. London: J. Barker, 1794. William B. Wood, 1813.

Folger Prompt F 23. Alter'd by David Garrick. *Florizel and Perdita*. London: Tonson, 1758.

Folger Prompt F 24. Altered by David Garrick. *Florizel and Perdita*. Theatre-Royal, Drury Lane. London: Tonson, 1762.

Folger Prompt Wint T 26. Adapted by John Philip Kemble. Theatre Royal, Covent Garden. London, 1811. Kemble ms. stage directions.

Garrick, David. *Florizel and Perdita*. MS #122. Larpent Collection, Huntington Library. San Marino, California.

Kemble, John Philip. *The Winter's Tale*. Theatre Royal, Drury Lane. London: C. Lowndes, 1802. MS #2240. Lilly Library. Bloomington, Indiana.

Morgan, MacNamara. *Florizel and Perdita*. MS #110. Larpent Collection, Huntington Library. San Marino, California.

—— *The Sheep Shearing, or Florizel and Perdita*. Dublin, 1755. Reprint. 1767. London, 1762.

Index